Facilitating Change Across Cultures

Praise for this book

At a time when polarisation and nationalism are on the rise it is important to redouble efforts to enable cross-cultural dialogue and exchange. Deborah Rhodes' timely new book provides a rich source of practical ideas and experience which will be of great interest to those engaging in such vital endeavours.

Professor Chris Roche, Director Institute for Human Security and Social Change, La Trobe University, Australia

Deborah Rhodes explores the key role of collaboration in progressing positive change – fraught with power politics and vested interests – and unpacks strategies and approaches that are mindful of context-specific cultural dynamics. With every page I found myself nodding, highlighting passages to return to, checking my own practice and principles, and learning from her deep insights into facilitation of change processes.

Sandra Kraushaar, Director, Pacific Islands, The Asia Foundation

This book provides a timely, thoughtful, and much-needed framework for facilitating change across cultures, particularly in today's polarised world. As a development worker from the global south, I have tried to mediate conflicts in understanding, values, and priorities between the cultures of donors and those who are actually engaged in development processes. It was a joy to read explanations for what I had struggled with. The concepts explored will be a paradigm shift in the development sector.

Gunawathy Fernandez, Independent Consultant and Former India Country Coordinator, Kindernothilfe (KNH)

Practical! This book highlights the very core element of development – the people – who are shaped by culture, values and social norms. It provides a clear reference for development practitioners on how to engage in 'development conversations', by discussing the fundamentals and methods of effective facilitation across cultures for positive and inclusive change.

Iwan Sriwidiyanto, Deputy Team Leader, Knowledge Sector Initiative, Jakarta, Indonesia

Facilitating Change Across Cultures
Lessons from international development

Deborah Rhodes

Practical Action Publishing Ltd
27a, Albert Street, Rugby,
Warwickshire, CV21 2SG, UK
www.practicalactionpublishing.org

© Deborah Rhodes, 2022
The moral right of the author to be identified as author of the work has been asserted under sections 77 and 78 of the Copyright Design and Patents Act 1988.

All rights reserved. No part of this publication may be reprinted or reproduced or utilized in any form or by any electronic, mechanical, or other means, now known or hereafter invented, including photocopying and recording, or in any information storage or retrieval system, without the written permission of the publishers.

Product or corporate names may be trademarks or registered trademarks, and are used only for identification and explanation without intent to infringe.

A catalogue record for this book is available from the British Library.

A catalogue record for this book has been requested from the Library of Congress.

ISBN 978-1-78853-209-9 Paperback
ISBN 978-1-78853-208-2 Hardback
ISBN 978-1-78853-210-5 Electronic book

Citation: Rhodes, D., (2022) *Facilitating Change Across Cultures*, Rugby, UK: Practical Action Publishing <http://dx.doi.org/10.3362/9781788532105>.

Since 1974, Practical Action Publishing has published and disseminated books and information in support of international development work throughout the world. Practical Action Publishing is a trading name of Practical Action Publishing Ltd (Company Reg. No. 1159018), the wholly owned publishing company of Practical Action. Practical Action Publishing trades only in support of its parent charity objectives and any profits are covenanted back to Practical Action (Charity Reg. No. 247257, Group VAT Registration No. 880 9924 76).

The views and opinions in this publication are those of the author and do not represent those of Practical Action Publishing Ltd or its parent charity Practical Action.

Reasonable efforts have been made to publish reliable data and information, but the authors and publisher cannot assume responsibility for the validity of all materials or for the consequences of their use.

Typeset by vPrompt eServices, India

Contents

Acknowledgements	viii
Preface	ix
1. Introduction	1
The context and key terms	4
A new concept: change facilitation across cultures	6
Complexity	6
A cultural values lens	9
Facilitators' roles	12
Facilitators' identity	12
Menu of methods	13

Part 1

2. Cultural values and change	17
Cultural values	18
What is culture?	19
What role do cultural values have?	24
Cultural value differences	25
Cultures' degree of comfort with change	28
Cultures' perceptions about power and leadership related to change	30
Cultures' perceptions about decision-making	31
Cultures' emphasis on tasks and relationships	32
Cultures' values related to gender egalitarianism	33
Cultures' values related to time and the future	35
Low- and high-context cultures	36
Working across cultures	37
Limitations	38
Implications	38
3. Development and change	41
What kinds of change?	43
A cultural lens on change	44
Framework to link cultural values and change	48

4. Implications for facilitators of the links between cultural values and change — 53
   Facilitating collaboration between people with different cultural values — 53
   Diversity and inclusion — 54
   A ladder of cultural awareness — 56

5. Culturally attuned change facilitation — 63
   Definitions of facilitation through a cultural lens — 65
   Power and leadership — 67
   Participation — 69
   Collaboration — 71
   Partnership — 73
   Inclusion — 75

6. Principles for change facilitation across cultures — 81
   Cultural understanding for facilitators — 81
   'Purpose' through cultural and power/political lens — 85
   Inclusion defined in culturally relevant ways — 88
   Trust and a shared culture are essential for collaboration — 90
   Adaptive and flexible ways of working are essential — 94
   Cultural understanding is relevant throughout a program cycle — 95
   Implications for practice — 96

Part 2
   Structure of Part 2 — 102

7. Strategies for change facilitation across cultures — 103
   A Cultural landscape analysis — 104
   B Build strengths-based collaboration — 115
   C Collectively choose and use a mix of facilitation methods — 126

8. Selection of methods — 129
   Criteria for selection of methods — 132

9. Culturally attuned change facilitation methods — 137
   Narratives and story-telling — 138
   Theatre — 142
   Music and dance — 144
   Appreciative Inquiry — 146
   Art and visual methods — 150
   Action learning and research — 152

Symbols	156
Village meeting style	158
Networks and movements	161
10. Contemporary facilitation methods through a cultural values lens	165
Workshops	165
Training	167
Advising	173
Coaching and mentoring	174
Strengthening knowledge systems	175
11. Cross-cultural conflict management methods	179
Building a shared culture	182
Cross-cultural dispute-management and resolution methods	183
Use of and support for culturally attuned mediators	184
Contestation methods	185
12. Evaluating change across cultures	187
Monitoring across cultures	188
Evaluation across cultures	190
Communicating findings from monitoring and evaluation across cultures	195
Skills for facilitators of monitoring and evaluation processes	196
13. Conclusion	199
Principles	200
The role of change facilitators	200
Strategies for change facilitation	201
Methods	201
Annex 1: Facilitation questions to consider through a cultural lens around a program cycle	203
References	207

Acknowledgements

Positive feedback received since writing a book called *Capacity Across Cultures: Global Lessons from Pacific Experiences* (Rhodes, 2014) has been a highlight in the last decade of my career: thank you to those who told me how they valued the book. It took me seven years to write, alongside full-time work and raising two sons. Now, with little paid work (thanks to the global pandemic) and two sons living independently, I was fortunate to be in a position to write another.

Since 2014, I have learned a lot more about 'how change happens' (Green, 2016), particularly through coordinating a course for NGO leaders called 'Making Change Happen' with Professor Chris Roche and Dr Linda Kelly, from the Institute of Human Security and Social Change at La Trobe University in Melbourne, Australia. Also, I have reflected about the role of facilitation across different cultures. I have also learned that writing a book with few other distractions takes less than seven years: it has been an enjoyable and intensely educational process over 18 months.

Huge thanks go to my husband Ernie, who has contributed greatly during the writing process, both in intellectual content and feedback, and practical and loving support. Our sons Sebastian and Jacob are now inspiring us, through their commitment to learning and making a positive contribution to a better world. Thank you, boys, for your contributions, listening skills, and tolerance!

I thank close friends and colleagues who have shared their perspectives, experiences, and advice over many years and encouraged me to write, particularly Lesley Hoatson, Sue Majid, Linda Kelly, Keren Winterford, and Diane McDonald. Your friendship and support are priceless and life-affirming.

Thank you to wonderful worldly people who agreed to read drafts and offered helpful suggestions, including Anne Wuijts, Linda Kelly, Jodie Kane, Perry Head, and Tamerlaine Beasley. Thank you also to Sumarlinah Raden Winoto and Antonia Mochan for working on the figures.

I would like to acknowledge the Black Lives Matter movement which particularly attracted the world's attention in June 2020. Placing issues about white privilege and systemic racism high on the agenda in countries such as Australia is long overdue: this is increasingly discussed in the international development context too. I did hesitate about writing this book in fear of being inaccurately seen as perpetuating 'us' and 'other' divisions. I took heart in messages from the Black Lives Matter movement about the importance of self-education and educating those around us. Hopefully, this book makes a contribution to building understanding, promoting respectful collaboration, addressing ignorance and inequalities, and supporting positive change.

Preface

Countless people and organizations across the world seek to bring about positive changes for others. They do so as funders, program managers, consultants, volunteers, or activists. They mobilize resources and come up with all sorts of creative ideas on how to 'make a difference'. Anyone from students to chief executive officers can commit to bringing about change for one group or another. Organizations, large and small, make extraordinary efforts to bring about change. The scope of change agendas is vast: at one end of the spectrum, the globally agreed Sustainable Development Goals (SDGs) offer a comprehensive plan; and at the other end, an improvement in the life prospects of one person or the well-being of one village may be the change sought. While some efforts succeed, many evaluations and analyses describe the complexities involved, slow progress or unintended negative consequences. Making a contribution to improving these efforts is the purpose of this book. The book offers a broad pathway towards achieving positive change, through a process of facilitation for cross-cultural collaboration.

There is no doubt that 'context matters' for change processes. The context in which change is sought has a major influence on every aspect of change – the processes involved, what is possible, and the likelihood of 'results'. Most factors that shape change have been widely addressed, but one area continues to be relatively neglected: the role of cultural values. Without engaging too deeply in the theoretical aspects, this book focuses on the implications of understanding about cultural values and change for the practical roles of change facilitators. By strengthening understanding about the influence of cultural values in locations in which change is expected to occur, as well as in the collaborative relationships and conversations which are necessary to bring about change, facilitators of change will be better equipped to make their contribution relevant and thus more likely to succeed. The premise for this book is that there are opportunities for significant improvement in the way facilitators contribute to change processes in multicultural settings and in cultural contexts different from their own.

While the people whose lives are expected to change should be central to each change process, the role of change facilitators is also crucial, for both those people and the partners with whom they collaborate. Facilitators from one cultural context who support changes in communities, organizations, or countries with different cultural values have to think differently and do extra work. While international change-oriented facilitation is often undertaken by people who have different values from the people whose lives are expected to change, this is not always the case. Variations within cultures, mentioned consistently throughout this book, as well as the complexity of many other factors that influence life and change mean that simple generalizations are always best interrogated. Even when facilitating within one's own cultural context, many philosophical and practical options need to be considered: when working across different cultures, the options are more complex and require different frames of reference and different knowledge and skills.

Cultural values play a significant role in the processes associated with change and development (Warren et al., 1995; Harrison and Huntington, 2000; Green, 2016). They interact with other influences, including politics and power, identity, class, ideas, organizations, relationships, and alliances. The extent to which cultural values influence the nature and scope of change is the subject of wide-ranging views and there are few shared frameworks across disciplines. The fields of economics and anthropology tend to be the most sceptical (Harrison and Huntington, 2000) while the disciplines of social psychology, organizational change, and business tend to give greater recognition of the influence. Existing theories can support thinking practitioners but they insufficiently link concepts of culture, change, and facilitation practice.

This book analyses relevant ideas from other disciplines through a cultural values lens and seeks to make them accessible for practitioners. Part 1 considers how change and development are understood differently between cultures and the role of facilitating change in this context. It identifies principles from this analysis to inform Part 2, which provides a framework to guide facilitation practice across cultures plus a menu of potential methods. The intention is to support facilitators to better understand the influence of their own and others' cultural values on their work and to enable them to engage better with people and organizations to achieve positive change.

Who am I?

I am a woman of English birth, living, and working on Wurundjeri Country, Australia. This land has never been ceded and no treaty has been signed, which means it always was and always will be Aboriginal land. I am deeply aware of my privilege and the benefits of life in a high-resource context. I have spent most of my life working in and learning about different countries. My cross-cultural marriage to Ernie has taught me a great deal. Learning from and providing training for thousands of people from many different countries about cultural values and their relationship to change and capacity has also deepened my emerging understanding about the complex world in which we live.

Professionally, I am a development practitioner, consultant, researcher, and trainer with 35 years of experience across hundreds of activities with multiple organizations in 30 countries. Over this career, I have been fortunate to learn a great deal, through listening, reading, practice, training, teaching as well as writing. My frames of reference have understandably changed.

Starting in government, I learned about policy, formal writing, and official national interests. In the non-profit sector, I learned about volunteering, advocacy, justice, inequality, inclusion, human rights, and different versions of national interest. In the contracting sector, I learned more about partnerships, managing the project cycle, and how to produce deliverables. As a trainer, I learned about the critical role of facilitation, adult learning, the power of interconnecting ideas from different disciplines, and the joy of contributing 'light-bulb moments'. These frames of reference have merged and been informed by diverse and sometimes challenging experiences. Through this career, and as I 'matured', I witnessed an increasing gap between contract-based systems and the reality of people's lives and hopes for the future. I felt the need to shift from technocratic approaches to respect-based collaboration for bringing about positive developmental change. I've benefited from the wisdom of many people and am humbled to have had so many opportunities to learn.

It has become clearer to me that 'development' is framed in many different and particular ways which neither resonate with each other nor with my own experience of the world. For example, portraying developing countries as problems to be solved, people who live in poverty as helpless victims, and programs and development agencies as only sources of 'solutions' and 'results' do not ring true for me anymore. Programs which seek to create economic growth at the cost of the environment, or protect the environment at the cost of communities, or build communities at the cost of positive cultural values, or change values for the sake of dominance and economic growth, all grate.

As an independent consultant, I have had the privilege of facilitating conversations and processes with many groups of people. As a trainer, program designer, evaluator, planner, or mentor, I have understood my role as facilitator, supporting collaboration between people, and generating shared commitment to a particular idea or approach or result. This experience enabled me to listen deeply to extraordinary and ordinary people, support people to see things differently, contribute new ideas, reflect on the big picture and the details of day-to-day life, and increasingly question many aspects of development practice. Over time, I began to formulate my own 'modus operandi' based on these rich experiences and the mistakes I made along the way. I learned that when one shows respect to others' cultural values, this immediately helps to build trust and respectful connections. I learned that when one acknowledges and values existing strengths in any context, this helps to generate good partnerships, increased agency and confidence, and the kinds of motivation and momentum necessary to achieve positive change. I learned that a safe space enables people to share their experiences and perspectives, so significant insights, and changes are possible. Of course, I have also witnessed a great deal of lack of respect, injustice, unfairness, ignorance, paternalism, exclusion, and what I regard as poor decision-making, and tried to use that as material for reflection, learning, and affirming the importance of particular values – integrity, transparency, justice, and respect.

Mistakes are common in this world of facilitating change and I have made my fair share. Sometimes I misread the room, made incorrect assumptions, gave too much emphasis to the foreigners' voice or a familiar group's voice, or was insensitive to power dynamics between people and organizations. Sometimes I did not bring my 'whole self' to a situation while expecting others to do so. Sometimes I cut people off in the interests of 'keeping time' or expressed my own views or reactions too didactically. I have learned that we are always learning. I have valued the benefits of mindfulness. *I now believe that being a development worker is about building relationships and working collaboratively and respectfully with other people, bringing, in one's back pocket, some useful principles, approaches, and tools to support people to understand, engage with, and respond to the complex situation in which we all live.* I feel uncomfortable with processes which assume things about other people, impose on, and extract from people. I feel more comfortable with those which quietly and respectfully enable and support people, organizations, and systems to make their own efforts to achieve their aspirations for a better, fairer, more inclusive life.

Writing this book provided me with an opportunity to share and reflect on my learning accumulated over many decades. I tried hard to include lots of examples, but most of my experience has been under client-written contracts that include confidentiality clauses. Without being able to name projects, countries, or organizations, draft case studies came over as uninteresting. I tried making up scenarios, but this did not sit well with the emphasis on 'context is everything'. After much thought, I concluded that I would simply state here that assertions and suggestions in this book are based on real-life experiences, my own reflections, interpretation of research from various disciplines, and feedback from people I've worked with over many years. Voices of participants are central to the process of facilitation: I have kept quotes from various people and events in mind when writing the book, though participants cannot be named or located as they have not given their permission.

Why now?

Facilitators' abilities to maximize the quality of collaboration between people and organizations with different values and priorities are essential to achieve the kinds of changes needed now and for the foreseeable future. At a time of unprecedented global turmoil, it is timely and appropriate to strengthen the role of change facilitators in addressing these issues as well as other ways to achieve positive change.

Over decades, globalization has contributed to much greater interaction between people of diverse backgrounds as well as increased understanding of differences and common interests, although the latter is neither uniform nor shared (Tett, 2021). There is scope for much better understanding about how change happens across various cultural contexts and how to support collaborative change processes. With shifts in national and international agendas in the 21st century and phenomena such as climate change and the COVID-19 pandemic requiring global responses, this is particularly timely. Issues of race, restricted movement across borders, and shared global challenges are high on everyone's agenda. How will people from different cultures collaborate to bring about the changes we all prioritize in this complex and dynamic world?

People are shaped by change and change shapes people in sometimes unexpected and unpredictable ways. For example, ways in which the world has responded to the massive changes brought about by the 2020–21 pandemic will influence people, organizations, relationships, and countries for decades to come. Given what is known about the success and failure of global efforts to date, it is clear that links between cultural values and the future of the world are central, not marginal. In response to COVID-19, one doctor noted:

> The pandemic has shown some interesting individualized responses in different countries and communities that highlight the effect of cultural complexities on the pandemic response. Culture plays a central role in determining attributions to illness, health-seeking behaviours and pathways, and community willingness to comply with measures to counter a pandemic spread. Therefore, cultural beliefs and values can contribute to the success or failure of global efforts to contain spread of an outbreak. (Rathod, 2020)

The same can be said about links between cultural values and all other issues and change agendas.

Who is the expected audience?

My expectation is that readers are a community of practitioners and facilitators interested in the processes of working successfully across cultures, towards positive change. Who is a facilitator? A facilitator is someone or an organization engaged in supporting groups of people through a process which enables them to achieve something: in this case, some kind of positive development-related change. A very important assumption underpins this book: that a facilitator's role is to partner, advise, support, or manage a process that contributes to others' achievement of change, which is relevant to them. A facilitator in this context is not a person or organization leading or driving change when working across cultures. They are both in front of and behind people in the change context: that is, in front of a room, but supporting people in a way that their voices lead. Nuances associated with the distinction between supporting/facilitating and driving/leading change can be easily overlooked, but are critical in both practice and theory, and thus to this book. Power issues related to the distinction are increasingly important in the context of localization and decolonization agendas in international development.

The book draws on the author's experience and others' work in three areas: international development, community development, and organizational change, but the potential audience is broad. Most examples in this book come from international development experience. This is a wide field, covering a vast range of ideas, sectors, and contexts, including community development and organizational change. Core messages will be useful for people and organizations involved in other positive change processes too. The author assumes readers are practitioners who want to think about their work in facilitation, as well as undertake facilitation tasks.

Every day, changes are initiated, implemented, and evaluated in many sectors, with people from various cultural backgrounds and in different cultural contexts. For example, staff from international development agencies call meetings to start new programs in topics as different as architecture and domestic violence. Community development workers in multicultural cities run workshops to build cohesion, strengthen resilience, or reduce marginalization. Government officials organize public consultations with multicultural communities to find out ways to increase engagement on environmental protection or prepare for new infrastructure, for example. Volunteers from non-profit organizations or activists with a shared agenda mobilize members and movements to lead and advocate for changes to global, national, or local policies that affect climate change or human rights. Professionals collaborate to bring about behaviour or attitudinal changes. The range of change-oriented initiatives is boundless.

A facilitator may run a single workshop or be engaged in a longer-term process with multiple elements. Facilitation may be explicit or implicit in a development worker's role. The level of complexity involved in applying and sustaining a cross-cultural lens could vary significantly between roles. The book's underpinning premises and approaches are potentially relevant to every context, but how they apply and what this looks like in each setting will vary depending on the specifics.

The book assumes those who want to support the achievement of change seek to maximize the relevance and positive aspects of change wherever they work. As many challenges faced by communities around the world are shared, there is always scope for and interest in collaboration and partnerships for change. Pathways to positive change cannot be superimposed from one context to another, as confirmed in community development, anthropology, international development, private sector development, and other disciplines. While many people still try to apply global approaches or insist on standardized models, those who have actually tried know that context is everything. This is not to deny the benefit of principles for collaboration, shared strategies for thoughtful engagement, and opportunities for sharing models, lessons, or ideas across borders. However, people in any context – 'insiders' – inevitably know the context better than 'outsiders'. Insiders have ultimate responsibility to bring about changes for themselves and success is more probable when leaders and drivers of change are from within communities and organizations.

Readers are likely to be well versed in the benefits of collaboration for achieving change. Genuine partnerships between external and internal stakeholders, combining multiple sources of knowledge and resources, are ideal, especially if they work well. Effective collaboration requires trust and other ingredients which cannot be assumed when groups come together from diverse cultures: trust and respect look different in different cultures. Whenever people and organizations collaborate, issues associated with power, politics, relationships, respect and contrary ideas about the 'best' pathways arise. For collaboration to be the most effective it can be, and for these issues to be effectively negotiated, cross-cultural conversations are essential. Facilitators of change can enable these conversations to take place: culturally capable facilitators in partnerships between insiders and outsiders are thus crucial.

This book seeks to build on existing literature about facilitation, cross-cultural engagement, and change, and in doing so fills a gap related to the intersection of these ideas for practitioners. Some readers may be familiar with two previous books (Rhodes and Antoine, 2013; Rhodes, 2014) focused on connections between cultural value differences and capacity development. Readers of those books will find that this extends those ideas into the broader world of change and roles of facilitators, and hopefully they will find new suggestions.

CHAPTER 1
Introduction

Why do people think that they can bring about change in others' lives? As a practitioner and trainer for community and international development workers for over 30 years, I often ask people what they think they or their organizations are trying to change. Some work on systemic level change, while most engage with people, communities, and organizations. Are they trying to change others' values or behaviour? When they realize both answers are problematic, the discomfort is often palpable. The rich discussions that usually ensue are in part a trigger for this book. If the aim of social and development programs is to change others' behaviour, then the chances of succeeding are low indeed, without both a respectful conversation and shared understanding about the links between values and behaviour in each context. If the aim is to change others' values, then this inevitably and hopefully raises discomfort about the idea of imposing one's own values on others. Like many other aspects of change and culture, of course this is not a binary choice but a complex navigation process with many ideas and people over time and space. This book seeks to contribute to the navigation process by supporting those who are involved in the practice of facilitating change to do so in ways which respect and take account of different cultural values.

Do change facilitators understand others' priorities? It is widely argued that those who have power over others do not understand the lives of people who are expected to change. How can those who seek to bring about change better understand the contexts in which change is sought? How can they better understand the values that are relevant to the context and to the relationships between people involved in change? How can change facilitators support better understanding of the connections between cultural values and changes in behaviour? How can they ensure the people for whom change is expected are at the centre? How can they build shared understanding of change processes and outcomes? Asking these questions and seeking answers will help change facilitators undertake their roles. In particular, efforts to deepen understanding about answers in each specific context will contribute to culturally respectful and effective contributions.

These questions are not new, but insufficient attention has been paid to them and the answers in international development (and to a lesser extent in organizational change and community development). Nearly three decades ago, Robert Klitgaard asked the question 'if culture is important and people have studied culture for a century or more, why don't we have well-developed theories, practical guidelines, and close professional links between those who study culture and those who make and manage development policy?'

(quoted in Foreword in Harrison and Huntington, 2000: xvi). In 2004, a World Bank report noted 'much of the discussion on the role of culture in development has either seen it as a primordial trip, a mystical haze, or a source of hegemonic power' (Rao and Walton, 2004: 3). The report stated that 'a focus on culture is necessary to confront the difficult questions of *what* is valued in terms of well-being, *who* does the valuing, and *why* economic and social factors interact with culture to unequally allocate access to a good life' (Rao and Walton, 2004: 4). More people study this topic now, but systems and structures which drive change-oriented practice in international development still largely ignore links between culture and change.

Achieving change with people from different cultures requires culturally attuned facilitators and collaborators. A key premise of this book is that change facilitators will be more likely to succeed if they have an understanding of their own values, the values of others, how the two may be seen from the others' perspectives, the implications for interactions between societies and people, and the connections between cultural values and how change happens. At a minimum, curiosity about cultural values and an openness to discuss them helps cross-cultural change facilitation. This book seeks to take facilitators beyond that initial level of curiosity (see Chapter 4 on various levels of cultural understanding).

While there is now greater awareness of political aspects of change reflected in more widespread use of political economy analysis in international development (Leftwich, 1995; Serrat, 2017), there is room for equally significant strengthening of cultural understanding. Little attention has been paid to ways in which facilitators contribute to change processes in multicultural settings and in cultural contexts different from their own. Improved awareness will have multiple benefits. First, it will help change facilitators and their respective organizations and funders to better understand their own cultural values and how they are seen from others' perspectives. Second, it will improve the quality of interactions and collaborations. Third, it will give due recognition to the agency and priorities of people whose lives are at the centre of change processes.

What methods are available to support culturally appropriate change and how can facilitators choose among them? Facilitators appear to use a relatively limited and familiar suite of methods, which have largely emerged from predominantly western cultural contexts (in this book, the term 'western' is used to loosely describe relatively high resource regions, such as Europe, north America and Australasia, but the limitations of the term are acknowledged). These methods reflect values of donor countries or funding or policy organizations, more often than not. What other methods might be more comfortable for people with different cultural values to surface and express their ideas and priorities? How might facilitators adjust standard methods to make them more culturally attuned?

To help answer these questions, Part 1 of this book builds a foundational analysis which integrates ideas about change, cultural values, and facilitation.

It broadly reflects double-loop learning (Argyris, 1977), used in organizational change, adult learning, and leadership development, as a means to encourage reflective practice. The reason it is useful here is that it supports the questioning of 'underlying assumptions, values and beliefs behind what we do,' (see Figure 1.1 below): in this case, facilitating change across cultures.

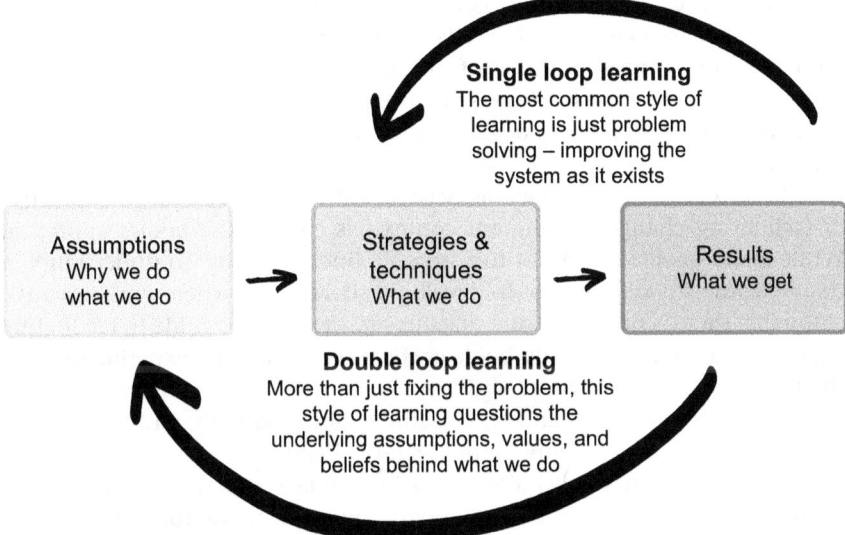

Figure 1.1 Argyris' model of double-loop learning

A cultural values lens is the primary frame of reference. First, cultural value differences and their implications for how people, communities, and organizations view and respond to ideas and experiences associated with change are considered. While this body of work is large, this book applies the lens to the phenomenon of change facilitation. Second, concepts related to the complexity of change processes are addressed through a cultural values lens, with recognition of the relevance of politics and power. This is important for many reasons but particularly because cultural perspectives are often accused of ignoring power issues. Third, facilitation practice and the role of facilitators is discussed, again through a cultural values lens. The concept of culturally attuned change facilitation is proposed as a response to this analysis.

Part 2 of the book takes this analysis and the idea of culturally attuned change facilitation to a practical level. It provides a set of principles to guide practice, a set of interrelated and mutually supportive approaches to deepen shared understanding among those involved in change, and a menu of methods to choose from which I have found from practical experience can support culturally attuned facilitation.

This chapter introduces key terms and frames of reference, drawing from broader community development, organizational development, and international development contexts. A picture to illustrate where facilitators may fit in a change process when working cross-culturally is offered (Figure 3.1).

The context and key terms

Several disciplines offer theories on aspects of the nature and role of change facilitation across cultures. There is no shortage of relevant evidence and guidance but synthesizing ideas from various disciplines, analysing them through different lenses, and relating them to the practical work of change facilitation are necessary to begin to answer the questions which introduce this chapter.

Acknowledging complexity associated with all aspects of the practice of facilitating change in different contexts is core to the book's approach. While many people search for five steps to 'bridge the gap' in understanding or 'overcome the differences' to develop a shared plan when working cross-culturally, there is no single, one -size-fits-all, step-by-step guide to facilitating change across cultures. This book encourages readers to experiment with shedding pre-conceived ideas and assumptions about themselves, the work they do, the communities and organizations they work with, and how change happens. It encourages more emphasis on collaborative learning and living with uncertainty than on building an individual's expertise in translation across cultures. It places more emphasis on how facilitators can support communities and organizations, whatever values they have, and wherever they might be, and how to build collaborative conversations in order to identify and achieve their own priorities, rather than how to get them to comply with others' notions of what is best.

Culture is one of the most complex words in any language. It is defined in multiple ways and used to apply to myriad phenomena. It can be used positively, neutrally, or in ways which are laden with judgement. It commonly encompasses day-to-day aspects of life – how we behave, interact, and communicate, what we wear, our food, ceremonies, our music, art, dance, and theatre. It also includes subjective aspects – what we believe and value, what we collectively determine to be right and wrong, good and bad, how we lead and follow, and how we expect people to behave and the world to be. The interactions between values, norms, and behaviour are complex, contested, inconsistent, and at the same time mightily powerful. Strong links between cultural values and understandings about change are discussed in Chapters 2 and 3.

Change is also one of the most complex and pervasive aspects of modern life and a key focus of many areas of academia, research, and practice. The concept has philosophical, psychological, political, and spiritual elements, as well as the cultural and practical elements which are the focus of this book. Change can be understood in vastly different ways across different disciplines (Krznaric, 2007). For this book, the kinds of change that might be relevant generally fall within the scope of the Sustainable Development Goals (SDGs), i.e. the aspects of life related to well-being, the planet's health, and prosperity for everyone. While some change-related goals are shared, different cultural values influence perceptions of these goals and how best to achieve them. Although the absence of a more definitive scope of change might be problematic for some readers, the principles and approaches included here are potentially useful for most topics and contexts (see Chapter 3).

Facilitation is usually defined in the western world as a process whereby a trained and experienced facilitator, who is not themselves a stakeholder, enables people who are stakeholders to achieve a particular result. The process involves supporting groups of people to undertake steps to achieve a result that is commonly understood and supported by all participants. The result may include a plan (at any level), new knowledge or skills, an agreed approach, a policy, or any other kind of jointly determined 'product'. Most commonly, facilitation is undertaken in meetings or workshops, where participants can hear each other's views and the facilitator can organize negotiations towards a shared outcome. It also may take the shape of longer-term interactions, from institutional twinning arrangements to individuals or teams working together over a certain period. The definition's emphasis on 'outcome' or 'result' suggests more western values, which emphasize task, performance, and achievement, than non-western values, which emphasize relationship and harmony. From the latter's perspective, facilitation processes can be used for building and maintaining harmonious relationships between various people or groups (and settling conflicts and disputes) or building shared understanding about a particular issue or idea. In the latter case, expectations that there will be a definitive product or new outcome may not exist. The term can also be used to describe the provision of leadership without taking the reins of power (Bens, 2005). Various definitions of facilitation and their implications are discussed further in Chapter 5.

People who facilitate change include individuals, teams, or networks operating in various contexts. Change facilitators could work within multicultural communities in their own country or internationally. They may work independently or within organizations such as non-profit agencies, non-government agencies, official development assistance donors, philanthropic foundations, and government ministries. Those who work within multicultural communities include community development workers, social workers, youth workers, and many kinds of service providers. Internationally, people involved in change facilitation include officials in development organizations, development workers, technical specialists/advisors, consultants, program team members, service delivery staff, and volunteers. Few people work as full-time facilitators, but many undertake facilitation as one part of their role. While many specialist facilitators come from western contexts, this book does not assume they all do: therefore, efforts are made to reflect varied cultural values and contexts among facilitators.

A new concept: change facilitation across cultures

A new concept, 'change facilitation across cultures', is offered in this book. It brings together three elements: the need to increase understanding about complex connections between change and cultural values in each context; use of this understanding to inform and shape collaborative engagement between people who are interested in achieving some kind of change; and support for the identification of change priorities and means to achieve them which are culturally relevant to each context. The theory, based on evidence from extensive experience and related literature, posits that this approach will more likely contribute to positive change than the dominant approaches used internationally. It acknowledges the role of power, relationships, and ideas in change, and focuses attention on the role of facilitators in navigating these and related elements.

Change facilitation across cultures encompasses a set of principles, approaches, and practices for facilitators to support positive change in contexts when social and organizational cultural values are not necessarily shared. It draws together existing evidence from relevant disciplines about cultural value differences and the link between values and change (Chapter 2), how change happens and what it looks like through a cultural values lens (Chapter 3), and the role of facilitation within these two contexts (Chapter 4).

Based on analysis of these interconnected elements, a framework to guide change facilitation practice across cultures is offered (Chapter 7). The framework seeks to assist those engaged in change-related facilitation, both to prepare for and undertake their roles. The framework supports facilitators who seek to enable groups of people to achieve the kinds of change they prioritize within their own cultural contexts. It also supports facilitators who work within partnership contexts, where there are cultural value differences and shared objectives across the partners.

For the purposes of this book, cross-cultural, change-oriented collaboration encompasses: a process of self-examination, based on understanding of history and culture and the value of humility; interrogation of the location of and distribution of power in change-related relationships; deepening shared understanding about value differences; and the selection of methods which support the progressive development of trust and more inclusive and egalitarian collaboration.

Complexity

> Human minds are full of concepts and constructs that have been developed and passed down over millennia to make sense of the world around us. The problem is that our world today is full of challenges that have reached unsurpassed levels of complexity and uncertainty, and full of complex systems that are increasingly connected and interdependent. ... systems are so extended and intertwined that it is

> not possible for any single person to have a complete understanding of the system as a whole. These systems still function despite our inability to understand them, for they are self-organising. (McKenzie et al., 2017: 2).

> What is needed is not the privileging of culture as something that works on its own, but the integration of culture in a wider picture, in which culture, seen in a dynamic and interactive way, is one important influence among many others. Attempts at integration have to pay particular attention to heterogeneity of each broadly defined culture, the interdependence between different cultures, and the vibrant nature of cultural evolutions. (Sen in Rao and Walton, 2004: 55)

Any consideration of change across cultures is inevitably complex. The process of bringing about change in order to make the world a better place, where there are different views about change, about what 'a better place' means, and about how to achieve improvements conjures up numerous ideas. Just about every aspect of cross-cultural change facilitation includes elements of unpredictability, with multiple influences across multiple systems interacting with each other differently at each time or place or with different people. The phenomenon or practice of cross-cultural change facilitation is, in effect, absurdly complex: a single and coherent approach or set of 'best practice' methods is unrealistic, unachievable, and inappropriate.

Ideas about complexity have entered into some aspects of development practice, but dominant approaches and most development systems cling to more linear, cause and effect, or results-based management-type thinking. What insights can complexity theory or complexity sciences provide about how to proceed in this area of work? They seem to have a great deal to offer, given that the SDGs encompass changes to social behaviour, systems, organizations, leadership, and partnerships, and that in every context in which change takes place, these and other elements and the way they interact vary widely.

Some attention has been paid to complexity theory in the development sector over the past two decades. Those who have addressed the connections between complexity theory and social change, such as Ramalingam (2013) and Barder (2012), have encouraged greater understanding of the reality of complexity for development programming. A fascinating map of complexity sciences (Castellani, 2018) describes the many threads of thinking since the 1940s, but few of these myriad models have been linked to development practice. Those that have been used more widely include the Cynefin model (Snowden, 2011), problem-driven iterative adaptation (Andrews et al., 2012) and complex adaptive systems (McEvoy et al., 2016).

Without diving too deeply into the world of complexity theory, there is value in recognizing that in almost all contexts in which change is expected to take place, links between ideas, actions, and results are unpredictable to varying degrees. Societies, social systems, and most contexts in which change occurs are empirically complex. It is obvious that many factors influence change and adaptation, and there is also plenty of evidence that the interaction of many factors differs between contexts, for multiple reasons. Cultural values are just one of the influences on change, with some cultures more comfortable with change than others. At the same time, change is often identified as a shift in cultural values themselves. In reality, it is not possible to find rules or approaches to predict with certainty when working in dynamic, non-linear, and emergent contexts and systems. For cross-cultural change facilitation, acknowledgement of complexity is essential.

Cross-cultural change facilitation encompasses ideas, systems, people, and relationships, many of which involve power, politics, and contestation. The first draft of nearly each paragraph of this book included a reference to 'many different perspectives', 'multiple views', 'diverse understandings' or 'contested ideas'. To minimize repetition, the use of these terms has been reduced, but in practically every topic area, complexities are involved. Change facilitators need to continuously develop the ability to work with uncertainty while supporting people and organizations to better understand the world around them to bring about change that makes sense to them (see Chapter 4).

The degree to which people understand and organizations deal with complexity is influenced by multiple factors. For individuals, these include cultural values, socio-economic status, access to education, genetics, psychology, and one's stage in life, for example. A person is not a passive recipient of these influences but has agency to interact with, reflect on, and form views about their role and how they may want to interact with and influence what happens. However, the degree to which individuals are expected to have agency varies across different cultural environments. For example, in an individualist society, a person is expected to exercise autonomy with respect to achieving their own goals or making a contribution to a better world. In a collectivist society, individuals are expected to collaborate with and show loyalty to their group members, make decisions based on their potential impact on others, and not leave members of the group behind.

The range of theoretical models, frames of reference, methods, and tools to help make sense of our world and its challenges can easily overwhelm a practitioner. Facilitators may have expertise in one or two disciplines but be required to grasp ideas and practices associated with other areas of learning. For example, a water and sanitation or public health education expert may build appropriate systems in their own cultural context but may not have been exposed to ways of facilitating systems development in another. A leader in one context may assume their proactive leadership skills are universally valued, and then strike issues when they practise these in a different context, for example one which is more or less collaborative and consultative.

Questions associated with cross-cultural change facilitation also involve varied levels of complexity. Depending on the context, big questions may need to be asked, such as 'why do we think we should or can contribute to changing others?'; 'why are we doing this?'; and 'what is the point of working at the community level when we cannot change the system that is causing this problem?' At other times, we may look for inspiration to work as a leader, a supporter, or in partnership with internal leaders to address a new issue, or seek a new way, or the 'right way' to facilitate or bring about a particular change. Perhaps, we may simply be faced with the question 'which method should I use?'

Acknowledging complexity is not an excuse to avoid clarity, but confirmation that a simple guide or set of steps or checklist of requirements is not possible. A cultural lens is one of several lenses that apply to any change facilitation process, not the only one.

A cultural values lens

> Many of the tools we have been using to navigate the world are simply not working well … problems have arisen not because those tools are wrong or useless. They are not. The problem is such tools are incomplete; they are used without an awareness of culture and context, created with a sense of tunnel vision and built assuming that the world can be neatly bounded or captured by a single set of parameters. (Tett, 2021: xiii)

This book seeks to deepen understanding of cultural value differences, including an analysis of power, as a basis for supporting positive and developmental change. In order to do this, the book applies a 'cultural values lens' to ideas about the facilitation of change. This reflects the premise that cultures have different values (cultures are often defined by these) which influence how people, organizations, and institutions (including government) function as well as how change is understood.

Change facilitators are predominantly engaged in issues related to behaviour, norms, or values, and how information changes these in one or many ways. Each of these are connected, as illustrated in Figure 1.2 below. Change-related agendas are often not clear about the particular level of changes sought or about the connections between one layer and another. For example, a public health campaign may seek to change the behaviour of people in their selection of food that contributes to health problems (e.g. obesity, diabetes), without understanding that food selection is strongly connected to norms about community cohesion or deeper values about mutual obligations within communities to traditions, leaders, or older community members, or about social change.

Facilitators who work across cultures need to be cognisant of their identity, their own values, and those of the people with whom they are working. Through a political historical lens, they also need to be aware of the kinds of racism, oppression, and discrimination inherent in relationships

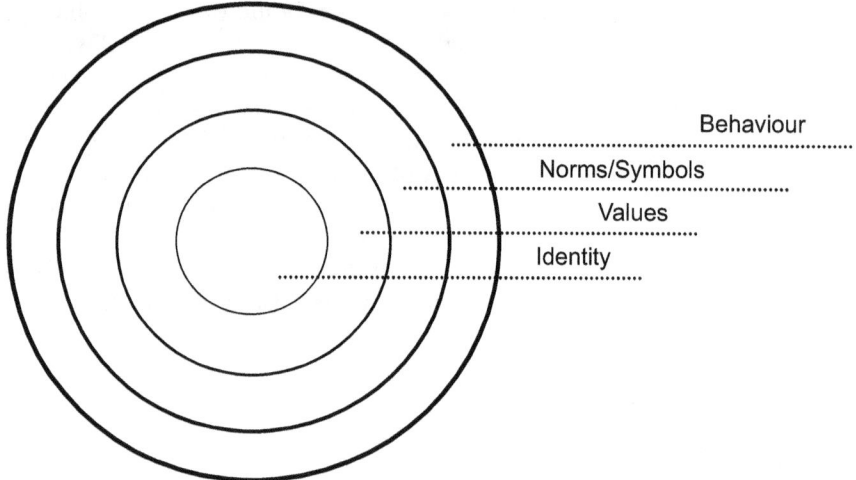

Figure 1.2 Relationship between cultural identity, values, norms, and behaviour

between different peoples of the world. They need to continue to uncover the unconscious values that they hold, which influence their behaviour, throughout their practice. This will help them become more effective facilitators. Through a cultural lens, they need to know how their identity and their intervention may be understood by others from different cultures in each setting. This recognizes that all cultures have values (even if different, dynamic, and contested) and these values influence perceptions of others with different values. A person from a culture which perceives hierarchy to be important is more likely to look at another through a hierarchical lens, while a person from a culture where egalitarian values are valued will more likely regard another through this lens.

For facilitators to work effectively across cultures, they need deep awareness of the links between identity, values, norms, and behaviour, and how these may differ in each context. In Figure 1.2, identity sits at the core, surrounded by cultural values: this could broadly apply to people, teams, communities, organizations, and societies. This implies that one's identity and values are at the centre of entities and that they inform the nature of each entity. This link is not necessarily absolute and consistent over time, nor agreed upon through different disciplinary lenses, but nonetheless highly significant. The only way to find out about the links in each context is to stimulate discussion with those who are there at the time, preferably in respectful, trust-based conversations. There is no text-book for this work, but plenty of evidence that respect and trust are crucial.

Norms in each context are shaped by deeply held cultural values and can be understood as 'the way things are done around here'. Symbols are also a powerful element of cultures, representing particular ideas that are specific to each cultural context (see Chapter 9 – section on symbols).

Behaviour in a society or organization is significantly influenced by norms (Green, 2016). Ignoring information about norms risks irrelevance at least, and failure at worst.

At an individual level, a person's core values have a significant influence on their identity and the way that person behaves. If they believe in gender equality, for example, they will likely behave in ways which demonstrate, illustrate, and confirm this belief. If they value status, and happen to hold a powerful or high-status position, then they are more likely to act in a way which demonstrates this power. If they do not hold power over others, then they are likely to act accordingly, deferring to others and holding their own views to themselves in order to avoid those in power losing face. If a person places a high value on the wisdom and authority of senior people, they are more likely to behave respectfully towards them, than criticize or undermine them. The consequences of showing disrespect to leaders in a hierarchical cultural context are often severe.

Core values of an organization influence the behaviour of its leaders and staff as well as what the organization looks like from the outside. For example, a community-based organization which values justice for marginalized people will more likely practise in inclusive ways than an exclusive one which values hierarchy. Leaders are commonly expected to set, influence, or uphold organizational values and therefore expected to have skills to communicate and promote particular values. When values are applied successfully, they can make an organization incredibly successful. Without them, 'anything goes' and the daily news is replete with stories of organizations which have poor or wrong values, poor leadership, or lack of consistent application of 'good' values.

At a community or society level, core values shape how people behave and thus what that society looks like from the outside (Hofstede, 1980). Communities and organizations are not always conscious of values: the values that may be on display may not be the sum total of a community's or society's values. Values emphasizing the centrality of maintaining relationships, for example, mean that within that society, there will be norms about appropriate behaviour and people are likely to behave in ways which prioritize the quality and maintenance of relationships. Values are not the only influence and the presence of particular values in a culture does not mean that they are consistently or universally applied, but they are a significant driver of life in every cultural context.

Are we explicit or underhanded in efforts to change others' values? If we are seeking to change others' norms or behaviour, are we aware of the links between core values and current norms and behaviour? Is it realistic to simply change others' values, norms, or behaviour because other ideas are perceived to be 'better' or more 'modern'? Do we respectfully engage in a conversation about whether values are still fit for purpose, considering our own values as well as others? Chapter 3 considers the relevance of cultural values for cross-cultural change facilitation.

Facilitators' roles

The phenomenon of change facilitation and its scope have changed over recent decades. Increased demand for and valuing of facilitation have altered expectations about what is possible, and the number of guides and specialists has proliferated. When a cross-cultural lens is applied to change facilitation, important questions arise which often do not appear in guides. They are rarely considered by government agencies and philanthropists, which largely determine change agendas around the world. Such questions vary from those that are critical to those worth considering. Also, since facilitators often represent a link between different cultures, their self-awareness and ability to translate and navigate between different cultural values are important. This is discussed in Chapter 5.

The focus of this book is on facilitators' many roles, including: to acknowledge and work with complexities; to understand contexts in which they are working; to work successfully with and support others to understand more about their situation and opportunities; to select a facilitation pathway; and set off, commonly without knowing the destination. Importantly, a facilitator is also likely to encounter different expectations about their role. Facilitators contracted by a funded organization may be expected to resolve complex issues which are not addressed by the organization itself through fear or lack of knowledge or skill. Participants in a workshop may expect the facilitator to drive changes which they wish to avoid themselves for a range of reasons. Cultural values in different contexts shape expectations of facilitators' roles, which need to be better understood by facilitators themselves, as well as by contracting and partner organizations.

Facilitators' identity

The identity of facilitators is worthy of consideration, particularly given current movements related to racism at a global level, localization, particularly in the humanitarian sector, and decolonization of the international development sector. The dominant pattern has been that facilitators are sourced from the country where funding originates, usually higher-resourced contexts. Thus, it is more likely that facilitators have cultural values which are found in donor countries and have good access to resources such as guides, and books like this one. It is also more likely, but not always the case, that facilitators are white-skinned and participants in facilitated change processes are not. Prior to the Black Lives Matter movement, which had a high profile internationally during the drafting of this book, this issue would not have been given much consideration. At a minimum, facilitators and the organizations which commission or employ them need to be cognisant of how they are perceived and the varied degrees of resource inequality between facilitators and participants in many cases. A view that facilitators are seen as 'neutral' may not be shared across different contexts.

Understanding cultural value differences is useful, if not essential, for building collaboration in any context. Change facilitators who work cross-culturally must examine the cultural and racial issues that influence their roles and the contexts in which they work. Collaboration between people from different backgrounds is essential for change and must be based on understanding of and respect for diversity. Differences between people that are based on skin colour and its relationship to power are important. Power is certainly one of the most important issues across all aspects of change and all cultural contexts, so facilitators must be deeply aware of these issues, even if they are still navigating how to address them. Different frames of reference produce different pathways towards change, but the end game is a world in which people are included, valued, respected, empowered, and have a sense of belonging.

Menu of methods

Many sources of methods are available for facilitators to use, but none appear to have been compiled and considered through a cultural lens. Part 2 includes approaches and methods which may be used with individuals, teams, partnerships, communities, organizations, networks, and other groups of people. Each has strengths and limitations and degrees of relevance. When working cross-culturally, it is not always possible to know in advance which methods will be best suited or to choose from a full menu of options. The menu of approaches and methods is intended as a resource for those who find themselves in a position of contributing to or supporting change. The author's examples of their use in the international development context are provided to illustrate benefits in different settings and are supported by others' studies and reflections.

The selected methods reflect this book's intention to contribute to deeper thinking and shifting practice that takes account of the fact that we do not all share the same world view, that the world is complex and dynamic, and that *cooperation between different people is the only way forward*. It seeks to support those who want to bring about, or more humbly to contribute to, change, as well as assist those who may be engaged in their own change processes or be the focus of others' change agendas.

PART 1

CHAPTER 2
Cultural values and change

> Culture is one of the most powerful forces in our world (Brownlee, n.d.)
>
> What people see as normal, desirable, or aberrant determines their sense of right and wrong, and can both drive and hold back the search for social justice. (Green, 2016)

Change facilitators need to be well equipped to make their contributions relevant and thus more likely to succeed. If they understand the influence of cultural values in the locations and in the partnerships within which change is expected to occur, their chances of making a useful contribution are greater. At a practical level, this means thinking, planning, and facilitating processes which take account of value differences. How can facilitators understand different cultural values? How can they take account of cultural differences when planning facilitation events?

An example might help: say you are asked to facilitate a two-day workshop to plan for a new phase of collaboration between an Australian non-government organization (NGO) and a group of medical personnel in the Solomon Islands, in the Pacific. The purpose of the program is to strengthen training for medical workers, to increase the ability of the health system to meet citizens' changing health needs. Imagine you are a facilitator from Australia, Canada, or New Zealand who has worked in the Solomon Islands before. You may have some experience with the medical profession so feel comfortable working with doctors. The NGO personnel want to participate as partners, rather than run the workshop themselves, so they seek a 'neutral' facilitator. In planning the workshop, there are many issues to consider. The influence of cultural values in the Solomon Islands context and on the particular organizational setting for medical personnel is just one of these. What values shape the way Solomon Islanders view power, status, decision-making, service, learning, and change, for example? How do Solomon Islanders prefer to participate in workshops and what cultural values influence doctors' approaches to training more junior doctors or differentiating between doctors of all genders? How might doctors' roles influence their engagement with a foreign NGO? How might a facilitated workshop maximize benefits for all those involved?

This chapter discusses the kinds of cultural values issues to be considered in planning a workshop such as the one illustrated above or other change-related process across cultures.

Cultural values

Cultural values can be understood from vastly different perspectives: these varied frames of reference are often contested. Even if one model is found which appeals, it is likely to highlight the diversity and dynamic nature of values. It may have been developed within a particular discipline and therefore is challenging to apply in others. Existing theories about cultural values have not generally been developed to support the practice of facilitating broad social change, although some reflect understanding about organizations and leadership.

Understanding cultural value differences is important for those who work with people and organizations in a modern world, and essential for those who seek to facilitate change. Even though there is no simple model to explain cultural value differences or pathways to such understanding, starting off on a learning journey is highly recommended. Continuous learning about oneself, one's world, and connections between values and behaviour is also essential. This chapter addresses contemporary elements in cultural values thinking and applies a values lens to change-related themes.

Ideas about cultural values are relevant to all aspects of behavioural, institutional, and systemic change. Cultural values are influenced themselves by many factors, such as geography, psychology, and history, as well as an influence on how societies, institutions, and organizations function. Interconnections between cultural values, power and politics, religious beliefs, ideas, and people – and thus the phenomenon of change – are myriad.

Understanding cultural value differences across the world is relevant to the ways that the concept of change is perceived in different contexts. Such understanding is critical to questions about who defines, leads, and drives change, what kinds of change are prioritized, and how change happens in different contexts. This is particularly the case when there is an expectation that 'positive' change is sought and must be delivered to meet certain goals, such as the SDGs. The same change can be seen positively in some cultural contexts and negatively in others, just as it can be understood positively and negatively by different disciplines and various individuals and groups within a country or community (see Chapter 3). Cultural value differences are just one set of influences on how change is understood or prioritized, but a powerful force in almost all cases.

In the academic world, economists and organizational change specialists give increasing attention to the role of social and cultural factors in shaping human behaviour. More analyses of globalization and universal concepts of human rights recognize the influence of cultural values on how change happens. For example, Rao and Walton noted 'in the world of policy, culture is increasingly being viewed as a commonplace, malleable fact of life that matters as much as economics or politics to the process of development' (Rao and Walton, 2004: 3). They argued that 'a focus on culture enables difficult questions to be answered about what is valued, who does the valuing and why economic and social factors interact with culture, resulting in access to well-being and the 'good life' being allocated unequally'. (Rao and Walton, 2004: 4).

Within organizations, there has been a great deal of study about connections between cultural values and change. In one of many similar studies, Yukl et al., (2003: 12), sought to understand the role of cultural value differences on tactics used for gaining approval from a boss for a proposed change, or for resisting a change initiated by a boss. They found:

> Most of the significant cross-cultural differences in perception of tactic effectiveness appear to be consistent with differences in cultural values and traditions. The Swiss and American managers had similar ratings on most of the tactics for which there were significant cross-cultural differences. In general, the western managers had a higher evaluation of direct, task-oriented tactics, whereas the Chinese managers had a higher evaluation of tactics involving personal relations, an informal approach, and avoidance of confrontation.

Putting neat boundaries around cultural values is challenging; however, research about cultural value differences is widely used to inform global trade, multinational leadership, and business development (Hofstede, 1980; House et al., 2004; Hofstede and Hofstede, 2005). Other disciplines use different frameworks and models to articulate differences. This book takes the basic elements included in research entitled *Global Leadership and Organizational Behavior Effectiveness (*known as The GLOBE Study) (House et al., 2004) and applies them beyond the original focus (leadership and organizations) to cross-cultural change facilitation. Focusing for a moment on what is meant by 'culture' is useful, before moving to an analysis of the connections between cultural values and change.

What is culture?

> Culture is shared understandings made manifest in act and artifact (Redfield 1948 quoted in House et al., 2004: xiii).

> Culture sets the rules for individual action (Hartley and Potts, 2014: 1)

Culture is one of the most complex words in the English language. It is understood differently between disciplines, including those which engage with change processes. This section considers key aspects of culture to inform facilitators' thinking and practice.

Anthropology, the study of contemporary human cultural lives, has different and sometimes competing schools of thought about culture, at least in literature produced within the English-speaking world (Tett, 2021). For example, social anthropology considers each ethnographic context to be unique so that theory cannot be drawn from them (Moore, 1993), while cultural anthropology focuses on the study of cultural variation among humans, implying patterns can be found.

In psychology, varied approaches for understanding culture also prevail. For example, Peng et al., (2001) consider three perspectives of culture in relation to human inference – the value tradition, the self tradition, and the theory tradition – and suggest a synthesis of these is 'both possible and preferable' for helping to understand how values and concepts of self interact. In lay terms, they suggest that there are strengths and limitations in the common frameworks for understanding how people and cultural values influence each other. This is useful to keep in mind for all disciplinary frames of reference.

Definitions from the development and change disciplines are relevant. For example, Rao and Walton (2004: 4) offer this definition:

> Culture is about relationality – the relationships among individuals within groups, among groups, and between ideas and perspectives. Culture is concerned with identity, aspiration, symbolic exchange, coordination, and structures and practices that serve relational ends, such as ethnicity, ritual, heritage, norms, meanings and beliefs ... [It is] a set of contested attributes, constantly in flux, both shaping and being shaped by social and economic aspects of human interaction.

Hofstede (1980: 1) defined culture as 'software of the mind' covering 'all those patterns of thinking, feeling and acting' which are 'shared with people who live or lived within the same social environment, which is where it was learned'. He distinguishes culture from 'human nature on one side and from an individual's personality on the other, although exactly where the borders lie between nature and culture, and between culture and personality, is a matter of discussion' (Hofstede 1980: 1). Hofstede's research about cultural values has been updated (Hofstede and Hofstede, 2005), is still dynamic, and used widely in organizational change, leadership, and business development.

The GLOBE Study is a seminal piece of research on the link between cultural values, organizations, and leadership undertaken by 170 researchers in 62 countries (House et al., 2004). Finding the study of cross-cultural research as 'tricky and difficult' the GLOBE Study identified and delved into many similar cultural dimensions identified by Hofstede. At the time of writing, the GLOBE Study is being expanded and updated. Hofstede and the GLOBE Study provide the main language and concepts related to cultural value differences included in this book.

Most will agree that cultural values and norms are dynamic over time. They can seem 'fixed' in the minds of those who hold them or those seen as 'intransigent' – illustrated by those who can see only one 'truth' or one definition of right or wrong – but are also influenced by other people and by experience. The idea that societies have these values or norms and that they can be negotiated and documented underpins the formalization of international treaties and agreements, including the SDGs. Agreements reached in these documents are often referred to as 'normative standards' in the sense that they represent apparent agreement about what is good or desirable or permissible. For example, UN Women report their work on youth and gender equality is 'guided by key global norms and standards that recognize the human rights of young women and girls' (UN Women, n.d.) which appears optimistic at best, given there are vast variations between countries on the rights of young women and girls. Similarly, the Convention on the Rights of Persons with Disabilities (CRPD) includes a series of principles and values that are not at all yet shared but which are expected to be applied progressively now that the Convention is ratified by most governments. While these values and norms may have been agreed upon by governments at a global level, all cultures do not necessarily share them at the national level: change facilitators are often tasked with bringing about changes related to these values.

Polyculturalism

Some change facilitators with relatively high levels of cultural awareness may find value in considering the concept of polyculturalism and how it might inform facilitation practice. Defined as the 'belief that cultures are dynamically interconnected and mutually influencing each other historically and in contemporary times' (Bernardo et al., 2019: 1), the concept is in part a reaction to the argument that multiculturalism creates more separation than inclusion. The concept includes the view that cultural contact and borrowing are the norm (Bernardo et al., 2013). Polyculturalism enables each of us to acknowledge that we may hold values from a range of sources, accumulated over generations and reflecting complex interactions between people and ideas. The term assumes that culture is an important part of a person's social identity, but that culture is not a rigidly bounded construct and, instead, that it is a dynamic concept that changes because of the interconnections and influences among cultures (Morris et al., 2015). 'Cultures have been forever fusing, exchanging ideas, and practices. As a result, each of us is a tangled skein of cultural influences, even if we identify with a single cultural group. Our music, cuisines, religions and folkways are all cultural mixtures' (Kelley, 1999; Prashad, 2001, quoted in Haslam, 2017: 1).

The implications of this concept are psychological at the individual level and potentially useful for those involved in team, organizational, and broader changes. As cultural intelligence requires ongoing conversations about cultural values, in each context, these discussions can consider polyculturalism as an idea to support shared understanding and achievement of shared goals.

Third space thinking

Facilitators with a high degree of cultural understanding may also consider 'third space thinking' as a frame of reference for understanding culture and applying it to practice. An early writer on this topic, Homi Bhabha, wrote *The Location of Culture* (1994) and it has now been considered in other disciplines.

Bhabha's post-colonial theoretical writing *inter alia* describes how cultures influence each other, in various ways, particularly those that have colonized and been colonized. According to Bhabha, the four main ways that cultures influence each other are: liminally, hybridity, mimicry, and ambivalence. Bhabha weaves philosophy, literature, cultural studies, and other disciplines into his writing; his explanations are described by some as dense and obscure and by others as enlightening and paradigm-shifting. He describes a third space, which is neither the culture of the colonizer nor the colonized but influenced by both. He questions the full dominance of colonizing cultures, saying that there was always a sense of anxiety, which enables the dominated to fight back and resist power (Bhabha, 1994).

The concept of hybridity is a central theme in Bhabha's work: he argues that each person is unique and their identity is a mix of different influences, shaped by the community in which they live, communicate, and learn. In an interview, Bhabha said that 'all forms of culture are continually in a process of hybridity' that 'displaces the histories that constitute it, and sets up new structures of authority, new political initiative. The process of cultural hybridity gives rise to something different, something new and unrecognizable, a new area of negotiation of meaning and representation' (Rutherford 1998: 211). Bhabha's premise is that categorizing people by particular identities is no longer meaningful, and there is a third space which is 'between' dominant structures and systems.

Both third space thinking and the idea of polyculturalism highlight that cultures influence each other. Third space thinking can potentially contribute to practical political change beyond the level of the individual, namely by acknowledging that there is a potential third space between cultures in which the 'baggage' of cultures (i.e. formal systems and definitions of identity and power) does not apply as constraints or limits. In broader social sciences, the term has come to refer to a space between different formal systems and settings, where people can operate without these constraints or limits.

The idea of third space thinking may be interesting for facilitators engaging in modern society, working 'beyond' categories which have been inherited from historical experience and identities imposed by others, but the practicalities are unclear. Bhabha's work can be variously interpreted, but is not readily accessible to most community development or international development organizations and systems. Given increasing awareness of post-colonial experience and shifts in world power, Bhabha's thinking supports facilitators to reflect on the fluidity of cultures, how cultures are influenced by others, and how boundaries between cultures and cultural identity can be contested at many levels.

While the rest of this chapter refers to frameworks for understanding cultural value differences, in order to promote better collaboration, Bhabha challenges the idea that such categorizations are useful and suggests the distinctions are not as defined as they may have been in the past. For example, he said that 'the assumption that at some level all forms of cultural diversity may be understood on the basis of a particular universal concept, whether it be "human being", "class" or "race", can be both very dangerous and very limiting in trying to understand the ways in which cultural practices construct their own systems of meaning and social organisation' (Rutherford, 1998: 209). Finding a practical way forward with this lens is not straightforward. Keeping in mind that boundaries between cultures and cultural identity are contestable and that change processes may be supported if this is understood more widely may be useful for some. That is, if people are in a position where they are supported to imagine a future without the constraints and limits of the systems and cultures in which they exist, they may be able to develop more creative and exciting ideas for change. Suggesting that power issues can be put aside in a third space is largely unrealistic, however. Facilitation approaches that seek to generate a third space which is different from dominant cultures and which may enable people to come together while limiting or avoiding the idea of one dominating the other may be desirable for some practitioners and not for others.

Third space thinking may also be a useful lens for considering complexities associated with poverty, social exclusion, and social inclusion, such as why people behave differently in various contexts. It could potentially help predict what sort of initiatives would more effectively ameliorate poverty and exclusion, but would require strong and deep relationships in which such analysis could occur. Without strong trust and in certain contexts, challenging the status quo could result in harm to those with low power. It can also be argued that when people from more egalitarian cultures are facilitating discussions in more hierarchical cultures about challenging those in power, they could be simply maintaining the colonial pattern of imposing values on other cultures.

Third space theory is used in a variety of disciplines for different purposes, including to explore and understand the spaces 'in between' two or more discourses, conceptualizations, or binaries. For example, in psychology, it is used to connect ideas about an individual's identity and the multiple societies in which they live. In education, it is used to promote the merging of students' cultural capital and the formal content of the curriculum in a classroom setting or as a potential research methodology (Jordan and Elsden-Clifton, 2014). In the discourse of dissent, third space has been interpreted as either the space where the oppressed plot their liberation; or the space where oppressed and oppressor are able to come together, free (maybe only momentarily) of oppression itself (Bhabha, 1994). Soja (1996) considered first space to refer to the material space, second space to refer to mental space, and third space is a space where everything comes together, extending beyond these spaces to intermesh the binaries that characterize the spaces.

In summary, there are multiple frames of reference on culture, each with something potentially useful for facilitators of change. At a minimum, these perspectives challenge us all to continually learn and reflect and to encourage others to do the same. Research by Hofstede (1980), Hofstede and Hofstede (2005), and the GLOBE Study (House et al., 2004) provides relatively accessible, evidence-based, and transportable theory about cultural value differences. It is used as a source of ideas and terminology for this book, and has been well tested in practice through training and consultancy practice in multiple settings. Importantly, efforts made to describe cultural differences simply as differences, without judgement about good or bad, right or wrong, are critical, as are efforts to explain why people may well see others' values as good or bad, right or wrong.

Terminology on interaction between people from different cultures

Terms used to describe relationships and interactions between people with different cultural values or identities vary widely. For example, the terms interracial, intercultural, cross-cultural or multicultural have proponents and critics. The concept of interracial collaboration focuses largely on redressing power relationships based on race. Other terms focus more on cultural value differences, building trust, and effective collaboration and seeking to address unequal power relationships in various ways. In this book, recognition is given to the limitations of each term, particularly in relation to unequal power. Emphasis is given to the benefits of understanding cultural values that differ between entities and how to support conversations about value differences that contribute to change-oriented action.

What role do cultural values have?

Cultural values influence a very wide range of human behaviour, as summarized in Figure 2.1

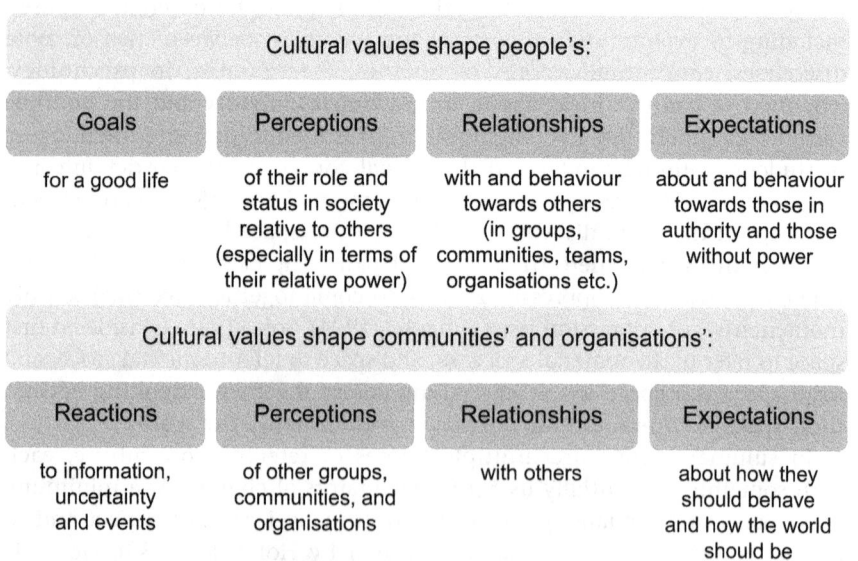

Figure 2.1 Key influences of culture on human and organizational behaviour

Box 2.1 Example of the value of raising cultural awareness in change contexts

A series of capacity development workshops was commissioned for nearly 100 Australian and Solomon Islands officials involved in a large multi-year change-oriented program in the law and justice sector. As part of the workshops, the facilitator included a basic introduction to cultural value differences. Discussions in the workshop were rich and informative: many reported 'light-bulb moments'. Several Solomon Islands participants reported afterwards that discussions about cultural value differences between Australia and Solomon Islands led them to understand the motivation of the Australian officials and the purpose of their presence, for the first time, after decades of collaboration. They said that this new understanding would significantly influence their future engagement with the Australian officials and their own sense of agency in their organisations and in relation to the priority changes sought.

Given their potential for wide-reaching influence, people involved in change processes should seek to understand both their own cultural values and the values of those with whom they are working. Since a large proportion of those involved in change processes work with people from different cultures, the skills to navigate differences across cultures, including collaboration, negotiating partnerships, facilitation, inclusion, managing conflict, and assessing changes over time, are also essential. Importantly, facilitators of change could also contribute to increasing cultural awareness of participants in change processes, so the latter are better able to understand the motivations of change facilitators. Box 2.1 is an example of the power of this idea.

In the business world there is now widespread recognition of the importance of culture for success, but other sectors are a little further behind. 'A business's culture can catalyze or undermine success' (Corritore et al., 2020) illustrates the kind of clarity on this point found in journals such as the *Harvard Business Review*. Hopefully, there will be greater recognition of the value of collaborating across cultures to counter increasing nationalistic tendencies in the early 21st century.

Cultural value differences

A body of research in the discipline of organizational change since the 1980s has sought to understand and describe cultural value differences underpinning societies, organizations, and leaders across the world. These values have been identified as shapers or influencers of many aspects of life, development, and change. Trompenaars and Hampden-Turner (1997); Hofstede (1980); the GLOBE Study (House et al., 2004), and Hofstede and Hofstede (2005) have all proposed various categories and labels to describe these differences. Cultural value dimensions from the GLOBE Study descriptions are illustrated in Figure 2.2 and briefly explained below (see also Rhodes and Antoine, 2013; Rhodes, 2014). The remainder of this chapter considers the consequences of various cultural value differences for change-related ideas.

26   FACILITATING CHANGE ACROSS CULTURES

Cultural dimensions globe study

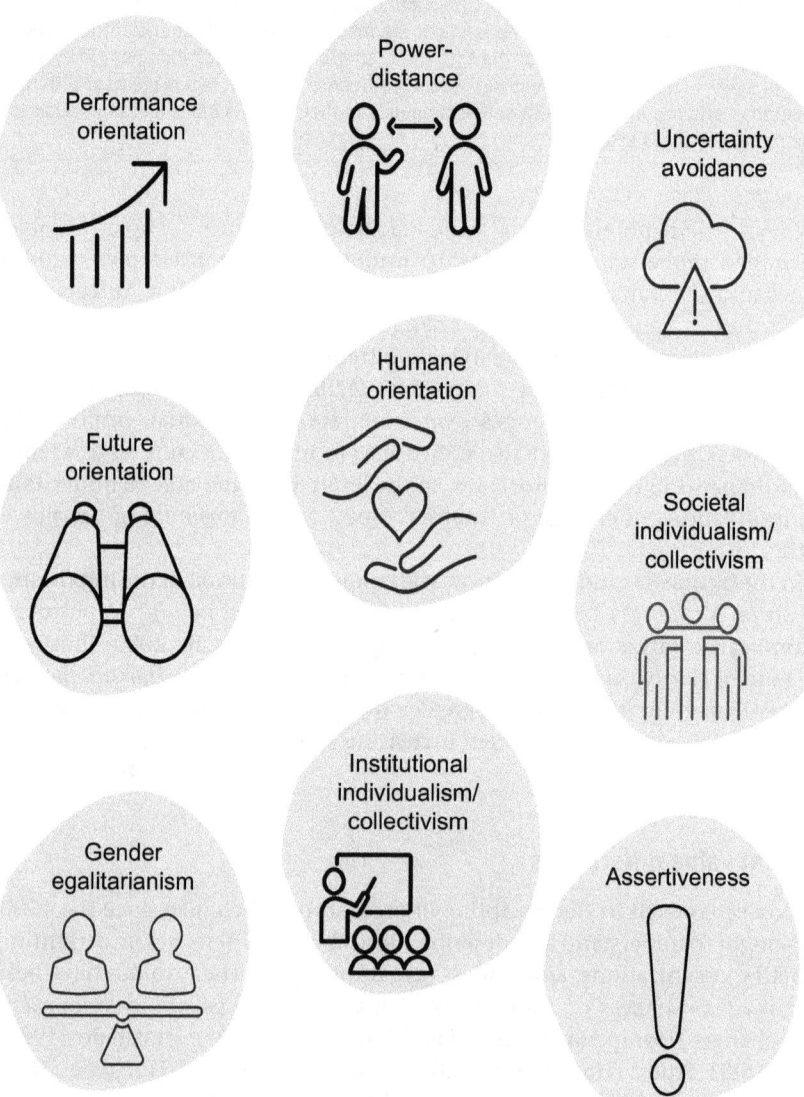

Figure 2.2 Cultural dimensions in the GLOBE study
Source: Graphic compiled by Sumarlinah Raden Winoto and Antonia Mochan, based on cultural values identified in the GLOBE Study (House et al., 2004)

Cultural value dimensions in Figure 2.2 are briefly explained below:

Power Distance (Low to High): the extent to which a community accepts and endorses authority, power differences, and status privileges.

- A low power distance culture generally seeks to reduce the gap between those with power and those without – through language, social, and political systems.
- A high power distance culture generally seeks to maintain order by defining and rewarding those with power.

Collectivism and Individualism: the extent to which decision-making is shaped and prioritized by individual or collective factors (either at social or organizational/institutional levels)

- An individualist culture promotes the belief that everyone is equal/ should be treated equally and is generally expected to make choices for themselves in their interests.
- A collectivist culture encourages people to make decisions which reflect a group's interests (an extended family, community, tribe, religion, or nation, for example) and where there is a sense of mutual obligation for members of a group.

Humane Orientation (Low to High): the extent to which concern for other people is prioritized.

- A culture with low humane orientation emphasizes more self-interest and self-enhancement.
- A culture with high humane orientation promotes fairness, more selfless behaviour, an emphasis on others' well-being, and stronger affiliation with others.

Uncertainty Avoidance (Low to High): the degree to which societies tolerate ambiguity or uncertainty about the issues affecting life.

- A culture which is low on uncertainty avoidance prioritizes risk-taking and innovation by people and organizations, on the basis that change is an expected and positive phenomenon and that it is okay to not know what might happen in reality.
- A culture which is high on uncertainty avoidance is more likely to prioritize the status quo and the maintenance of existing processes and systems, on the basis that the 'devil we know is better than the devil we don't!'.

Assertiveness (Low to High): the degree to which societies support and encourage people to be forthright, tough and direct when expressing views, including about cultural values.

- A culture which is low on assertiveness prioritizes humility, modesty, subtlety, and indirect communications and consider that competition is largely undesirable.

- A culture which is high on assertiveness prioritizes more direct communications, competition, tough behaviour, and the articulation of success.

Gender Egalitarianism (Low to High): the degree to which societies define roles for people based on gender.

- A culture which is low on gender egalitarianism has highly defined roles for different genders.
- A culture which is high on gender egalitarianism is relatively less patriarchal in all spheres of life and decision-making.

Future Orientation (Low to High): the degree to which societies are prepared to forgo short-term gratification for long-term rewards.

- A culture which is low on future orientation tends to prioritize short-term spending, plans and gains or 'instant gratification', and promote leaders who focus on maintaining routines.
- A culture which is high on future orientation tends to prioritize saving for the future, flexibility and adaptability and longer-term planning, and promote leaders who are visionary and lead people through uncertainty.

Performance Orientation (Low to High): the degree to which a society encourages innovation, high level performance, and quality outputs.

- A culture which is low on performance orientation tends to prioritize seniority in the selection of leaders, as well as maintaining stability of existing systems and ideas.
- A culture which is high on performance orientation gives more attention to merit-based systems, quality standards, the contestation of ideas, and the achievement of 'better results'.

These dimensions of values are all relevant to the phenomenon of change. Deeply held cultural values shape ideas about and responses to the phenomenon of change, as well as the nature of particular changes in each context, including multicultural settings. The discussion below addresses aspects of cultural values deemed most relevant to the phenomenon of change.

Cultures' degree of comfort with change

Hofstede (1980) first described the concept of *uncertainty avoidance* to distinguish between values found in different cultures related to change. He defined this to mean the extent to which a society, organization, or group relies on social norms, rules, and procedures to alleviate unpredictability of future events. He identified that cultures could be found along a spectrum from those which were relatively comfortable with uncertainty and change (low uncertainty avoidance) to those more likely to prefer the status quo and stability (high uncertainty avoidance). After much critique of his work, he repeated his studies and in 2005 published again, confirming and expanding evidence related to differences in uncertainty avoidance between cultures. The GLOBE Study also confirmed this phenomenon, defining this concept as 'the extent to which members of collectives seek orderliness, consistency, structure, formalized procedures and laws to cover situations in their daily lives' (House et al., 2004: 603). The GLOBE Study found a positive and significant correlation between uncertainty avoidance and intolerance of ambiguity.

According to these researchers, cultures can be found along a spectrum ranging from those which are lowest on uncertainty avoidance values to those which demonstrate high uncertainty avoidance. Members of low uncertainty avoidant cultures are more comfortable with change and while there may be initial resistance to change, this is often short-lived. In contrast, members from high uncertainty avoidant cultures rely on informal relationships rather than formal policies and prefer to work with unspoken group norms so that behaviours are predictable. They tend to resist the imposition of change and are intolerant of norm-breaking behaviours. People in these cultures tend to look to the past in order to navigate the future. A senior public leader from Papua New Guinea told the author 'the past is in front of us and the future is behind us; we have to use the past to navigate our future'. A village leader in Samoa expressed similar sentiments, saying: 'democracy is bad for community, as it causes uncertainty and instability: people have to work out new ways of relating to each other and that creates fear'. How can a leader be inclusive if it both undermines their power and creates fear and uncertainty?

In cultures with low uncertainty avoidance values, change and innovation are regarded as positive phenomena. In these contexts, there are explicit ways in which change and innovation are encouraged and many strong systems that support ongoing change. For example, change processes are highly and widely described and promoted; governments promise and seek to bring about change; leaders are judged by the extent to which they bring about change; individuals who seek to bring about change are promoted and rewarded; and organizations which are constantly changing are deemed more successful than those that stay the same. In these contexts, a professional industry of facilitators and change management specialists has emerged, dedicated to supporting change processes. At this end of the spectrum, transformational change and innovation are regarded much more positively than incremental change.

In cultures with high uncertainty avoidance values, dominant ideas in society and institutions are about maintaining stability and minimizing uncertainty. In these cultures, leaders are more likely to discourage dissent, curiosity and questioning, limit the voices of those who challenge the status quo, and reward those who maintain existing power structures. Cultural events and practices in these contexts tend to emphasize the importance of past events, current leaders, and strong institutions. Organizations in high uncertainty avoidance cultures tend to seek to stay true to their history rather than change to suit the times. In this context, preferred changes are likely to be incremental in nature, rather than transformational: major changes may be seen as threatening to the natural order, undermining of existing power structures, and challenging to people's sense of comfort.

The key issue here is that values differ in relation to perceptions of and comfort with the whole idea of change. Anyone involved in change therefore needs to find out about these perceptions and experiences before they start engaging in facilitating change processes, so their efforts are informed. If these value differences are not understood by external facilitators (e.g. external to the organization, culture, or community), then they may find their efforts are irrelevant, misplaced, and thus less likely to succeed. At worst, they may be harmful, threatening, placing people at risk of further exclusion, undermining existing coping mechanisms, or alienating those who can contribute to positive change.

While there may be relative differences between cultures overall, of course people and organizations within a cultural context are also likely to hold different perceptions of change: ideas may be contested and dynamic over time. Some leaders and organizations may be more oriented towards change than others as a result of education, personality, exposure to different ideas, and other factors. There may be diversity within groups and contested ideas about both the concept of change and the ways in which change processes occur. People at different stages of life can be more or less open to change. Major events, crises, and challenges can also have a major influence on perceptions of and tolerance for change at individual, community, national, and global levels.

When visiting or working in a new culture, it is difficult for outsiders to ascertain whether a particular leader, organization, or community is more or less comfortable with change and uncertainty, even though they may recognize certain types of familiar behaviour as being innovative and change-oriented through their own cultural lens. Thus, skills to facilitate discussions, to listen to multiple perspectives, and acknowledge the role of cultural values on a person's, community's, or organization's ability to change, are worth generating.

Cultures' perceptions about power and leadership related to change

Values about uncertainty and change are connected with other cultural values, including perceptions about power, decision-making, the achievement of tasks, and the importance of relationships. A spectrum of values in relation to power distance across cultures was found by Hofstede (1980) and Hofstede and Hofstede (2005), and the GLOBE Study (House et al., 2004). At one end of the spectrum, cultures seek to minimize the gap between those with and those without power. A low power distance culture appears relatively non-hierarchical compared with those at the other end. In low power distance cultures, leaders and people talk about and apply the concept of equality, albeit imperfectly in many cases. Manifestations include: flat organization structures, equal opportunity policies, non-discrimination policies and 'tall poppy syndrome'. In a low power distance culture, such as Australia, good leaders are those who are inclusive, tend towards consulting staff, share information, and involve others in decision-making processes. Calls for gender equality, disability inclusion, and participation of marginalized groups are consistent with a belief that gaps between those with and those without power should be minimized. When these values are transgressed, there is often a negative public reaction.

At the other end of the spectrum, cultures consider hierarchy is essential for stability and certainty, power is retained in a few hands, and a threat to leaders is portrayed as a threat to order and everyone. In these contexts, dominant cultural values are relatively more hierarchical, with some in extreme contrast, described by those from low power distance cultures as authoritarian. In such settings, leaders who are perceived to have wisdom, access to resources, and spiritual power are seen as best placed to make decisions on behalf of those without (e.g. usually younger people, women, less educated people, minority groups, and the 'masses'). Based on this context, leaders are expected to maintain social order, stability, and harmony on the basis of their status, concentrating decision-making among those who 'know best'. Critique of those in power tends to generate negative public reaction in such contexts and suggests there are challenges to prevailing values.

Cultures' perceptions about decision-making

Cultural values have a big influence on 'who participates?' when it comes to decision-making about change. In a highly individualist culture, people place a great deal of value on their own choices and agency. People in these cultures want to make their own choices according to their own interests and priorities and will more likely drive their own change agendas, like going to university, moving jobs, moving countries, setting up a new app, or starting a family. Individualist societies often describe a person's success as being related to their independence, initiative, and self-drive. Education systems in such cultures teach children to become independent at an early age, emphasize critical and original thinking, and promote individual initiative and free choice. Government policies tend to assume people will act individually, make their own decisions, and use government systems to suit themselves. Governments establish complaints systems so people can express their views about service quality, for example. Institutions are often a platform for individuals to make their mark.

In a highly collectivist culture, on the other hand, people are more likely to make decisions which take strong account of the impact of their decisions on others in their own group, however defined. People from a village or church group will consider their choices in terms of what would be seen by the group to be the best. Education systems in these cultural contexts teach children to make decisions that reflect the potential impact on others and emphasize rote learning and compliant behaviour rather than independent initiative. Government policies in collectivist cultures are more likely to reflect the assumption that people will identify and comply with their group-determined norms and will not complain about or to those in authority. Institutions are seen more as a newly constructed 'collective' where people work with each other in mutual obligation.

In multicultural communities and organizations, dominant values will likely reflect the interface between cultural values and the particular mix and experience of leaders and community/team members. Many factors shape and are shaped by different perceptions of change and how it can be achieved or avoided.

When it comes to international development cooperation, individualist cultural values in western donor countries usually contrast with collectivist values in countries where development programs are implemented. In individualist cultures, one's identity is generally defined by oneself and is separate from the group's identity. Individuals in these cultures tend to be motivated by self-interest, communicate more directly, and are members of multiple groups. This helps in part to explain why many people seek to 'save the world' in their own way, setting up new organizations and go-fund-me pages for a particular cause. Individualists expect to be included in public processes and do not tolerate the opposite. In contrast, in collectivist cultures, one's sense of self is more likely to be defined by one's group's identity (e.g. racial, religious, language, island, family, dynasty) and one's obligations and goals are more connected to a defined group than oneself or a whole nation or 'the public good'. In these contexts, people may not expect to be included or heard, and when asked to speak up, many feel threatened and fear showing disrespect to those in power. Communications between group members are more indirect, group rather than individual activities are more important, and distinctions between in-groups and out-groups are pronounced. This tends to explain why development agencies often struggle to access or find differing views among community members about priorities or issues.

Cultures' emphasis on tasks and relationships

The difference between task and relationship-oriented cultural values is significant in the context of change orientation. The GLOBE Study (House et al., 2004) identified different ways to describe these basic distinctions: assertiveness (high to low); performance orientation (high to low); and humane orientation (high to low). Generally, cultures which are high on the task end of the spectrum place great value on setting and achieving plans and objectives, or 'getting things done'. In these cultures, people prioritize 'to do' lists and determine success by the number of tasks completed. In organizations, success is strongly measured by achievement of set targets which require task completion. In government, success is measured by achievement of change agendas, reflecting political leadership reform targets, for example. In task-oriented cultures, the concept of project management was invented, whereby particular objectives are achieved through detailed planning according to pre-determined definitions of tasks, budgets, and timelines. Task-oriented cultures are generally focused on achieving change, and they have invented many complex performance management systems to ensure changes are achieved – at individual, team, and organizational levels. The many measurement aspects associated with monitoring and evaluation reflect task-oriented cultural values.

In contrast, relationship-oriented cultures, or those high on humane orientation, prioritize the maintenance of harmony between people within groups. These cultures accord high value to connections between people, to the extent that belonging and affiliation are stronger motivators than getting a job completed. In relationship-oriented cultures, more emphasis is given to people's well-being than to professional success, and more emphasis is given to processes associated with community and social support than independence and self-sufficiency.

Change defined from the perspective of a task-oriented culture may simply represent a process of setting tasks, initiating the tasks, ticking them off when completed, and then assessing whether they achieved the expected result. From a task-oriented perspective, this is 'success' but from a relationship-oriented perspective, such a process may not only look absurdly mechanistic, but is also a sure-fire way of threatening relationships between people and causing great disorder and chaos. In relationship-oriented cultures, the driving forces in a society are to ensure that harmony prevails, so this may mean there is a strong emphasis on settling disputes (e.g. sorry ceremonies, peace-settlements) and on communications which do not cause others to lose face or be embarrassed. From the perspective of a relationship-oriented culture, an acceptable or desired change may be one which neither causes offence to existing leaders nor disharmony between groups of people. It is not surprising that from the perspective of task-oriented cultures, it appears not a lot of change occurs in relationship-oriented contexts.

Cultures' values related to gender egalitarianism

Commitment to and interest in achieving changes in gender relationships, gender equity, and many other related aspects of life are core priorities and area of focus for many governments, organizations, movements, networks, and people in the 21st century (e.g. Grown et al., 2016). In this context, understanding connections between these kinds of change and gender-related cultural values is critical. This is not the place to try to summarize or synthesize the huge body of work on gender equality. Here, the focus is on cultural values associated with gender egalitarianism, which are highly relevant to change facilitators, including those who specifically engage in processes which seek to change values, norms, and behaviour related to gender roles and responsibilities, gender equality, equity, and justice.

Hofstede (1980) found that one of the most fundamental ways in which societies vary is the extent to which each prescribes and proscribes different roles for different genders. While his particular categorization has been critiqued, it is clear that cultures consider gender roles differently and that there is a distinction between those which are oriented towards equality and those which are less so. While there are massive variations in the manifestation of those values, all cultures fit somewhere between those two ends of the spectrum: differences are relative to another rather than categorizable into a box.

Given this book's focus on facilitating change, cultural value differences relating to gender egalitarianism are particularly pertinent, not just for those who focus exclusively on gender equality, but for all those engaged in change. The GLOBE Study (House et al., 2004), identified that cultural values could be distinguished and compared by the degree to which gender role differences are minimized. Their detailed research identified seven culturally related drivers of gender egalitarianism: parental investment; climate, or geographic latitude; religion; economic development; social structure; and resource control, mode of production, and political system. Links between gender egalitarianism and other cultural elements are highly complex, interconnected, and sometimes contradictory.

Facilitators of change are likely to be involved in processes which either implicitly or explicitly engage with gender egalitarian issues, from the formation of gender-balanced small group discussions to society-wide changes in values. Understanding the cultural context in which people hold values about gender roles is relevant to processes which seek to change roles and values. Knowing that approaches which might work in one context will not necessarily work in another, means that context-specific understanding is necessary for determining efforts to support change. While people may not agree with another's values, that does not mean these values can be ignored: values are one of the most critical influences on societies. Just as citizens may not agree with their government, that does not make the government go away. Acknowledging that values influence people's understanding of the world and their place in it is a good start when engaging with change-related processes. Working respectfully with values to engage in conversations about whether they are still 'fit for purpose' and how they might be changed is an appropriate role for change facilitators.

When facilitators are involved in processes which seek explicitly to change gender-related values and inequality, they may more likely succeed if there is shared understanding about values underpinning the existing situation and whether these values are still fit for purpose and collaboration between people with shared values. Similarly, views about the status of people with disabilities or those identifying as LGBQTI+ vary widely across cultures, based on values related to power distance and collectivism, for example. These values can be used positively to help bring about more inclusion rather than 'blamed' for the lack of inclusion. For example, in Fiji deeply held collectivist values mean that people with disabilities may be included as members of the village group, but when they leave the village and reach more individualist settings (towns and cities), they face barriers to inclusion. Pitching inclusive efforts to suit each cultural context is essential.

Cultures' values related to time and the future

Cultures vary in their perceptions of and approach to time and the future. Some consider time as linear, paying attention to setting and meeting deadlines, for example. Others consider time to be circular, cyclical, and endless. In cultures which prioritize the setting of deadlines, work is organized in order to meet deadlines and success measures are often associated with the pace of change. In cultures which consider time is circular, the idea 'there is no need to work too hard today, as what we don't achieve today can be done tomorrow when the sun comes up again, as it has every day in history', is more likely to prevail. In these contexts, meeting deadlines is not necessarily prioritized, but other values are, such as harmony with colleagues. Change facilitators' awareness of dominant values' influence on perceptions of time and the future will make a significant difference to both strategic and day-to-day work.

Since change agendas often articulate long-term changes, different values about the future are relevant to understanding what is prioritized and what is possible. Future orientation has been identified as a basic value of all cultures. Cultures can be compared by the degree to which a society encourages and rewards future-oriented behaviours such as planning and delaying gratification (Ashkanasy et al., 2004; Javidan, 2007). A popular view is that countries with lower socio-economic status encourage a focus on immediate concerns for survival, and those with higher socio-economic status allow for savings and investments for the future. However, the research by Ashkanasy et al. (2004) found the opposite. They explain this as higher-income nations enjoying the present more and not being overly concerned about future orientation because they have already accumulated substantial wealth and material resources. A long-term perspective taken by communities in lower-income contexts may reflect needs to cope with scarce or limited resources to sacrifice for the future.

Change facilitators' awareness of dominant values related to time will help inform expectations about the timing of possible changes at planning, implementation, and evaluation stages as well as expectations about leadership related to change in each context. Cultural perceptions about the future can influence the selection of leaders: for example more visionary leaders are desired in cultures which give higher priority to the future, whereas more compliant and controlling leaders may be desired in cultures which are less future-oriented. In a hierarchical culture, if leaders have endorsed plans for change, there may be no expectation that the details will need to be explained, but the focus is on simply making the changes as the leaders have determined. In contrast, in more egalitarian and individualist cultures, people seek to know all the details of any change that may affect them, but they may be more comfortable with negotiating uncertainty over time, since they are more used to being part of constant change.

A particular manifestation of different cultural perceptions of time relates to the time allocated for relationship building. In a task-oriented, future-oriented cultural context, initial greetings between people in new teams are likely to be perfunctory: the main focus is getting on with the job as quickly as possible so deadlines can be met. In cultures which see time as more cyclical, there are also likely to be strong relationship-orientation values, so the process of getting to know new team members is highly valued and significant for success. The time for team members to build up knowledge of each other and develop trust is seen as essential for success: its absence is more likely to lead to failure. Facilitators who do not pay attention to different perspectives on time will find their processes can easily override norms in ways which negatively affect the likelihood of success.

Low- and high-context cultures

In anthropology, some cultural analysts refer to the distinction between low- and high-context cultures, and though not discussed in great detail in this book (until Chapter 11), this concept is relevant to change facilitation processes. The distinction between low- and high-context cultures is commonly found in cross-cultural communications advice and particularly relevant to conflicts across cultures (Hall, 1976). The distinction refers to the extent to which people within a culture are explicit about the context in their communications.

In low-context cultures, there is a reliance on clear, comprehensive, explicit, and direct communications, so little is left for interpretation. In these contexts, which tend to be more individualistic, successful communicators are those who express messages completely and directly. The listener does not have to guess what the person is talking about or read between the lines.

In contrast, in high-context cultures, the preferred ways of communicating rely on more implied messaging and existing knowledge about the context. In these contexts, fewer words are exchanged, because the key elements are assumed, based on shared knowledge and more collectivist values. People in high-context cultures tend to be able to use less direct verbal and non-verbal communication using small gestures, body movements, symbols, or metaphors, for example, and the listener will need to be experienced and skilled in reading between the lines, interpreting the silence, or giving deeper meaning to subtle hints. While some intercultural communications studies reference this distinction, and it is easy to identify examples from many contexts that may fit one or the other, critics have questioned the absence of evidence for the distinction.

When those from low-context cultures engage in change-related processes with people from high-context cultures, different communication styles can result in miscommunications, laboured interaction, embarrassment, insults, awkwardness, and sometimes conflict. Being too specific, for example, can be regarded as being rude or patronizing from a high-context cultural perspective. In studies about conflict, those from low-context cultures were found to seek to offer solutions when any conflict arises, while those from high-context cultures prefer non-confrontational ways of engagement, avoiding naming the conflict or causing others to lose face (Chua and Gudykunst, 1987). Facilitators' awareness of low-/high-context cultures can reduce misinterpretation at least.

Working across cultures

Multiple guides and books have been written in English-speaking countries, particularly the US, to support those who work across cultures in various sectors. They are commonly written for business people or missionaries working internationally. Others are written for those engaged in social work or community development in multicultural settings (e.g. Brownlee, n.d.; Song, 2016; Padilla et al., 2020). While settings and purposes vary, overlapping suggestions are found and some may be broadly useful for facilitators of change. A summary of the kinds of general suggestions in these guides includes the following (based on Brownlee, n.d.):

- Learn about other cultures but avoid stereotyping, generalizing or assuming ideas about other people – when you are trying to learn about the complexities of people and communities, keep the ideas about cultural value differences in your back pocket.
- Listen actively and with empathy, trying to put yourself in the other's shoes, even if this means being on the edge of your own comfort zone.
- While recognizing there is no 'right way' to communicate with everyone and there is always room to improve, keep questioning your assumptions and keep practising.
- Develop skills to keep communications working rather than finding someone to blame when there is a miscommunication, but if people do not want to engage with you, respect their choice.
- Develop the ability to separate observation from judgement.
- Develop the ability to consider yourself through another cultural lens – where appropriate seek to adjust your norms and behaviour that may be disrespectful or ineffective.
- Develop the ability to understand the connection between history, including oppression, power imbalances and mistreatment, and contemporary understanding of relationships between cultures and countries, being open to hearing different perspectives.
- Remember that the behaviour of any particular individual or organization is influenced not just by cultural norms, but by many

other factors (family, education, personality, ethnic background, geography) and people are more complicated than any cultural norm could suggest.
- Remember that we all have values, norms, and behaviour that could be seen as 'different', depending on where you are standing.

Limitations

The validity and limitations of Hofstede's cultural dimensions, widely referenced in the GLOBE Study, have been extensively criticized, including by people from different academic disciplines. McSweeney (2002) is the most cited critic and Ailon (2008) is another. The GLOBE Study discussed, largely endorsed, and expanded the range of cultural value differences found by Hofstede, and as noted above is being repeated with a more extensive coverage during 2020–21 (<https://globeproject.com/> [accessed 22 September 2021]). Others have identified different models and language for describing cultural value differences between organizations (e.g. Trompenaars and Hampden-Turner, 1997).

While terminology from the GLOBE Study (House et al., 2004) is used in this book, the disciplinary context in which the research was undertaken is organizational change and leadership. It refers to cultural values and social contexts in a broad sense and was not necessarily intended to support social change facilitation.

As mentioned frequently in this book and in others which consider cultural values, there is no claim that cultural values are the only influence on individual, community, and organizational behaviour, let alone national behaviour. Cultures which share similar values may express them in highly varied ways, the result of multiple influences over time. Being culturally aware is not about definitively knowing or categorizing any particular culture, but about being curious and open to learning, reflecting, respecting, and seeking to understand the connections between values and people in different contexts, including one's own culture. Being culturally literate is not about claiming more status than others, but extending awareness to the way one engages with others, with humility, respect, and commitment to generating shared understanding of a complex world.

Those interested in cultural value differences and their implications for change are encouraged to follow threads in the continuing debate and research, recognizing there is never likely to be one universally agreed single frame of reference at any level for understanding differences between people and communities across the globe.

Implications

> Our understanding of others has not expanded at the same pace as our interconnections. (Tett, 2021: xiv)

The benefit of understanding value differences, for everyone involved in change, is that it creates opportunities for initiating and stimulating respectful discussions that can help to actually generate agreed changes. Everyone in this field strongly advises against the use of cultural value differences to 'put people or cultures in boxes'. Rather this analysis is intended to encourage exploration and generate approaches which not only take account of value differences (rather than determine particular paths of action or impose one set of values on another culture), but use shared understanding about differences to bring about change.

Cultural values are described as dynamic and diverse, meaning that within a culture there can be many different values held and they can be changing at different paces. Young people in some cultures may react in various ways against the values of their elders, for example some quickly, some slowly, and some not at all. When facing a crisis, previously nascent values may surface or be subsumed by other values. Progress on gender equality can be slow in some settings and fast in others too, subject to a whole range of influences, perceptions, and experiences.

This chapter confirms that awareness of cultural value differences is essential to inform the relevance and effectiveness of change-related efforts. While some may consider that cultural values can be construed as a hinderance to development, awareness **of** values is necessary in order to bring about any kind of change, including **to** values. The application of a cultural lens to aspects of organizational and social life generates a more complex understanding of how different people engage with the world than is generally available from other forms of analysis. In the next chapter, this lens is applied to ideas related to change.

CHAPTER 3
Development and change

> Effective change is a collaborative, inclusive and participatory process (Canadian Observatory on Homelessness, n.d.)

Change facilitators focus on bringing about some kind of positive change. In practical terms, the particular change that facilitators are asked to address can either be already determined by the commissioning organization or the source of funding, or more open to being shaped by the priorities of those whose lives are expected to change. In any case, facilitators play a major role in influencing the scope for people to express and negotiate agreed priorities for change and determining the processes for doing so. The facilitator is often a key link between different definitions and expectations and thus plays a translator or interpreter role. The role of facilitators in contexts where people can control their change agendas or where they have little control can be crucial. How well they play that role can influence the quality of change processes and the nature and scope of change in reality. This chapter assists change facilitators to think about change through a cultural lens.

A change facilitator may be asked to design and facilitate a process to prevent human trafficking from remote districts in Laos or Cambodia or Myanmar, or to make disaster responses more disability inclusive in a Pacific country or to encourage women to attend ante-natal care services in rural Indonesia. Logistical questions may be the first to be asked, such as how much time is available, who needs to be included, what content needs to be communicated, what are expected outcomes, or what venue is available. However, bigger questions need to be considered about the cultural values which shape current behaviour in these contexts, the cultural value differences that exist, and how changes to these values and behaviour might be understood in each setting. This chapter considers ideas about change and cultural values and the links between them to enable practitioners to navigate these complexities.

Ideally, change which is determined and prioritized by people whose lives are expected to change should be the primary focus of change facilitators, but in reality, this is often not the case. The agenda for change is often interpreted and set by others and imposed on people who have little choice. International treaties and national policies negotiated and worded far from the villages where their implications flow often determine the nature and scope of changes. In a context where different values influence the nature and scope of change, a facilitator can support those involved to navigate the differences.

Recognizing the complexity of influences on the definition and perceptions of change and of factors that shape change processes and outcomes, this chapter focuses on just one aspect: the relevance of cultural values for change. It seeks to help facilitators avoid or at least minimize the potentially harmful effects of 'making a difference'. It also seeks to help facilitators avoid change-related efforts which are irrelevant, ineffective, or unsustainable, particularly for people whose lives are affected by change, but also for the organizations who allocate resources to bringing about change.

Change is an extremely widely used term in the 21st century: there is value in briefly reflecting on its meaning and how it might be understood differently from various cultural perspectives before getting into how to facilitate and achieve change. In English, change can be a verb: 'to make or become different' or 'to exchange one thing for another thing'. It is also a noun, i.e. 'the act of becoming different, or the result of something becoming different' or 'something that is pleasant or interesting because it is unusual or new' (*Cambridge Dictionary*). It can also refer to the coins or banknotes received after a purchase, when more money is handed over than the price of the item! In other languages, the term 'change' can also be interpreted in different ways, with more or less neutrality or judgement.

Awareness of and efforts to respond to ongoing and new global challenges of inequality, injustice, and climate change confirm the need for change in terms of the systems which cause and sustain them. As illustrated in Chapter 2, different cultural values influence perceptions of the concept of change more or less positively, reflecting different degrees of comfort with perceived uncertainties. The distinction between good and bad change is relevant. Facilitators generally do not set out to bring about 'bad' change, but positive change from one cultural perspective may be easily interpreted as negative from another.

The concept of change is drawn from and relates to elements of philosophy, sociology, and history. It is also a central theme in more contemporary disciplines, such as economics, organizational development, and psychology. Krznaric (2007) summarized perspectives about the idea of change through the lens of many of these areas of study. His work helps explain ways in which different disciplines consider, articulate, and thus measure change, and difficulties when disciplines interact.

In many disciplines, the term 'development' is used to define a certain nature or type of change – as in community development, organizational development, capacity development, national development – which implies some kind of positive, beneficial shift that improves the relevant entity. 'Developmental change' is sometimes used, though this can have different meanings in business (low level change which contrasts with transformative change) and psychology (the process of change that occurs during a person's lifetime), for example. When a multidisciplinary framework is used to consider change and development, it is clear the terms are understood in different ways.

The relationship between actions and change is studied in great depth in many disciplines, from engineering to psychology as well as complexity sciences. Ideas that help facilitators to make sense of the potential for change and the source of potential expertise to bring about or support change in any context are useful. The Cynefin framework (Snowden, 2011) developed to support decision-making has become widely used for the distinctions it makes between different levels of complexity in change-oriented processes. The framework draws on research into systems theory, complexity theory, network theory and learning theories, and potentially enables those involved in change processes to understand the context in which they are operating. It distinguishes contexts between: those where there is a clear or obvious connection between actions and results and 'best practice' is likely to succeed (simple); those where the connections are not so linear and 'good practice' is most appropriate (complicated); those where the connections are highly complex, so 'emergent practice' is appropriate (complex); or those where the links between actions and results are unknowable in advance (chaotic). The distinction is highly useful for those involved in change processes to understand how links between actions and results may be understood and which kinds of approaches are more likely to be appropriate.

What kinds of change?

The nature and types of change to which this book applies are not limited or pre-prescribed. The ideas in this book are applicable to social, community, and organizational change, including behavioural and value change, which is deemed, at least primarily, to be a beneficial or positive result to people's lives and societies. Suggested approaches and methods are relevant to processes which support positive change as well as the achievement of positive results. Highly technical or specialist changes, such as adoption of particular technology or shifts in scientific endeavour are best left for others to ponder and support, though generic concepts and methods may be relevant.

A vast body of work relates to change in the international development discipline and is relevant to change across cultures. Examples include ideas about how change happens (Green, 2016); the role of politics, power, and leadership in shaping change (Leftwich, 2011; Leftwich and Wheeler, 2011; Carothers and de Gramont, 2013; Booth and Unsworth, 2014; Hudson and Marquette, 2015); and 'doing development differently' (Booth et al., 2016). In contributing to broader understanding about change in the English-speaking world of development practice, this work is largely a reaction against previously disproportionate emphasis on technical solutions to particular problems and responds to evidence that complexity, power, context, and values are major factors in change.

It is a challenge to find an appropriate balance between the application of expertise in a particular sector (which may be changing rapidly itself), understanding and engaging with political/power/partnership-related issues, responding to different frames of reference and ideas, as well as cultural values, norms, and beliefs in any change context. The effort inevitably requires a highly informed and skilled approach and potentially a large team, committed to ongoing learning and reflection, as well as a great deal of humility and goodwill.

The kinds of change which dominate current development practice include: better leadership and governance; more inclusion and greater equality of and access to opportunity; improved protection of human rights and greater justice; better service delivery (in terms of inclusion, reach, coverage, or quality, for example); or better environmental protection. Almost any other aspect of well-being and sustainability may be sought by those involved in change. Whatever the change, there is no single pathway, answer, or solution.

The pace of change and development appears faster than ever before. Information flows more rapidly and much further than in previous decades. New ideas, both positive and negative, are taken up in varied and unpredictable ways. When some change happens in one place, like the adoption of a new piece of technology, consequences may be global, but the impact can be positive or negative, depending on many factors, with cultural norms and values just one frame of reference.

Some development-related issues and challenges stay the same or are worsening, such as inequality, global warming and climate change, injustice, and conflict. On the other hand, a long list of positive changes can be described across the globe related to health, education, employment, inclusion, understanding of and agreements about human rights, and other aspects of human life. Some say the problems left to be tackled are the most intractable. Others consider the human race is already living beyond the planet's means and faces the biggest challenges ever. People of all ages from many countries are keen to contribute to making the world better than it is now. While there are some shared ideas about how this can be achieved, there are also contested notions. There are plenty of opportunities and plenty of lessons and experiences to draw from, but no 'right' answer.

The globally agreed SDGs address most, but not all, aspects of contemporary social, economic, and environmental life. While these goals are global and apply to all countries, cooperation between people from different cultures can focus on almost any aspect of life. There is broad agreement about the value of achieving SDGs, but little agreement about the nature of changes envisaged and how each will be actualized in every context. Cultural value differences are relevant to assumptions that people and organizations have about what these changes look like and how to achieve them.

A cultural lens on change

> Culture, not politics, determines the success of a society. (Daniel Patrick Moynihan quoted in Harrison and Huntington, 2000: xiv)

> Tunnel vision is deadly. We need lateral vision. (Tett, 2021: xiii)

While the idea that culture is relevant to 'how change happens' remains a relatively marginal frame of reference, it has been increasingly acknowledged since the mid-1990s (Warren et al, 1995; Harrison and Huntington, 2000; Rao and Walton, 2004; Bicchieri and Mercier, 2014; Green, 2016; Hudson and McLoughlin, 2019). Following the publication of Harrison and Huntington's work (2000), a high profile and major contribution to understanding of links between culture and development was published by the World Bank in 2004 (Rao and Walton). In their book, *Culture and Public Action*, they compiled voices from various disciplines and called for more culturally attuned practice. More than a decade later, Green (2016) identified social norms, complexity, and power as three major elements in how change happens. Most recently, the Development Leadership Program (DLP) communicated its research interest in the expression of leadership in different cultures in late 2019 (Hudson and McLoughlin, 2019), representing acknowledgement of cultural value differences. Questions such as 'how does culture matter for development?' (Rao and Walton, 2004) and 'how does history and culture affect perceptions of leadership?' (Hudson and McLoughlin, 2019) seem obvious, but they have not been asked frequently in international development research and not yet taken up by many practitioners.

Using a cultural lens to consider the concept and practice of change helps to build understanding about why different cultures define and respond to change differently and what this means for cross-cultural practice. Just as Kyznaric (2007) pointed out that different disciplines understand social change in various ways, cultures also consider change differently (Hofstede 1980; House et al., 2004; Hofstede and Hofstede, 2005). Those working across cultures to engage with change-focused ideas in effective and respectful ways therefore need to reflect on how change may be seen differently through this lens (see section within Chapter 2 on cultures' degree of comfort with change).

While change, by definition, is the opposite of consistency, by the 21st century, constant change is the norm rather than the exception. People, communities, and countries which cannot keep up with the rapid pace of change are quickly left behind or excluded. Organizations cannot risk staying the same if their competitors forge ahead with changes. Escaping from the onslaught of new ideas, ways of working, and frames of reference (good, bad, and indifferent) is harder than ever: interconnections between countries through businesses and information technology are pervasive. At the level of the internet, trying to quantify the sharing of ideas across the world, even in one day, would be an impossible goal. The planet is criss-crossed by planes carrying people and ideas in every direction: on one day in 2018 alone, there were 250,000 planes in the sky, though two years later the COVID-19 pandemic resulted in a dramatic drop to fewer than 6,000 on 2 July 2020, for example, according to <https://www.flightradar24.com/40.31,-103.39/4> [accessed 24 September 2021].

The idea that change does not just happen by itself but is deliberately sought and facilitated through individual or collective action underpins a great deal of human effort. As Green (2016: xi) noted: 'for the last several thousand years at least, human beings have tried to imagine a different world from the one they live in, and worked together to create it'. The achievement of positive change to improve the lives of people and communities, over different periods of time and in different locations, is central to the work of millions of people and thousands of organizations, the investment of billions of dollars and other resources, all within different cultural contexts.

Over the past 70 years of international development practice, there has been a positive but incomplete swing away from the idea that people from wealthy countries know what is best for those in low-resource countries, in terms of the 'necessary changes'. Hopefully, fewer people and governments now believe that with the right amount of money and other resources, sustainable, and significant change will happen. Acknowledgement of the complexities involved, the shared challenges, and the interconnections between one place's wealth and another's poverty contribute to this recognition. On one hand, there is increasing understanding that collaboration between people and institutions from different contexts is necessary to achieve positive change, rather than replication of models from one setting in another. Learning and working together, bringing together respective strengths, and testing to see what works in different contexts are now considered essential. Those with experience have stopped seeking some silver bullet response to complex challenges. However, on the other hand, there are still signs that people from well-resourced countries believe they know what is best for those with fewer resources. A proliferation of new donor priorities, new civil society organizations, new volunteer-based programs and new ways of transferring cash and goods from 'rich' to 'poorer' countries illustrate this ongoing practice.

The degree to which different perspectives on change and development are incorporated in official development assistance or community-level cooperation varies. The shift away from stand-alone government donor agencies to integrated development and foreign affairs agencies in the early 21st century suggests that the domestic interests of donors (perceptions of change) are more likely to prevail than the priorities of the countries where development programs are implemented (Gulrajani, 2018). Efforts are now more usually made (or at least considered) to design and implement programs that reflect the economic and security priorities of the governments of countries which provide development programs. In the non-profit sector, development agencies generally (but not always) seek to respond to change priorities expressed by communities in which they work, based on degrees of understanding about the specific context. These approaches recognize that leadership and ownership of any change agenda is critical for the achievement of change, from reformed financial management or new attitudes towards people with disability.

Politics, power, social status, education, geography, personality, and many other factors influence different perceptions of change: whether something is seen as positive or negative. A new maternal child health service in some contexts could be seen as positive for health outcomes but a threat to the status of grandmothers, older women, or traditional midwives who have traditionally provided information and support to new mothers. Improved access to education could be seen as positive for the potential future lives of individual children and to nations, but reduce the number of hands available to grow food for a rural subsistence farmer's family for a time. At a systemic level, a government may be seen as more efficient if it introduces a merit-based new procurement process, but well-connected business leaders could see that the change makes their work less efficient and their business less profitable. An overseas scholarship may bring great learning opportunities and potential earning for an individual member of a family or staff member, but it may contribute to envy as well as future issues when the person returns with new ideas which challenge the status quo and those with power.

The speed of change (as noted in Chapter 2 above in relation to uncertainty avoidance) and degree of predictability of change are judged differently across cultures. Communities and organizations will vary in their comfort with different paces of change and perceptions of urgency. The extent to which changes are embraced could vary between age groups, institutional affiliation, or genders as well as the characters of leaders and the style of leadership.

Cultural values within teams and organizations are now widely understood as critical for both overall success and an ability to drive or respond to change. There is no shortage of advice on how organizations can strengthen their internal values to ensure success. Within work-related teams and organizations, perceptions about change can also vary widely, subject to the values that prevail, leadership styles, and many other factors operating within and outside the context. A great deal has been written for organizations working in western cultures about how organizations can or should change their values or better apply their values. Much has also been written for western organizations about how to succeed in other cultures, particularly where there are markets to exploit and businesses to merge and take over.

In summary, understanding the role of cultural values on conceiving and driving change is critical to any change process. Whether change involves people's behaviour, an organization's capacity to bring about a particular result, or a community's norms, an understanding of values is crucial. It may be easy to dismiss existing values in the rush to bring in new ideas and ways of seeing the world, but the pathway from the old to the new is more likely to be smooth when there is some clarity about the starting point. When people and organizations collaborate, navigating different cultures is a core task for all involved, both those who seek to bring about change and those who are expected to change. Setting and keeping an eye on shared cultural values across different networks and partners can be both exciting and challenging.

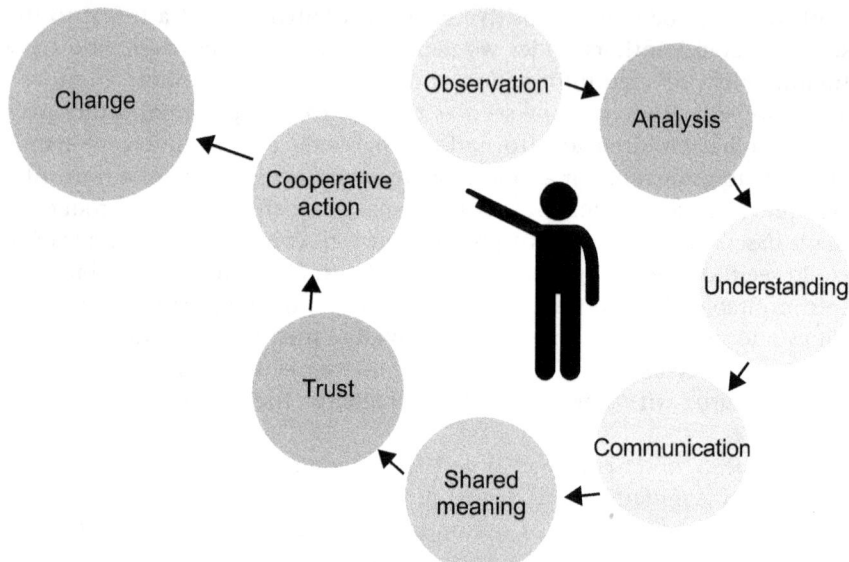

Figure 3.1 Elements linking cultural values and change

Framework to link cultural values and change

A framework to draw together ideas about cultural understanding and how change happens is offered here (Figure 3.1). It is similar to the framework which describes links between cultural understanding and capacity development, developed by Rhodes and Antoine (2013). Elements in the framework (Figure 3.1) reflect themes associated with cross-cultural change facilitation. The framework links **cross-cultural understanding** (comprising the first three circles: Observation, Analysis, Understanding) with the skills of **engaging with people** (the next two circles: Communication, Shared Meaning), and the processes essential for **bringing about change** (the last two circles: Trust, Cooperative Action).

The elements in Figure 3.1 are explained below. The first three – Observation, Analysis, and Understanding – are broadly addressed in Part 1 of this book. The second two – Communication and Shared Meaning – link Part 1 and Part 2, where analysis and understanding translate into defining strategies for cross-cultural collaboration. The last two elements – Trust and Cooperative Action – are addressed in Part 2 which focuses on 'how to' build the collaborative relationships essential for bringing about change.

Cross-cultural understanding

Observation involves gathering data or information about a particular context, setting, or process, without making value judgements. Asking questions such as 'what, when, who, and how' will help in this observation process. Avoiding the 'why' question at this stage is important, as asking why tends to direct the observer away from objective data gathering into more subjective explanations of observable events. Objective data gathering may be difficult at first, as it often challenges deeply entrenched habits and behaviour. For many, distinguishing between the separate processes of observation and judgement is difficult because the two appear seamless. When the two are separated, people are more likely to be able to engage in constructive cross-cultural interactions.

Analysis involves making sense of what has been observed, using some kind of framework. This book uses the GLOBE Study cultural dimensions (House et al., 2004) as a means to encourage reflection and discussion about cultural value differences, but there are other frameworks. Whatever context the change process is located within – a topic, a place, a discipline, an organization, a movement – will likely have other critical frameworks to assist analysis. These may be considered themselves through a cultural values lens, to help shape understanding. For example, a power analysis or a gender analysis will need to take account of different cultural values relating to hierarchy and equality.

Understanding in this context refers to understanding similarities and differences in the cultural values that underpin behaviour, whether that be how people work together, interact with each other, lead, follow, practice respect, learn, or respond to information. Similarities are strengths because they enable shared and implied understanding of the world. They also assist in the development of trust and collaboration. Differences offer opportunities for partners to explore and leverage complementary strengths. Using a strengths-based approach will help people to appreciate what they have analysed. Using a problem-based approach will often lead to portraying the 'other' in negative terms, which is unhelpful for subsequent steps in the cycle.

Cross-cultural engagement

Communication in this context means effective cross-cultural communication about value differences. Where language is shared, this is obviously easier: value-related words are often not readily translated between languages, so effective communication is required. Active listening, checking, re-checking, and use of translators and cultural guides may be required. Conversations may involve introducing opportunities for checking understanding about observations or concepts or ways of working. They may involve asking lots of questions, explaining the reasons why people have different values and perspectives, and careful and respectful discussions about differences. Encouraging others to ask questions and providing respectful answers is also essential at this stage.

Shared meaning is the critical link between effective communication and trust. It suggests that those involved in the process agree on the definitions and interpretations of key concepts being used: in this case, the changes sought and means to achieve change. Co-creation of shared meaning is critical: without this, trust cannot easily be achieved. Identifying and discussing values that people already hold in common, despite cultural differences, can be a cathartic experience as well as help to bond members of a team or group. Negotiating how to manage different values and discussing how to navigate complexity and conflict, when working together, are also critical in this step.

Cross-cultural cooperation

Trust is the key ingredient for achieving collaboration and is more likely to be achieved as a result of the previous processes than without them. Implicit trust can start to evolve during early stages of an interaction, if there is goodwill and a shared commitment to collaboration. Trust is likely to be implicit because a new group does not usually set out to engender trust. To achieve trust that is sufficient to proceed to cooperation (the next stage), group members are likely to need to demonstrate a degree of vulnerability, self-disclosure, openness, mutual support, and a willingness to listen. Facilitators and group members will need to pay attention to such behaviour in order to deepen the level of trust between them. Essentially, there are two types of trust – swift trust and deep-level trust. Swift trust is forged between team members who are thrown together, often at short notice. There may be little time for team members to get to know each other but they are asked to work collaboratively to carry out complex and sometimes dangerous operations, such as rescuing survivors after a tsunami. Deep-level trust is more relevant and necessary in long-term collaborative engagement, particularly where changes in behaviour and values are envisaged.

Cooperative action is the key ingredient to achieve any form of change, although other ingredients are also necessary. Facilitation of cooperative activity, the focus of this book, thereby acknowledges that many steps are required before cooperation is possible. Without genuine cooperation, sharing risks and successes, the chances of achieving sustainable change are extremely low. Other success factors, including long-term engagement, a shared goal, political will, and sufficient resources are also very important, but without cooperation may be less critical.

While Figure 3.1 uses a simplified cycle to explain the connection between these elements, they can also occur in parallel, or be useful in a different order. Sometimes, previous steps may need to be repeated. For example, a partner in a cooperative activity may believe that trust levels are high, but subsequently find they are not (or never really were), so efforts to build trust may require going back to the first step or later steps before proceeding to genuine cooperation. Change facilitators may find this model useful for locating their efforts at different times. At minimum the model confirms the impossibility of turning up in a new context and expecting cooperative action at the outset and a quick step to change.

This chapter confirms that ideas about change facilitation are relevant to all kinds of change. Connections between understanding cultural values and achieving change are explained, using a simplified cycle of reflection and interaction. The cycle is useful for enabling facilitators to understand elements of cross-cultural engagement and to help move groups of people towards well-founded collaboration. Implications for practice are considered in the next chapter.

CHAPTER 4
Implications for facilitators of the links between cultural values and change

> The true voyage of discovery lies not in seeking new landscapes, but in having new eyes. (Marcel Proust, quoted in Ramalingam, 2013)
>
> Listening to someone else's view, however 'strange', does not just teach empathy for others, which is badly needed today; it also makes it easier to see yourself. (Tett, 2021: xiv)

Change facilitators who work across cultures are in practice accompanying groups of people on a journey from one point to another, from where they are now to where they seek to be at a time in the future. As the definition of facilitation suggests, their role is to help make this journey possible and easier. In practical terms, this covers every aspect of planning and facilitation, from negotiating terms of reference with clients and organizational or community leaders, to writing up outcome documents or other products. This chapter considers the implications of links between cultural understanding and change for facilitators' own cultural awareness and their practice. While acknowledging not all facilitation processes are undertaken by relatively well-resourced westerners, this chapter addresses different levels of cultural awareness for anyone working with people in this increasingly globalized world. Chapter 5 applies a cultural lens to other aspects of cross-cultural facilitation.

Facilitating collaboration between people with different cultural values

> Professional success is largely dependent on cultural intelligence or knowledge about similarities and differences between cultural norms, and personal interest and motivation in knowing other cultures. (Costin, 2015)

Understanding cultural values and the quality of intercultural collaboration are more critical to the achievement of developmental change than is acknowledged by most technical approaches. In this increasingly interconnected world, the most obvious way for facilitators to maximize the quality of their work is to contribute to deeper intercultural understanding and collaboration. This requires a level of cultural understanding on the part of the facilitator. In this section, the commonly used terms are discussed and a ladder of cultural understanding is proposed, which draws on literature from various disciplines on this topic. The first rung of the ladder is basic cultural awareness and each subsequent rung represents increasingly complex cultural analysis and engagement. The ladder symbolizes that striving to reach the highest rung will maximize the quality of cross-cultural change facilitation. Many factors shape the learning and experience which enable people and organizations to 'climb the ladder'. There may be a question about what can be found at the top of the ladder, but metaphorically it could be described as global harmony!

Capabilities for cultural understanding are described in a variety of ways in the literature, with researchers and practitioners espousing benefits and critiques associated with particular terms. For example, authors refer to cultural awareness, cultural understanding, cross-cultural or intercultural competence, cross-cultural communications skills, cultural intelligence, and cultural mindfulness. The terms used to describe this phenomenon have emerged largely since the mid-1990s, in parallel with increasing demand within multicultural contexts and increasing recognition of the importance of intercultural engagement. For change facilitation practitioners, the broad ideas can be summarized as 'being culturally literate'. The nature and degree of literacy varies for each of the steps of the ladder. While some levels of understanding are more transactional in nature, higher (or deeper) levels represent more transformative and sophisticated engagement with concepts of culture and identity.

In a world where interactions with people and ideas from other cultures are significantly more common than ever, having the ability to 'make sense' of others in order to address shared issues is helpful for everyone (Tett, 2021). In the world of development-oriented change, this applies to people who work as facilitators, the organizations engaged in supporting and bringing about change, and anyone whose life is expected to be touched by engagement with people from different cultures, or touched by change that comes about through this engagement. When facilitators encourage participants in collaborative development processes to strengthen the quality of their interaction in culturally informed ways, the likelihood that benefits will occur is maximized.

Diversity and inclusion

The concepts of 'diversity and inclusion' emerged in mainstream literature in western cultures in the 1970s to describe the idea that people with different characteristics and qualities should be empowered through respect for and appreciation of their differences. Primarily seen as a means to maximize business success by applying diverse views on problem-solving, it has spread to other sectors and now, 50 years on, is guided by legislation and policies in many jurisdictions (Robertson, 2006). The two terms are different but related as follows:

> *Diversity* is understood as the mix of differences that exist within people who may find themselves working together. This mix includes people with visible and invisible differences such as thinking and

leadership styles, religious background, sexual orientation, age, ability, experience as well as cultural values. The 'practice' of diversity now informs recruitment strategies in many countries and includes efforts to promote the exploration of differences in safe, positive, and nurturing environments.

Inclusion refers to systems that ensure different perspectives are actually surfaced and incorporated into decision-making, and is strongly linked to leadership practice which explicitly supports the valuing of different perspectives. Inclusiveness is the quality of the organizational environment –values, leadership, systems, approaches, and attitudes – that maximizes and leverages the diversity of talents and perspectives of all those involved.

Two core elements of inclusive practice are: facilitation of *belongingness* (supporting individuals as group members, ensuring equity and justice, shared decision-making) and *valuing of uniqueness* (encouraging diverse contributions and helping group members to fully contribute) (Rhodes and Antoine, 2019). With most diversity and inclusion models based on US experience, they largely reflect low power distance and individualist cultural values. Other countries adjust the models to suit their particular social and economic contexts.

Claims for the success of diversity and inclusion approaches are often remarkable. There is now widely quoted evidence that inclusive organizations are 35 per cent more successful than others (Hunt et al 2012). The CEO of Qantas reported on a spectacular turnaround from 2013 to 2017 because of its diversity and inclusion qualities: 'we have a very diverse environment and a very inclusive culture'. According to the CEO, Alan Joyce, those characteristics 'got us through the tough times ... diversity generated better strategy, better risk management, better debates, [and] better outcomes' (Bourke, 2018:1). Researchers in the private sector have found that 'organizations with a highly diverse workforce that do not pay attention to an inclusive environment are likely to be more dysfunctional than those without a diverse staff. Research suggests that one can find the answer not so much in policies and procedures as in the mindset of leaders in creating an inclusive culture' (Janakiraman, n.d.). Inclusive leadership is now increasingly promoted as a means to ensure diverse and inclusive workplaces succeed (Randel et al., 2016, 2018) (see Chapter 5 for more discussion).

Diversity and inclusion are regarded as positive phenomena in this book, through a cultural lens, but they can be understood to be limited or have negative connotations. For example, Hudson (2017: 10) noted 'the paradigm's centering of inclusion as a core anti-racist strategy has tended to inhibit meaningful treatment of racism as a structural phenomenon'. This reflects the view that efforts to build more inclusive organizations can ignore the need to eliminate racism, and that efforts are required to do both. A focus on the potential for these efforts to support each other exists, but requires considerable effort at many levels.

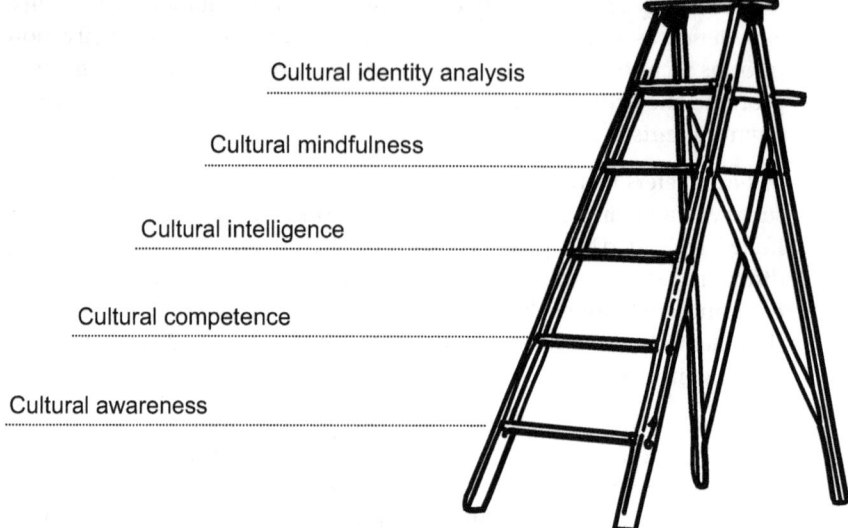

Figure 4.1 Ladder of cultural understanding

A ladder of cultural awareness

> We can all embrace some of the principles of ethnography: to look around, watch, listen, ask open-ended questions, be curious like a child, and try to walk 'in someone else's shoes', to cite the proverb. (Tett, 2021: 27)

A ladder of cultural awareness is proposed in Figure 4.1. The analogy represents the idea that over time, one can step up to higher levels of understanding and ability to apply this understanding about cultural value differences.

Each of these steps in cultural awareness is described below.

Cultural awareness

- Lowest level of awareness which includes understanding that people are different from each other and that they behave in ways which are distinctive.
- Essential as a building block for deeper levels of understanding.

The most basic level of cultural understanding is commonly labelled 'cultural awareness'. This refers to a person's understanding of the differences between themselves and people from other countries or other backgrounds, including differences in attitudes and values. It can also apply to organizations, in the sense that their policies, systems, and processes can reflect cultural awareness, either of their context, their customers and clients, or the way in which they develop relationships with others. Even though the idea of cultural awareness is easily critiqued for its over-simplicity, having some cultural awareness is better than having none, and at least it is a start.

In the context of international and community development practice, as well as social work and education, a myriad of researchers have considered issues related to cultural awareness. An industry of consultants and a library of guides seeks to increase cultural awareness: from Lonely Planet travel guides to parts of international consulting companies offering training for staff of multilateral organizations. In the international development setting, while work has been undertaken at the level of individual development workers, little evidence can be found of systemic consideration by development organizations of cultural value differences in their strategic or programming processes. The small number of relevant references include: Lensu (2003) who investigated cultural respect in humanitarian work; Reis and Bernath (2017) who mentioned cultural awareness among qualities for humanitarian workers; and Chang (2007) who researched cultural competence among Taiwanese development workers. Ang (Ang and Van Dyne, 2008) argued that if development workers are not culturally skilled and do not apply relevant work practices, their work is likely to be unused or misapplied. Leaders and staff in most development agencies do not appear to have read such research.

Deeper understanding than 'cultural awareness' is necessary for those working across cultures on processes which expect people to change their behaviour, organizations to change their ways or working, or communities to change their values or interactions with the world.

Cultural competence

- Ability to apply awareness to the practice of engaging with others from different cultures.
- Widely considered in social work, health, education, and other sectors.
- Includes cross-cultural communications skills and potentially language skills.

Cultural competence describes how cultural awareness is applied to the practice of engaging with people from different backgrounds. It is most widely considered in social work, health, education, communications, and related sectors. The history of the concept highlights a number of different perspectives (for a summary, see Ruben, 1989).

In the discipline of social work in multicultural contexts such as the US, Canada, and Australia, cultural competence is both widely valued (e.g. see Jackson and Samuel, 2011) and roundly critiqued (e.g. Pon, 2009). A dominant emphasis in the literature is the ability of social workers to bridge cultural gaps, understand clients' needs, and support integration. The expectation is that social workers will adjust their efforts to reach clients from different cultures, but the broad systems in which they operate are premised on the expectation that people from other cultures will adjust to dominant values and norms in the new country of residence. While social work practice operates largely at individual and community levels, some elements apply at broader systemic levels. An organization in London, Sydney, or New York could be described as culturally competent if it engages effectively with communities from cultural backgrounds that differ from the dominant national culture.

In change facilitation, cultural competence could refer to the application of cultural awareness in practical terms. For example, this might include incorporating culturally respectful welcomes, ensuring recognized leaders from the relevant context are invited and given key roles, or including cultural symbols in presentations. It may include ensuring that no language or terms are used which could be seen as insulting or disrespectful or that the selected strategies for bringing about change are not harmful. Cultural competence training can provide various frames of reference for strengthening skills. The online courses offered by Australia's Special Broadcasting Service (SBS) are a good example of contemporary emphasis on cultural competence (SBS, n.d.).

Cultural competence may be one step further up the ladder than cultural awareness, but risks being seen, as described by Sakamoto (2007) and Pon (2009), as lacking acknowledgement of power. It is founded on the idea that one group, largely people from predominantly white cultures, can get to know 'others' in order to overcome the differences, sell more products, convince them of the validity of ideas from their own culture in the context that the 'others' are often found to be 'lacking, inferior, deviant or abnormal' (Pon, 2009: 59). A way of deepening understanding of culture that acknowledges power in the context of intercultural relations is therefore necessary. Before stepping up to that level, a note on cross-cultural communications skills is useful.

Cross-cultural communications skills

Paying continuous attention to communications is one of the most critical elements for those involved in facilitating change across cultures. This requires personal sensitivities and professional skills as well as a suite of methods. Change-makers often assume that their shared focus on a particular outcome is sufficient to link people from different backgrounds, and at many levels this can be true. However, greater consideration of the values, communications styles, and ways of working that influence collaboration will significantly strengthen the quality of engagement and thus the likelihood of success. This effort can particularly help reduce or manage clashes along the way towards achieving the desired results.

Cross-cultural communications skills are often taught independently or separately within business, health, communications, and education courses. A substantial proportion of modern position descriptions ask for these skills though there is little consistency in the way the skills are understood, demonstrated, and assessed. Employers may provide professional development courses to strengthen skills, but they use a range of terms, focus on different skills, and take students to different levels of understanding.

In the international development context, an early study recognized 'seven interpersonal communication skills often mentioned as being important to cross-cultural adaptation: empathy, respect, role behavior flexibility, orientation to knowledge, interaction posture, interaction management and tolerance for ambiguity' (Ruben and Keally, 1979: 16). Some of these skills are more like qualities, while others can be understood at individual as well as organizational levels. Teaching these and related skills is the focus of many professional development courses.

Language competency is linked to this level of skill and as facilitators are inevitably working with people who speak and/or write in many languages, cognisance of the implications of this for change facilitation is crucial. Learning languages, a huge field of endeavour and research, is related to cultural understanding and awareness of cultural value differences. Efforts to understand and speak the language of participants in a change process are always valued. Similarly, efforts to ensure that information shared in change facilitation processes is not just accessible in the language of participants but adjusted to be culturally relevant and meaningful will make a contribution to the quality of collaboration. Employing co-facilitators with fluency in the language of participants is recommended (see Chapter 7).

When people come together from different cultures to discuss change processes or set shared goals, it goes without saying that effective communications are crucial. Some research from the business world may be useful for those involved in facilitating change for social benefit. The way messages are spoken, heard, and read between the lines differs widely between cultures (related to low- and high-context cultures, see Chapter 2). In some cultures, direct language is preferred and promoted, while in others, messages are implied, nuanced, and potentially ambiguous. Body language is a critical aspect of communication and differs widely between cultures. A related issue arising in change-oriented cross-cultural communications is the management of silence (Brear, 2020).

Cultural intelligence

- Capability to relate and work effectively across cultures in order to effect a desired change.
- Sometimes equated with cultural competence.

Cultural intelligence is sometimes used interchangeably with cultural competence, but is defined as the capability to relate and work effectively across cultures *in order to effect a desired change*. Since the term emerged in the early 2000s (Earley and Ang, 2003), cultural intelligence has been used in business, education, government, and academic research. The concept draws on earlier work on cultural competence and has been more recently described by Dolan and Kawamura (2015).

Cultural intelligence encompasses a set of capacities to understand and effectively respond to the beliefs, values, attitudes, and behaviour of others for the purposes of bringing about change. These capacities include cognitive, motivational, and behavioural elements. While most of the literature on this topic focuses on individual competence, similar concepts can also apply to organizational or group competence, linked to values, norms, and ways of working. Given the high value accorded to cultural intelligence for business, researchers have dedicated considerable efforts to developing tools for measuring and predicting cultural intelligence (e.g. Ang and Van Dyne, 2008). This has confirmed the link between cultural intelligence and effective collaboration across cultures, but may need to be adjusted to suit engagement outside the business sector.

In the international development field, while cross-cultural skills are often included as requirements in position descriptions for development workers, cultural intelligence is not generally prioritized. Few organizations explicitly target the development of cultural intelligence or support its application at systemic or programming levels. However, for facilitators of change across cultures, a high level of cultural intelligence is beneficial for all aspects of the process, from planning to evaluation. Cultural intelligence is key to building trust, the most crucial element for meaningful and enduring collaboration on change-related processes and outcomes.

Cultural intelligence helps facilitators to identify and draw out the rich and often underlying dynamics of groups of participants. Being aware of one's own values and others' values enables a facilitator to ask questions and interpret the responses through a cultural lens, to dig deeper where appropriate, and encourage shared understanding of each other's differences and the positive benefits these differences can evoke. The intention is to leverage the richness, complexity, and depth that can be found in a room of people with different cultural values and perspectives, to identify a new future, plan for its achievement, and motivate action.

Culturally intelligent change facilitators recognize the importance of knowing their own values and power as well as valuing different cultural perspectives 'in the room', including those related to power and leadership. A mix of methods is available to draw out and negotiate shared values, particularly those which deliberately surface the wide range of perspectives in multicultural or cross-cultural teams for the purpose of generating various options to achieve change. Facilitators' ability to apply cross-cultural understanding themselves and support those involved in change processes to understand the role of cultural values when combined will enable groups of people to focus on the potential for synergy, cooperation and, ultimately, desirable improvements.

Cultural mindfulness

- State of being mindful of own cultural construct and others at the moment of interaction.
- Forming reactions and responses without stereotyping.

Cultural mindfulness is a relatively recent concept, which more explicitly includes reference to one's own values. Perhaps first coined by Kabigting (2017:1), it is defined as: 'a state of being mindful of, first, your *own* cultural construct, and second, the cultural constructs of the other person you are interacting with *at the moment* of such interaction. It simply means basing your reaction or response to the actual stimuli (the other person) without the baggage of cultural stereotyping'. Connected to the broader concept of mindfulness, cultural mindfulness focuses one's attention on the current emotional, psychological, spiritual, physical, and other aspects of the 'here and now' through a cultural values lens.

Cultural identity analysis

- Transformative level of understanding.
- Examination of changes to cultural values in self or others through interaction with others.

An even deeper and potentially transformative level of understanding about culture includes the examination of one's own cultural identity in a way that goes beyond recognizing that one has cultural values, to analysing how these are changed, shaped, or influenced through the interaction with others. This reflects psychological aspects of culture, but also responds to interaction between cultures, through both colonialism and globalization more broadly. The crossing of boundaries between cultures, however porous, and the influence of this on contemporary life is related to third space thinking and polyculturalism (see Chapter 2). A facilitator who is conscious of their own identity within this context, and is also able to support others' consciousness about this phenomenon and its implications for ideas about change, is perhaps at the highest level of understanding about the interface between culture and change. An organization which is able to integrate this understanding into the way it relates to the world is more likely to be able to navigate the complexity than one which holds and seeks to hold true to a single set of values.

How far up the ladder?

Facilitators operating in their own culture may not need to get off the ground onto this ladder, but most will need to take at least the first step. Even the most highly experienced cross-cultural facilitators may not, however, reach the top step. In practice, some individuals and organizations may demonstrate qualities and expertise across several levels of cultural understanding at the same time. It is unlikely that they could reach the highest step without taking a journey through the other steps. At a global level, aspiring to higher levels of intercultural collaboration seems a reasonable goal, but in the contemporary context of states, borders, nationalist and racist leadership, and divisions exacerbated by a global pandemic, chances of reaching this level currently seem remote.

This chapter suggests that finding language to describe the nature of cultural understanding which appeals to a wide audience is not easy. It uses a number of terms found in the broader literature to describe different levels of understanding and encourages facilitators to aim as high up the cultural literacy ladder as they can. For the remainder of this book, the term 'culturally attuned' is offered as a catch-all phrase to cover the idea that efforts taken are considered through a cultural lens in a way which maximizes harmonious understanding, and assumptions are continuously reviewed, consistent with double-loop learning (Argyris, 1977: see Chapter 1).

CHAPTER 5
Culturally attuned change facilitation

> We also need to develop a greater understanding of the impact of culture on participative process. Can the Western concepts of participation and democracy inherent in many participative technologies really be translated into a different cultural environment? (Blunt, 1995 referenced in Hailey, 2001)

The practice of facilitation for change is relatively new in historical terms, with most material produced in high-resource settings since the 1990s. It could be seen as one of many reactions against (or means to ameliorate the negative effects of) top-down changes and decisions imposed by leaders or external powers deemed out of touch with others' reality. It could also be seen as an inevitable way to respond to negative aspects of discipline specialization. It could be a manifestation of egalitarian values that dominate in the cultures where traditional development programming has developed. It could also reflect increasing evidence that models and approaches developed in one cultural context do not necessarily apply in another.

The discipline of community development has a lot to offer the practice of facilitation for change. Other disciplines, such as organizational change, leadership, psychology, behavioural science, anthropology, human geography, politics, peace and conflict studies, and legal studies also contribute theories, frames of reference, and research evidence. Contemporary change facilitation sources tend to reflect a convergence of ideas from two main sources: community development and organizational change. This chapter draws ideas from various disciplines to assist facilitators' reflection and practice.

Given that through a cultural values lens a facilitator is expected to support others' efforts to bring about their prioritized change, rather than drive or lead change, understanding about the distinction is important. This chapter discusses expectations of a facilitator through a cultural values lens. It considers concepts of facilitation, power and leadership, participation, collaboration, partnership, and inclusion through this lens. It seeks to contribute to understanding about how to avoid causing harm in cross-cultural facilitation practice.

When facilitators are working in cultures other than their own, understanding their own values and how they may be understood by participants in change processes is important. It is common for people to be unaware of their own values, even throughout their whole lives, particularly when they are not exposed to societies with other values. Even those exposed to others' values may remain blissfully unaware. While facilitators in high-resource contexts understandably promote the positive aspects of facilitated change, they need to be aware how some of the key aspects of facilitation and change may be understood differently in different contexts, and how they might therefore adjust practice to suit each context. If facilitators come from largely egalitarian, individualist, task-oriented, and low uncertainty avoidance cultural values, and they are facilitating groups of people with more hierarchical, collectivist, relationship-oriented, and high uncertainty avoidance cultural values, the differences can be significant. The implications of these differences are worthy of consideration, and are also relevant to people working with diverse groups within cultures.

When facilitators are working in multicultural contexts, recognizing and responding to dominant cultural values means that more complexities are involved in change processes. For example, a community development program in urban Melbourne or Manchester which includes people from many different cultural backgrounds and seeks to bring about some kind of health or education related behaviour change is more likely to reflect cultural values which dominate life in Melbourne or Manchester, as well as potentially seek to understand other values. This may involve facilitating two-way discussions about how different values shape behaviour and what this means for the messages and communications methods which suit people with different cultural values, in addition to discussions about the particular change topic. Facilitators who understand that all values have strengths and limitations, depending on one's point of view, will be better able to engage respectfully.

Evidence in evaluation reports and research papers in every sector confirms that positive benefits accrue when there is greater, rather than less, inclusion in facilitated change processes. This evidence explains the emphasis on participatory methods in community, organizational, and international development. Holman et al., (2007: 7) identified eight reasons which drive the use of participatory change methods, from their ability to accelerate action to their communication of a message about what could be better. In summary, the practice of facilitation of collaborative change reflects the following premises:

- Better results are achieved when multiple ideas are pooled, different perspectives are taken into account, successful partnerships are forged and collaboration takes place.
- People who have been involved and heard are more likely to feel valued and committed to achieving the changes they agreed to and motivated to take action.
- Marginalized groups will benefit from positive change, improved lives, and economic or social development if they are included and not left behind.
- Whole societies will be better off when all members are valued and included.

Researchers have addressed various aspects of this phenomenon. For example, some have considered: the pedagogy for facilitation across cultures drawing on Hofstede's work (e.g. Jelavic and Salter, 2014); learning and teaching across cultures (e.g. Leask and Carroll, 2013); general facilitation approaches (e.g. Bens, 2016); and methods to facilitate change (e.g. Holman et al., 2007; International Facilitation Association, n.d.). This chapter seeks to make key elements of this literature accessible.

When shared meaning (element 5 in Figure 3.1) is missing or when those involved in change do not understand the context in which they are operating, things go wrong: there is no shortage of formal and anecdotal evidence to confirm this. Green (2016: 235) refers to some of the many challenges inherent in facilitating change in different contexts: 'such stories of failure to understand culture and context are unfortunately common in the world of aid and development, and among activists more broadly'.

Definitions of facilitation through a cultural lens

The process of facilitation and its results can be understood differently through a cultural values lens. For example, in a low power distance culture, ideal facilitators may be viewed as skilled but 'neutral' people who set up an environment or run a process whereby others with expertise and knowledge in the particular topic area can express their varied views. This suits an individualist culture, since people are expected to express their ideas, choices, and preferences, and to excel in their field of expertise. As noted above, it also suits a task-oriented culture, since facilitation usually produces some kind of product, plan, result, or outcome. While there is usually some recognition that the facilitator is 'influential' in terms of how ideas are framed and what opportunities are made available, they are not generally seen as leaders.

In a high power distance culture, a facilitator may be seen as coming from a particular position of power (they may be appointed by one group or speak only one language, the language of the dominant, ex-colonial power or another authority), or they may be more educated or older than participants, so they may be seen more as a leader in a hierarchical context, rather than as a neutral person. They may also be seen for the particular values that underpin their practice, for example they may be focused on a task (such as negotiating to get a result or outcome) rather than the maintenance of relationships. From the participants' perspective, those with a low sense of power in a hierarchical culture are likely to have low expectations that there can be an equal weighting given to all those in a room, just as those with a high sense of power in this context would expect their voice to dominate.

In some collectivist cultures, sophisticated processes have been developed over thousands of years to achieve outcomes. For example, in Fijian and Samoan communities, complex norms determine who speaks first, next, and last, based on perceptions of relative status. This results in strict processes for negotiating agreements that avoid the sense of winners and losers, but generate consensus and give greater power to particular people. While those from more egalitarian cultures may witness exclusion or judge the process to result in 'lowest common denominator' decision-making, less egalitarian cultures may witness chaos and selfishness and wince at the loss of face associated with some groups winning over others (as occurs in voting) in an 'egalitarian' facilitation process. Navigating these expectations is feasible for a skilled cross-cultural facilitator, but highly challenging in practice.

Facilitators in organizational development in some countries have access to vast resources about what makes successful organizations and how to get there. A large global industry exists to promote frameworks, models, learning, and expertise in these areas. Organizational development lessons and principles are largely drawn from western cultures, and based on western values. They tend to emphasize the importance of including everyone, of facilitation towards shared objectives, and related decision-making and inclusion processes. In western cultural contexts, such approaches are more likely to work well but, in others, challenges may arise. In multinational companies, head office culture may be the source of theory, approaches, and tools to support organizational change across the whole organization. Facilitators from head office are often sent 'out' to run sessions about organizational change, including aspects of organizational culture. Some are better than others at recognizing different cultural values and using culturally attuned approaches.

Expectations and definitions of a good facilitator may differ. Assumptions that facilitators need to come from high-resource or well-funded cultures are best questioned. In a high power distance culture, people who stand up at the front of a room are more likely to be seen as those with power, rather than those who are neutral. If a facilitator takes the approach that they wish to empower those in the room, they may struggle to engage participants who see themselves as holding low power as they do not wish their seniors to lose face. Efforts to encourage participation may make participants feel uncomfortable. In a collectivist cultural context, plenary discussions often fall flat because most participants will want to consult their colleagues or members of their group before saying anything that may be seen (unintentionally) to have negative consequences for others. Efforts to generate a new result may not bring about agreement because participants are concerned about the loss of face implied for their leaders, which may be associated with changing tack.

Most community development and international development practitioners know the most effective leaders and drivers of positive and sustainable developmental change come from within the context where change happens, i.e. within communities, organizations, and countries. People in a context inevitably know it better than those from outside. If changes are imposed by or seen to be imposed by outsiders, particularly those whose values are different, the chances of them being relevant, accepted, and sustainable are substantially reduced. The subtleties and complexities of each context need to be understood. For example, in post-colonial settings, some people may pay automatic respect to ideas that come from the previous colonial 'masters' (consistent with high power distance), while others may automatically reject ideas from this source (consistent with collectivist values about self-rule, for example). These reactions can also vary over time. In cultures where one gender, ethnic, or religious group dominates others, expectations that plans can be generated and agreed upon by all those in a room, as if they are equal, may be unrealistic. Some change-oriented programs in the 21st century seek to overcome these inequalities, but doing so without an understanding of the values and beliefs in each local context can result in harm. Local guides are often critical in helping determine how to facilitate processes in such contexts.

Navigating complexities within each context and within each partnership is often the role of facilitators: issues of power and different expectations of the facilitator always need to be considered. A great deal of international cooperation is founded on the premise that when locally determined and led priorities are supported by external sources (e.g. funding, specialist personnel and/or other resources), then significant changes are both possible and more likely to be sustainable. Complexities associated with 'locally determined' and 'locally led', i.e. power and leadership, across cultures are therefore important for facilitators to consider.

Power and leadership

Understanding core concepts about power and leadership is critical for everyone involved in change. Even if facilitators believe or acknowledge they are not the drivers and leaders themselves, they may be seen by others as having power and leadership influence, and therefore potentially displace or undermine the leadership of others. The concept of leadership can encompass the element of 'influencing' others, which facilitators and advisors are doing when selecting tools and supporting particular conversations. Navigating the subtleties of leadership, influencing, driving, and supporting takes considerable self-reflection and skill, as well as cultural understanding. Few are likely to be fully comfortable with the phenomenon of imposing cultural values on others, even when they may be perceived by others to be doing so. Avoiding the perception of white privilege and colonialist approaches is not easy in a globalized world where change is rapid and identities are shifting.

Cultural identity plays a significant role in community perceptions of leaders' ability to bring about change (Hudson et al., 2019). The wielding of power and the exercise of leadership are integral to ideas about change and facilitation. Power can be seen as corrupting or positive, depending on one's cultural values. A great deal has been written about power and leadership in different cultural contexts and how critical these are to understanding and engaging with change (e.g. Leftwich, 1995, 2009, 2011; Green, 2016; Developmental Leadership Program 2020b). It is easy and common for those from one culture to critique the leadership style of those from another. People in individualistic cultures, where critique is a strong value, and in low power distance cultures, where power is expected to be widely shared, are quick to decry autocrats who 'stifle' critique and hold power to themselves, often ignoring the social contracts between leaders and followers. Those with collectivist and high power distance values are less likely to critique leaders within because of deeply held values about respect and order. They may see leaders in low power distance cultures as 'weak' and chaotic because of their lack of apparent authority, expressed through their ongoing consultation with others and inability to be decisive and control others.

In cultures where change is positively valued, a good leader is someone who achieves change. Conversely, in cultures where stability is more highly valued, a good leader is one who maintains stability. Crises highlight many negative and positive aspects of leadership, and the connections between values and leadership expectations. For example, research efforts by the Developmental Leadership Program (DLP) during the COVID-19 pandemic in 2020, illustrated the complexities involved and synthesized leadership lessons emerging in different cultural contexts (Developmental Leadership Program, 2020a).

Many frameworks have been developed for describing and strengthening leadership (e.g. Mendenhall et al., 2008). These reflect varied values about how individuals should behave in relation to others, how a society should operate, how an organization can succeed, and how changes can be achieved. Expectations about power and leadership reflect cultural values generated over long and complex histories, through revolutions, wars, and overthrowing of various social systems. In western cultures, the presence of myriad guides in bookshops on 'how to be a leader' illustrates the view that everyone is seen as a potential leader. Suggestions that leadership will be effective if seven particular steps are taken or five selected characteristics are nurtured reflect the values in such cultures. In hierarchical cultures, leadership roles are bestowed upon the inherited few, the wise older citizens, the highly esteemed religious leaders, or the existentially powerful autocrats, not the common majority: in this context, fewer books are written to share ideas about leadership. Citizens are less likely to buy books to teach them to lead, but rely on others who have status, wisdom, and experience, and perhaps some loyal advisors.

Distinctions between different types of power (first raised by Rowlands, 1997 and since elucidated by others such as VeneKlasen and Miller, 2007 and Mathie et al., 2017) are helpful when considering the concept through a cultural lens. The differences between power over, power to, power with, and power within are now more widely discussed: each may be understood differently within varied cultural contexts. Facilitating discussions about the differences is potentially a useful contribution to understanding change in different cultural contexts.

How power is understood is relevant to how leaders work with others. Cultures which are low on power distance, individualistic, task-oriented, and open to change are relatively more oriented to the idea of including different people in decision-making and access to social and economic opportunities, regardless of characteristics. However, in high power distance cultures with collectivist, relationship-oriented, and change-averse values, such as India, Samoa, or Indonesia, it may be assumed that people are relatively less likely to embrace major changes, including some of those associated with inclusive leadership (see Inclusion below). While the point about comparisons has been made above, it is worth reiterating here in particular that like all statements about cultural values, this does not mean that all people within specific cultures share these views, but that in overall relative terms, there are differences between cultural values. Ideas associated with inclusion may not necessarily be explicitly or consciously prioritized because values that dominate are about 'in-groups' and 'out-groups'. Social contracts exist between leaders and followers which bind them to mutual rights and obligations, and provide stability and opportunities for those who are parties to the contract. In this context, for a leader to be more inclusive, they need to bring an 'out-group' into a social contract. However, this requires changes in core values as well as behaviour for everyone concerned. The idea of reconciling notions of stability and predictability with the provision of opportunities for all and expanded civil liberties requires significant changes in core cultural values. Such a process may take decades even with the best political will, efforts by younger generations, and highly managed peaceful change processes. Without such changes in core values, sustaining inclusive leadership may be unrealistic.

The power associated with systems which support change facilitation (i.e. government and philanthropic donor systems) often have limits on the extent to which genuine participatory and inclusive practice can occur, as discussed further below. Their values are likely to dominate, since these systems determine the kinds of support to be provided, the ways in which funding will be determined and allocated, and the nature of what success looks like.

Participation

> This would imply that the process of participation is not universal and is contingent on different cultural norms or assumptions (Hailey, 2001: 97)

Participation is the other side of the coin to facilitation – without the former, the latter has little meaning. Change facilitators need a good understanding of the concept of participation, how it is understood in different cultural contexts, and how to achieve the best process in each context.

In the western world, a major paradigm shift began in the 1960s across several disciplines, including social work and international development, which can be broadly characterized as *away from* top-down and technical approaches *towards* participatory approaches. The large body of work by Robert Chambers is well known, highly influential, and has shaped much contemporary practice (for example, Chambers, 1983, 1994, 2002, 2005, 2008, and 2013; Bennett and Roberts, 2004; Barefoot Guides, n.d.). Most international and national NGOs apply participatory methods in their development cooperation practice. When reflecting on participation in 2013, Chambers (2013: 75) wrote:

> Participation in development-speak is used to cover a multitude of practices, some inspiring and good, and some depressingly bad. I shall not define it but simply say that participation has implications for power relations, personal interactions, and attitudes and behaviours and that participatory can apply to almost all social contexts and processes, not least in organizations, education, research, communities and the family. For its part, development can be taken to mean good change, raising questions of power and relationships concerning who says what is good and who identifies what change matters — whether 'we' professionals do, or whether it is 'they' — those who are poor, marginalised, vulnerable and excluded.

It is easy to critique the reality of participation in the modern world, as it has been commodified and distorted over time. By the 1990s, participation was viewed as a central tenet in development practice at many levels, from the World Bank to the smallest of civil society organizations, even if not applied evenly. The practice of maximizing participation has been nominally sustained since then, but critique of its dominance, practice, and use by donors is found in many quarters (e.g. Blunt, 1995; Fowler, 1997; Cooke and Kothari, 2001; Hailey, 2001; Cornwall, 2006; Cornwall and Coelho, 2007). There remains considerable debate about the concept at historical, philosophical, political, and pragmatic levels, including the idea that the promotion of participatory approaches is akin to imposing western models of democracy in contexts which may not have sought or prioritized these ideas. Only some of this debate has considered participation through different cultural perspectives.

The link between participation and cultural values is worthy of consideration for those involved in facilitating change across cultures. It is reflected in the sub-sections of this chapter and potentially connects to the 'depressingly bad' aspects of participatory practices, i.e. where they are applied without understanding the cultural values which shape participation in decision-making in each context. Hailey (2001: 97) suggested 'this would imply that the process of participation is not universal and is contingent on different cultural norms or assumptions'. While the literature on this topic is complex, and is linked to other areas such as political participation, it generally leads to two sets of implications for practitioners: first, the need to think deeply about one's own culture and to carefully analyse the different cultural contexts in which participatory approaches will be used; and second, to consider the types of participatory approaches which will be culturally relevant in practice. These implications are reflected in the two parts of this book.

Collaboration

> Collaboration is a process involving organizations working toward a goal they can't reach alone. The process requires long-term commitment and an understanding that there will be shared risks, responsibilities, and rewards. Successful collaboration must be based on mutual respect, a valuing of difference, trust, a plan, lots of patience, determination to adopt new attitudes and pull in partners not usually involved, and, most of all, a sense of common purpose. (Brownlee, n.d.)

Collaborative partnerships are among the most important mechanisms for achieving change. Very few changes are brought about and sustained by a single person, even great leaders. It goes without saying that collaboration and partnerships are most likely to be successful if effective conversations take place. Successful communications about what changes are sought, how they will be achieved, and what success looks like inevitably require a high degree of shared meaning. Meaningful communications and the achievement of shared meaning across cultures are not easy when people and organizations have varied cultural values. Cross-cultural understanding is crucial for collaboration.

In an English language dictionary, the word collaboration has at least two general meanings: the situation of two or more people working together to create or achieve the same thing; and (interestingly) the situation of people working with an enemy who has taken control of their country (*Cambridge Dictionary*). The first meaning is applied to this work, and it is interesting that the definition includes the element of creating or achieving something, rather than simply people working together for the sake of working together. Also, the fact that the definition refers to two or more *people*, rather than groups of people (or organizations), can be seen as a manifestation of individualist cultural values. This helps illustrate how cultural values (in this case task orientation and individualism) shape language (in this case the meaning of a very common word about why people work together).

Links between ideas about collaboration and cultural values are vast, rich, and complex. At one level is the idea of collaboration *between* people from different cultural values. For example, it is often reported that cross-cultural collaboration is the key to achieving major development changes and that a large proportion of business mergers and acquisitions across borders fail because of a clash of cultural values (e.g. Gelfand et al., 2018). At another level, one can consider how the idea of collaboration is understood differently in different cultures as more relevant to this book.

Cultures vary on the values that shape the nature of interactions *between* people within communities or other defined groups. This is particularly evident on the 'individualism-collectivism' dimension described in Chapter 2. Interestingly, a great deal of literature has been generated from more individualistic cultures on the concepts of collaboration and effective communications, based on research that suggests that cooperation is critical for achieving successful organizations and effective change. Most western literature uses the formation of collective action as a means to achieve a particular result, or achieve a task, in the form of change or development, rather than for its own sake. In contrast, collectivist cultures have ideas about working collectively deeply embedded in community life, so collectivist practices are undertaken for their own sake and not necessarily to 'achieve' a particular result, other than ongoing harmony and inclusion. It may seem amusing that people from individualistic cultures commonly seek to build the capacity of people and organizations in collectivist cultures on how to work collectively, but on the other hand, collaboration *across* different groups can actually be quite challenging in collectivist contexts.

Change facilitators are well advised to engage with community development literature: collaboration is central to this discipline. For example, Barr and Huxham (1996) defined community development as involving people from different sectors and organizations *collaborating* to improve a specific area. Collaborative efforts can be initiated and variously facilitated or supported by community organizations, individual leaders (in the broadest sense of the word), government, service providers, foundations, or businesses, to address particular issues. Challenges associated with genuine collaboration across sectors, or between various groups, are well documented in many disciplines. Barr and Huxham (1996) note the ideal community development process involves all those who may be affected by a particular intervention, but in reality this is rarely the case. A range of factors prevents such inclusion, including cultural values about power and decision-making.

Ideas about collaboration in the context of organizational change are largely shaped by western cultural values and seek to generate better results. A key driver of change is often the demand for increasing individual and team productivity, rather than collaboration for its own sake. More recent interest in diversity and inclusion reflects a reaction to the reality that many change processes in fact neglect or exclude particular groups, a phenomenon found across most of the world.

In the world of international cooperation, the nature of collaboration has changed over time, but there remains relatively little recognition of cross-cultural aspects. Since the 1970s, government and major philanthropic donors have sought to generate a sense of collaboration with governments of countries where development programs are provided, for example through the series of international agreements on development effectiveness. The true extent of collaboration during implementation and evaluation varies widely. As in the business and organizational development sectors, more recent focus on inclusion has begun to influence collaborative effort across more groups. The SDGs' new emphasis on 'leaving no-one behind' and the inclusion of Article 17 on partnerships (see next section) illustrate the changing nature of collaboration.

By definition, collaboration is different from the more dominant competitive and contractual systems associated with capitalist economies. While achieving change requires collaboration, arrangements put in place between people and organizations to achieve change are often based on competition and compliance with contracts. Which organization can achieve the desired change for the lowest price? Which organization can achieve the biggest change for the set price? The extent to which these systems contradict each other varies across different contexts and times, and collaboration is indeed possible within a competitive and compliance-driven context, even if challenging. When navigating this aspect of complexity, there is value in recognizing the cultural values that shape collaboration.

Partnership

Contemporary organizations use the term partnership to describe a wide range of relationships. Partnership is now promoted as a key to success and a critical means to design and bring about changes that individuals or organizations cannot typically achieve themselves, or to extend benefits further. A world of support for brokering partnerships, cross-sector partnership development, business partnerships, and monitoring partnerships has emerged since the early 2000s. How do different cultures consider the idea of partnership or practices associated with partnership management? How do partnerships address and respond to different cultural values? How do partnership facilitators ensure their work is culturally attuned? What can facilitators learn from the practice of partnership brokering across cultures?

More formalized partnership development approaches generally originate in relatively individualist cultures. Is this a reaction against some of the limitations or excesses of individualism? When a society's key values encourage everyone to compete, become successful individuals, strive to reach their own potential, and take all steps possible to achieve, then it is easy to see that this has downsides. Individuals can try their best but are limited by having only one brain; they can be left behind while others strive for and achieve great success; they can be exhausted by trying to understand so many different and new ideas on their own. Not everyone can achieve their potential, not all organizations can be best all the time or save the world, and not all businesses can be the top business in their sector. When evidence of change processes consistently highlights the critical importance of effective collaboration and quality partnerships, then it is not surprising that a movement has grown to support them.

Collectivist cultures by definition are those which place a high value on collective action, which in theory suggests there is a greater affinity with the concept of partnership. Interestingly, collectivist values emphasize collaboration based on mutual obligations within a particular group, rather than collaboration with just anyone or with people outside the in-group. When there is an expectation that people from one self-defined group should collaborate with those from another, the natural reaction may be bemused resistance or lack of engagement. For example, when a community leader from one island in Vanuatu was asked why the national office of an organization did not include staff representing other islands, he responded 'why would we set up an office that could not possibly succeed? The trust that we need to run a successful office is simply not there when people are from different islands'. When the purpose of such a collaboration is to achieve a particular task, and the cultural value emphasizes the maintenance of harmonious relationships over the achievement of a particular task, then there is a double limitation on the chance of success.

Task-oriented cultures tend to see that relationship development is largely for the achievement of particular results or tasks. Perhaps, therefore, the interest in partnership development can be seen in the context of the value of task orientation: an underpinning premise is that 'more can be achieved if we work in partnership', prioritizing the idea that 'achieving more' is the ultimate goal. For cultures which prioritize the maintenance of harmonious relationships as a goal, partnerships can be either ho-hum, or rather confronting if there is some expectation that some actual task is seen as more important than maintaining harmony between people.

From an egalitarian cultural perspective, where individuals are broadly expected to be relatively equal and everyone has the right to have a voice and be listened to, a partnership mechanism makes sense as a means to allow for shared expression of ideas and enables people to consider the difficult questions. Relatively low power distance values suggest that partners in a partnership have a roughly equal stake in a particular situation, so it's a matter of 'brainstorming' and negotiating the different interests and frames of reference to develop a result. In high power distance cultures, values emphasize that those with power are the ones whose voice should be prioritized over others, and those without power do not have an equal voice. This means that those without power do not expect to have an equal voice, be listened to, or to raise any concerns they have that may embarrass their leaders and contribute to a loss of face. The idea of asking the hard questions about interests of leaders, challenging the status quo, or other aspects of partnership may be particularly challenging in high power distance contexts.

Finally, partnerships often encourage participants to be comfortable with uncertainty, encouraging systems which support high levels of flexibility and adaptability, as well as continuous monitoring to identify emerging issues. The practice of partnerships supports partners to set off on a path, sometimes without really knowing where the path will go and how to trust the process and the other partners, and to bend with the wind as the various issues emerge. For cultures which place a high value on uncertainty avoidance, this approach can be uncomfortable or sometimes confronting.

A growing pool of skilled partnership brokers work across many countries as a result of formal training by groups such as the Partnership Brokers' Association. These approaches and lessons have the potential to support change-oriented change facilitation practice, particularly if good attention is given to cultural values in cross-cultural partnerships.

Inclusion

The practice of facilitating change, by definition, raises the question of who is included in a process or in a room. It also raises questions related to power and leadership (see Power and Leadership above) and particularly inclusive leadership (see below). The idea of inclusion is now referenced in many disciplines and the SDGs, which emphasize 'leaving no-one behind', the first time such a sentiment has appeared in a global agreement. This reference now implies an inclusive approach is necessary in all aspects of public policy and international cooperation.

New, global, and complex challenges require collective and inclusive responses. In western cultures, business and organizational psychology disciplines promote inclusion widely as the key to maximizing organizational success. In international development cooperation, achieving human rights, reducing inequality, maximizing justice, and using participatory approaches to economic and social change require inclusive approaches. Participatory approaches (see Participation above) also encompass ideas about ensuring everyone, particularly the marginalized, is involved in making decisions about matters that affect their own lives. A blend of effectiveness and justice imperatives underpin inclusive effort.

Western literature on inclusion provides models and strategies to engage and benefit people with backgrounds and characteristics that differ from dominant or mainstream populations (see Chapter 4). In the US, where much of the diversity and inclusion research originates, the emphasis is given to gender and multiracial workplaces. In the development world, characteristics related to gender, race, ethnicity, ability, religion, and class are incorporated, as well as geographical isolation. Current US research is finding some evidence that inclusive organizations outperform non-inclusive organizations, largely because the inclusive organizations benefit from the views of people from varied backgrounds. In the development discipline, little evidence yet exists about the consequences of inclusive approaches, though Carter (2015: 2) found:

> The strength of the empirical evidence varies for the range of societal benefits from inclusive development approaches ... This brief review finds evidence of broader benefits to society of lower income inequality, improved human development outcomes, women's and girls' empowerment and inclusive growth approaches. There remain, however, evidence gaps and ongoing debates over findings. There is a gap in evidence on the impact of voice, empowerment and accountability approaches on long-term, transformative change. Empirical cross-country evidence on the impact of inclusive economic and political institutions on economic and other development indicators is contested. The evidence on the macro-level economic and social impacts of social protection and increasing service delivery is limited and inconclusive. Lastly, with contested concepts, indirect effects and long-time horizons, it is perhaps

inevitable that evidence linking inclusive development approaches and peacebuilding and state-building outcomes is scarce.

Consideration of the concept and practice of inclusion through a cultural lens raises important questions: 'how do different cultures consider the concept of inclusion and its application in practice?' and 'how culturally feasible is it for less inclusive countries to shift towards more inclusive development?' Just as positive change and development in one cultural setting (or from one disciplinary lens) can be seen as destruction in another, aspects of inclusion can be seen as positive from one perspective or undermining order from another. From those cultural values discussed in Chapter 2, the most relevant are power distance and individualism/collectivism (Hofstede, 1980; House et al., 2004) and gender egalitarianism (House et al., 2004), discussed below.

Inclusion and power distance

As noted in Chapter 2, in cultures with low power distance values, organizations and societies appear relatively non-hierarchical and ideas about inclusion and equality are relatively more widely applied. Good leaders tend towards consulting staff, sharing information, and involving others in decision-making processes, consistent with egalitarian principles and inclusive policies. Calls for inclusion are consistent with a belief that gaps between those with and without power should be minimized. Of course, even in relatively more egalitarian cultures, inclusion is not necessarily afforded to all people, as attested by the experience of indigenous populations in Australia, the US, and Canada.

Inclusion in cultures with high power distance values may be understood differently. In such contexts, power is retained in the hands of a few, and a threat to leaders is portrayed as a threat to everyone with whom the leaders have a social contract. Leaders with wisdom, access to resources, and spiritual power are seen as best placed to make decisions on behalf of those without: inclusion of everyone is neither prioritized nor seen as appropriate. Usually many or most younger people, women, less-educated people, minority groups, and the 'masses', who are in some kind of social contract with their leaders, do not expect to be included in decision-making. Of course, there are many exceptions, particularly with globalization, but in relative terms this is more likely to be the case. Leaders are expected to maintain social order, stability, and harmony on the basis of their status, concentrating decision-making among those who 'know best' rather than those who are marginalized. In most Asian and Pacific cultures, the clear presence of and (general) respect for hierarchies and authoritative leaders, such as kings, chiefs, sultans, big men, and village leaders, suggests ideas about inclusion are not necessarily prioritized. Of course, when these patterns are threatened, such as when there are widespread protests or challenges to power, they are the subject of considerable attention, and are not the norm. It is worth reiterating that generalizations described here are certainly generalizations, and do not imply that all people within a culture share the same values or that values do not change over time. The benefit of the differences is for comparison purposes and to help cross-cultural interactions reflect potentially different frames of reference.

Inclusion and individualism/collectivism

Differences between individualist and collectivist cultural values (described in Chapter 2) influence views about inclusion. In individualist cultures, people expect to express their own ideas and preferences and be heard: whole systems and workplaces are built on this value. Individuals in these cultures tend to be motivated by self-interest, communicate more directly, and are members of multiple groups, without feeling any particular obligation to any of them. People expect to be included and do not tolerate exclusion. Competition of ideas is both expected and often highly valued in these contexts, thus inclusion is important. Interestingly, in individualist societies, people tend to see themselves as citizens of a country and have a clear sense of 'the public' as a phenomenon, which implies some form of obligation. For example, in the COVID-19 pandemic, individuals were implored by their governments to take particular action for the 'public good'. And individuals who broke the rules were taken care of by the legal system 'for the public good'.

In contrast, people in relatively more collectivist cultures tend to negotiate decisions and goals within their own groups, where they already know preferences, priorities, and expectations of group members and especially the groups' leaders. The premise that individuals' views are equal or that people from other groups have equally valuable ideas are an anathema to highly collectivist cultures. Interestingly, while collectivism implies strong bonds to the members of a particular group, this does not necessarily apply to a whole nation or 'the public'. This is because obligations to the particular group absorb so much attention, and other groups within the public comprise 'others' who cannot be trusted upon to the same degree as those within the group. In these contexts, people do not expect to be included or heard, and when asked to speak up may feel threatened and fear showing disrespect to those in power. Bad behaviour by people in other groups is often seen as consistent with stereotypes and 'othering': including 'others' is not seen as important.

One implication of different values related to inclusion is that it cannot be assumed that everyone is equally comfortable with the idea and its practice. In low power distance and individualist cultures, people are socialized about inclusion from early in school life, while in high power distance and collectivist cultures, people are more likely to be comfortable with communicating with or understanding the nuances and metaphors which have developed among members of their own group, but not so comfortable to engage with other groups. Thus, the latter may be less inclined towards expressing their own opinions outside their own context. In collectivist societies, distinctions between in-groups and out-groups are often quite pronounced, so the idea of including out-groups in decision-making may be seen as 'odd', 'dysfunctional', or outright 'dangerous'.

Interestingly, Australia is one of the most individualistic cultures in the world according to Hofstede's contemporary research (Hofstede, 2020), so its national interest in and commitment to inclusion is understandable. Inclusive approaches also reflect rights-based thinking, whereby all people are understood as having equal human rights (even if they are not necessarily protected). Inclusive approaches are certainly an appropriate goal in individualist societies. In collectivist cultures, people largely have a deep understanding about how to thrive and survive **within** their own variously defined particular groups, but not necessarily **across** different groups or at a national level. This means that when people from individualist and collectivist cultures collaborate, discussions about how inclusion is understood and how it can be achieved in different contexts are essential.

Inclusive leadership

Inclusive leadership is a relatively recent concept, which brings contemporary ideas about diversity and inclusion (Mor Barak, 2000 and 2015; Randel et al. 2016 and 2018) together with understanding about the practice of leadership. Initially based on research about how to strengthen private sector organizations (Wuffli, 2016), inclusive leadership ideas are now applied to broader development change agendas (Roche, 2019) and are directly related to achievement of the SDGs (Mohammed, 2019). While inclusive leadership has become a popular topic in recent years, it is an emerging field of study and practice: it may be the next phase in, or type of, leadership development (e.g. Bortini et al., 2016).

Inclusive leadership promotes approaches which include and consider the voices of diverse members of a society or organization. The major themes in inclusive leadership are: whether the 'followers' feel a sense of belonging, and whether followers' unique contributions (e.g. different abilities, traits, perspectives, qualities, and efforts) are valued. An analysis of the extent to which these elements are found in a change-oriented context may be useful for planning for facilitation processes (see Chapter 7).

This discussion certainly does not argue against inclusion at all, but for considered approaches to inclusion. Rhodes and Antoine (2019) described examples where inclusion-related ideas have 'caught on' in different cultures, which are not inconsistent with other approaches described in this chapter. They found the following approaches have been used: respectful engagement with cultural values and appreciation of how they influence behaviour (see Cultural understanding for facilitators in Chapter 6); use of strengths-based approaches (see Chapter 7); use of authoritative leadership in high power distance cultures to require inclusion; and acknowledgement that inclusive leadership may be messy and unpredictable (see Chapters 11 and 12).

This chapter has confirmed the benefits of using a cultural lens to consider core aspects of facilitation, particularly power and leadership, participation, collaboration, partnership, and inclusion. The use of participatory methods is well documented in many contexts, but whether they have caused harm, despite the many benefits, is not well researched. There are plenty of critics but in the practice of international development cooperation, a commitment to participatory approaches has been accepted as a central tenet of good practice since the 1970s and 1980s, even if not always applied in reality. These approaches developed largely as a response to research that showed local people know their context best, and that marginalized people are excluded in high power distance cultures. Whether participatory processes change values and address systemic exclusion or negative aspects of low power distance cultural values in sustainable ways is not often the focus of research and may not be a reasonable expectation. Despite the many other benefits of participatory approaches, double-loop learning (Argyris 1977 – see Figure 1.1) encourages continuous reflection about the underlying assumptions, including the values which underpin their use.

As noted above, complexities associated with achieving positive systemic, organizational, or other kinds of change across cultures are significant. External people and funding can at best facilitate and support leaders and people within their own context to achieve positive changes that have meaning for them. While there may be different degrees of influence and contribution, they largely cannot control or engineer change. Where there is a possibility of a confluence of ideas about the priority accorded to change, the broad nature of change, and the ways in which the change is likely to occur, then there is a greater chance of success. A facilitator can make a difference, but where there are contradictory views in these elements, the chances of achieving positive change are significantly reduced. Long-term collaboration, based on respectful and trust-based relationships, and shared responsibility for success and risks are thus key ingredients for success.

The assumption that all cultures have the same values in relation to change and how to facilitate is flawed. This is not an argument against inclusive, participatory, and facilitated approaches. It rather calls for greater effort to understand the context in which inclusive approaches are applied. It also calls for increased efforts to reduce any harmful and negative effects, particularly for the marginalized people who are so often intended to be the beneficiaries of such approaches. Part 2 of this book seeks to support those involved in the facilitation process to reflect on cultural assumptions, reduce potential harm, and maximize positive benefits.

CHAPTER 6
Principles for change facilitation across cultures

How can facilitators of change contribute 'meaningfully', when meaning can be understood so differently from different cultural perspectives? How can facilitators maximize the cultural relevance of their contributions, while recognizing the complexities of power and their own cultural 'baggage'? How can they maximize the quality and benefits of participation and inclusion when working with people from different cultures? How can facilitators approach their work to achieve both successful processes and relevant change-related results when working cross-culturally or in multicultural settings?

This chapter proposes a set of six principles to support and inform the specific practice of facilitating change across cultures, reflecting discussion in previous chapters. These principles are:

1. Change facilitators who work in multicultural or intercultural contexts require a high level of cultural understanding.
2. Cultures have different perceptions of the purpose of facilitation and the nature of change and these need to be recognized.
3. Defining inclusion in context-specific ways is necessary to bring about greater inclusion.
4. Generating shared culture and building trust are key to effective collaboration.
5. Adaptive and flexible ways of working are essential for intercultural collaboration.
6. Cultural understanding is relevant throughout a program cycle, including in monitoring, evaluation, and learning processes.

These principles are strongly interconnected and mutually supportive, though discussed separately below. When collectively considered and applied, these principles support effective cross-cultural engagement more generally as well as successful transition through different stages in a change-oriented programming cycle.

Cultural understanding for facilitators

> We humans are fundamentally all the same species and feel common human emotions and each of us also has its own unique personality. Yet the culture in which we grow up has a profound impact on how we see the world, how we see a communication style effective or

undesirable, how we show disagreement, how we consider certain ways of making decisions natural or strange. (Lastennet, 2015)

In the modern world, change facilitators need to have the deepest level of cultural understanding possible. When facilitators operate in contexts where cultural values differ, there is value in them continually stepping up the ladder (Chapter 4) towards deeper cultural understanding about connections between cultural values, change, and facilitation and stronger abilities to apply such understanding in practice. As stated earlier, it is not always the case that this applies only to westerners working in other contexts. The extent to which individuals and organizations involved in facilitating change can understand and apply cultural understanding will vary in different settings.

In practical terms, a culturally attuned facilitator is one who serves all the people in the room in the best ways possible. This includes ways which maximize benefits for all, reflect understanding of the different frames of reference that influence people's views of the world and of change, and recognize that a level playing field is extremely rare. A culturally attuned facilitator can support the development of more nuanced strategies than could be found within a single cultural context. They can engage respectfully and effectively with people from different backgrounds, facilitate complex conversations, generate shared understanding, and support participants to find the kinds of pathways that they are willing to take towards a better future.

Taking account of the power issues so explicitly expressed by Pon (2009), cultural understanding should not imply some kind of higher status given to those from dominant cultures to perpetuate inequality with those from 'other'/non-white cultures. Being aware that race, power, and cultural values are interconnected and crucial to the way the world works brings with it a responsibility to work respectfully, humbly, and in a constant state of listening and learning. Building understanding about connections between cultural values and change is a shared responsibility and does not require any particular model, but rather a combination of curiosity and an ability to create opportunities for reflection and respectful discussion about these links.

Change facilitators have at least three major opportunities in relation to working in culturally attuned ways. First, they need to be aware of their own values and power, and how they may be seen by others in relative terms. Second, they need to be curious and constantly seeking to learn about cultural values and norms, and how they are relevant to the contexts in which they work. Third, they need to create opportunities to help raise awareness among participants of change processes about the links between cultural values and change, since understanding how people other than ourselves see the world will help to address the kinds of divisions that cause harm to us all.

Primarily, change facilitators need to be aware of their own values and those of the people and organizations with whom they work. When facilitators are self-aware, they have a better chance of maximizing the relevance of their work with all participants. Several layers are involved here: individual, organizational, and cultural/systemic levels of understanding. Interactions between the layers can be highly complex, as illustrated by different ways of understanding cultures (see Polyculturalism and Third space thinking above).

Generating awareness of one's cultural values is not always easy, simply because values are usually hidden 'underneath' norms and behaviour (see Figure 1.2) and may not be obvious most of the time. One's own values may not be easy to articulate, can change over time, can surface differently at challenging times, and obviously cannot be found in a book or on the internet! Interestingly, the degree to which people are aware of their own cultural values can be influenced by broader social cultural values. In individualist cultures, for example, people do not necessarily see themselves being influenced by social norms and values because the cultural value is that individuals should be original, independent, and freethinking. In collectivist cultures, members of groups are explicitly taught the group's values because this is what defines and holds the group together, which is highly valued. In one workshop, an Australian official expressed the view that his values were personal and private so he preferred not to talk about them, and his I-Kiribati colleagues reacted with amazement, noting that in their more collectivist culture people were raised to speak openly and confidently about their values, and to do so proudly when meeting people from different cultures.

Awareness of one's own values often increases when one leaves one's home country, realizing and experiencing the implications of the idea that core beliefs are not necessarily shared. If born and raised within a culture where the values are broadly shared, where systems and leaders confirm these values, and where daily life is consistent with these values, then questions about values are less likely to be raised. For those who move beyond their own values to seek to understand others and raise questions about 'core beliefs' through education, intermarriage, or some other experience, the awareness-raising journey about one's own and others' values often begins.

Learning about another culture and adopting or adapting to another culture can be a lifelong pursuit. For example, say a person raised in India moves to Australia at the age of 20 and becomes fluent in Australian English, works in an Australian workplace, and marries someone born in Australia. They may adopt or adapt to some Australian cultural values but will also likely retain deeply held cultural values from their upbringing, especially when challenges arise. Similarly, an Australian-raised person may move to India at the age of 20 and learn Tamil or Hindi language and seek to embed themselves in Indian culture in many ways. Having not been brought up with Indian values, they will likely always retain some core Australian values, even if they try hard to change their behaviour and comply with Indian norms. Social and cultural values can be dynamic and at the same time remarkably stubborn and deeply rooted.

Holding and supporting respectful conversations about values and how change happens is one of the most important roles a change facilitator can play. Being culturally aware also means continually asking questions about values and their influence on people's behaviour and their aspirations. Those who have developed maturity in their cultural awareness may be more confident and capable of asking really key questions which are related to changes in cultural values. Questions such as 'are my/your/our cultural values still fit for purpose?' or 'how might other cultural values help in achieving the kinds of change I/we/they want?' are best asked only when there are high levels of trust and mutual respect, and by people who are NOT seen to be imposing their values on others.

According to US-led research (e.g. Kelley and Myers, 1995), people who are highly culturally aware and adaptive tend to have certain qualities and preferences. They are open to reflecting and continuous learning about themselves and others and about the broader world of ideas, and demonstrate curiosity and a sense of adventure. They tend to have strong interpersonal skills, such as an ability to engage with and learn from people with different cultural values and an ability to initiate and maintain relationships with people who may be different from themselves. They also have the ability to monitor and manage their own thoughts and reactions in intercultural contexts, using largely positive frames of reference and emotional resilience. Equivalent research from more hierarchical, collectivist, and relationship-oriented cultural contexts has not been found although similar or different qualities may apply.

Culturally aware organizations recognize that they not only have values, expressed in their vision statement or strategic plans and the way they engage with the world, but also recognize, respect, and seek to collaborate with organizations with different values. It is common for organizations to collaborate and compete with others with similar values, but rare to find organizations seeking to collaborate with others whose values may differ markedly. NGOs working with the private sector, for example, recognize the critical nature of cross-sectoral collaboration, but are often highly challenged both within their own organization and in the implementation of partnerships.

At a national level, some cultures appear more interested in applying, exporting, or enforcing their values on other cultures, either explicitly or implicitly, implying their own values are 'better' than others. This is reflected in colonialist and neo-colonialist behaviour which continues in many ways in the modern world. For example, US democracy institutes explicitly seek to promote ideas about the value of democracy to other countries, Chinese institutes promote Chinese cultural values, and France supports the Alliance Francaise, which is dedicated to the promotion of French language and culture. Other cultures tend to keep their values more private, except when travellers or visitors come to join celebrations, events, and festivals.

Culturally aware facilitators of change are interested in thinking about and preparing for how people may behave differently in a process like a workshop, a planning meeting, joint research, or other participatory event. Those who are culturally aware themselves are more likely to know how to engage respectfully with people, groups, and organizations with different cultural values. They are open to learning how values influence expectations about behaviour in organizations and society. Since power and leadership are so critical in the context of change, being culturally aware helps facilitators to initiate and support conversations about what makes a good leader and how people feel included in each cultural context. It involves listening carefully to responses in order to understand the drivers and values which inform views about how change is understood and the pathways to achieve change in inclusive and culturally relevant ways.

Simply demonstrating an interest in others' values, an understanding that people, organizations, and countries have different cultural values, and respect for different values, can often be enough to start to build trust. Since trust is one of the most essential ingredients for collaboration on almost any change or development-related topic (see Figure 2.2), including inclusion itself, this has to be an easy win. Recognizing that prospects of inclusion can be interpreted as a threat to those with power in a hierarchy can help generate more respectful engagement. It is probably inappropriate to assume that everyone agrees inclusion is 'good' and just needs funding/training to make the change. Good facilitators take people from where they are to where they can get to on their own journey, without assuming shared values and understanding of change. Tools and methods to address these and other aspects of facilitation are provided in Chapters 9 and 10.

'Purpose' through cultural and power/political lens

Facilitation processes focused on some kind of change can be initiated by different people or groups and undertaken for myriad reasons. Given the huge variety of potential topics and levels at which facilitation takes place, permutations are endless. Consideration of three particular elements of facilitation through a cultural lens is useful: the source of an initiative; its purpose; and the power/political aspects of the facilitation agenda. Awareness and analysis of these elements through a cultural lens should help inform the selection of appropriate approaches and methods as well as other aspects of facilitation, such as who would be the best facilitator and where the process should take place. Reflection on these questions could result in different types of engagement from those which could work in another cultural context. For example, if it became clear that an external facilitator would be seen as a person who would wield inappropriate power over the participants, then a local facilitator may be substituted, or vice versa. Similarly, if it became clear that treating all participants from a hierarchical culture as 'equals' could cause harm to some marginalized groups (during or after the event), then the event could be restructured or revised.

The source of an initiative may have a significant role on the nature of the facilitation and how it is seen by participants. Before attending a workshop, participants may ask 'who wants this to happen?' or 'why does x want this workshop?' or 'who seeks to benefit from this facilitation process?' The answers, variously interpreted, may well influence the nature of participants' engagement. For example, say a State Government agency operating a service in suburban Sydney or San Francisco wishes to test a new policy which will affect people from different cultural backgrounds and hires a facilitator to run a workshop about the proposed policy. Migrant groups may respond to the fact that a government body is asking the question, reflecting deeply held views about power and authority. For example, those who come from higher power distance (more hierarchical) cultures may be reluctant to question or challenge those in power, compared with those from low power distance (more egalitarian) cultures. Those from individualistic cultures may be happy to turn up to the event and express their own opinion about the policy, whether founded on evidence, experience, or their whim on the day. Those from collectivist cultures may feel they must listen to the voices of the people from their group and form a shared view on the matter before even participating in the process. They could be reluctant and stressed if asked to respond to unforeseen questions on the day, in case other members from their group may not agree.

In international cooperation, say a development agency initiates a facilitated process with the purpose of designing an innovative new development activity or preparing for a bold new project. Those from a high uncertainty avoidance culture may prefer options which imply less risk, smaller-scale changes, or more manageable changes than bigger transformative changes proposed by a donor from a low uncertainty avoidance culture. Those from the donor country could be frustrated by the apparent lack of enthusiasm for high level change and push for 'higher-level results' than the participants. This occurs frequently in the author's experience.

The purpose of a facilitation process may be to enable external facilitators to hear from various groups on the assumption that those who are more or less marginalized (i.e. those with lower power) will have different ideas. While facilitators from low power distance cultures could assume this is a good idea, and that participants will appreciate the opportunity to express their individual ideas, participants from high power distance cultures may find this purpose highly challenging. In a hierarchical culture, questioning, challenging, or expressing different views from those who hold power can be, at minimum, highly disrespectful, a risk to one's well-being, or, at worst, life-threatening for those who have less power. They are therefore not likely to raise ideas that they consider may show up or appear to undermine those perceived to have power in their context.

In collectivist cultures, people are expected to consider others in their group when expressing views and making decisions. Women in collectivist cultures, for example, may not necessarily see themselves as members of a disadvantaged gender first, but as members of a particular village, language group, or religious group, where the values of gender egalitarianism are shared. They may not consider they need to have different ideas from men in their group, since they are members of that same group. Similarly, people with disabilities in a village community may share similar views and ideas about their status as everyone else in their village and not necessarily consider themselves to be marginalized or discriminated against within their own value context. Their identity may be largely based on their membership of a village, clan, family, or language group, rather than any particular impairment. Thus, engagement in a facilitated process is highly likely to reflect their view of power associated with the initiator of the process, their obligations associated with group membership, their culturally informed view of the purpose of the workshop, and their view of the relationships and changes implied.

When the source of a facilitated change process is within a culture itself, then it's likely that existing traditional systems already exist and have existed for some time. For example, in most Pacific cultures, there are clear processes for engaging community members, led by chiefs or other community leaders, with widely understood protocols about who speaks first and how to find unanimity of decisions. Bringing in an external facilitator may or may not be useful, depending on many factors. While people from more individualist cultures may critique these traditional processes, for example for apparent inegalitarian attributes, better results may be achieved from adjusting traditional processes that people are familiar with, rather than introducing methods from completely different cultural settings.

As noted in the previous chapter, links between ideas associated with cultural values and political/power analysis are strong. Change facilitators familiar with the contemporary and emerging body of work which supports more context-sensitive and politically attuned practice will find that it does reference cultural values. The body of work includes 'thinking and working politically' (Development Leadership Program, n.d.), 'doing development differently' (ODI, 2014), and 'working flexibly and adaptively'. In summary, this work suggests that for development partners to facilitate genuine and sustainable changes, they require better understanding about three aspects of the context in which they are working: the complexity of intersecting influences on how change happens in that context; the politics and power aspects of change (leadership and coalitions, for example); and the cultural values which underpin societies' preferences (about change and government responsibilities, for example) and the nature of organizations. These elements are now seen as critical for understanding how developmental change actually happens and thus the purpose and nature of development-oriented programs. Proponents for reform (including, for example, Andrews, 2013; Andrews et al., 2012; Booth and Unsworth, 2014; Rocha Menocal, 2014), generally aim to support more effective development practice through more politically and culturally informed and responsive efforts (Valters et al., 2016).

Being aware of the source of the initiative of a facilitation process and analysing its purpose through a cultural and political/power lens will help facilitators prepare for their contribution. They should prepare for different reactions and types of engagement among participants, particularly those who may be systematically, traditionally, logistically, or otherwise excluded. Since the application of culturally and politically attuned approaches inevitably requires learning and responsiveness to emerging lessons about what works and why, there has been a shift, to some extent, in expectations about the agility of programs to respond to changes in the context and emerging lessons. This is further considered under the fourth point below (Cultural understanding is relevant throughout a program cycle).

Inclusion defined in culturally relevant ways

As noted above, the question of 'who' participates in a change facilitation process is universally relevant. Facilitators may or may not have a role in the selection of participants, but they will always have a role in determining how they will be included. The discussion here is intended to encourage culturally attuned approaches in relation to inclusion, since shared values about the nature and practice of inclusion cannot always be assumed. This is not to suggest that facilitation processes should not be inclusive, but that thoughtfulness is required in determining the 'who' and 'how' aspects of inclusion in each context.

As noted in Chapter 5, benefits of inclusive practices are now widely promoted in western and multicultural organizational contexts. In cultures where egalitarian values are widely understood, if not consistently applied, the idea of gender inclusion is now rarely questioned, for example. A shift in the argument from 'why' to 'how' women and men should be included equally in facilitated change processes has largely occurred in most western cultural settings and among western facilitators. At the global level, there is much attention to and engagement in gender equality issues, including inclusive approaches to change.

The selection of participants in a participatory and facilitated process is generally a political and cultural phenomenon, though it is often perceived as a technical, efficiency, pedagogical, or compliance issue. Selecting the 'right' participants is often identified as critical to the success of a change-oriented process and, because of its importance, development agencies often seek to influence the process. Whether the practice of including equal numbers of participants by gender actually addresses deeply held cultural values about gender equality is questionable, but it can illustrate a development agency's values and have benefits for participants at various levels, as well as potentially negative side effects.

Determination of the 'right' people in a facilitated change process reflects cultural values about power, access, and membership of in-groups or out-groups. From an individualist and low power distance culture, selection may be made primarily on the basis of perceptions about individual agency/merit, official responsibilities (job description), representation of a demographic type, and equity. From a collectivist and high power distance culture, selection may be made on the basis of ethnic/religious/other group membership, past or future obligations to others, and relative status (informal or formal). Negotiating different values like this requires cultural awareness, communications, and respectful negotiation skills.

Official development assistance agencies have increasingly insisted on gender equity in funded workshops and training events since 1975. It appears to be easy to impose a requirement that participants should comprise equal numbers of men and women – reflecting ideas about diversity. However, in many cases, culturally respectful conversations about why equal numbers of participants were required, how to support gender equity, and genuine inclusion at more systemic levels did not take place. Now these conversations are more common, expectations are more shared, and there is more global understanding about and commitment to gender inclusion. Some development partners are also now applying similar approaches to disability inclusion and youth participation. Without supporting conversations about power, equality of opportunity, and assistance in translating the relevance of participation for those who may not be the most appropriate participants, for example, the imposition of externally determined requirements about diversity may not have all positive results. Providing support for people to participate in new processes and roles may be necessary, and may take time, particularly in cases of systemic exclusion.

The actual inclusion of participants within facilitated change processes is complex and subject to a wide range of context-specific as well as broader political and conceptual issues. The methods described in Chapters 7 to 12 address specific aspects of inclusion, but at a systemic level, inclusive practice requires inclusive leadership (see Chapter 5).

Inclusive practice requires both politically attuned facilitators and accessible, safe, and comfortable spaces. The creation of an accessible workshop venue, for example, can make or break the degree of inclusion. If facilities are inaccessible in terms of location and space, people with disabilities are likely to be excluded. If information is not provided in accessible and inclusive ways, then people who have sensory impairments will not be able to participate equally. In some cases, carers are necessary, so ensuring they are also able to participate appropriately is an important aspect of inclusion. Facilitators who understand how to work inclusively with people from different backgrounds, in terms of impairments, or any other kind of characteristics, will more likely succeed.

Many organizations which fund community development and international development activities increasingly monitor and measure success using evidence about the extent to which women and people with disabilities are included. From the perspective of those in power in some cultures, some leaders and their in-groups may see this as a 'threat'. Without direct engagement with and support from the leaders whose power may be seen to be undermined, an inclusive approach may not be sustained, regardless of the interests of marginalized groups, once a development partner leaves. Support from local leaders for any kind of change may require renegotiating social contracts with members of their particular in-group, potentially resulting in diminished power and influence for existing in-groups. As a result, leaders themselves may risk losing support.

Facilitators can play a key role in contributing to inclusive leadership, and changes in views about the benefits of inclusion, especially if they are able to work respectfully and sensitively. Values about leadership and followership are learned from a young age, and people, societies, and organizations use them as road maps to conduct relationships. Any attempts to change these maps involves careful analysis, planning, negotiation, and support, which requires culturally attuned facilitation.

Trust and a shared culture are essential for collaboration

Different cultural perspectives on the concept and practice of collaboration suggest that consideration is needed about the ingredients for success across cultures: trust is the most critical of these. As noted in Chapter 2, in highly collectivist cultures, the idea of cooperation with people from other groups (defined differently in each context) may seem counter-intuitive and counter-productive. For example, some organizations in many countries include staff from only one area, or tribe, or religious or ethnic group because the level of trust and mutual obligation would be too low if staff were mixed, leading to significant ineffectiveness and inefficiency. Within western cultures, there are also differences. For example, in a comparative study of US and Scandinavian coalitions, Polley (1989: 165) found:

> There are significant cultural variations in patterns of coalition formation and interpersonal behavior across cultures. American groups tend to be either unified or highly polarized while Scandinavian groups are more likely to maintain mild polarizations. In addition, Americans tend to be more individualistic and self-centered than Scandinavians and are more likely to polarize around issues of alienation versus involvement, while Scandinavians are more likely to polarize around issues of authoritarianism versus nurturance.

With increased globalization, regional and international collaboration has been a clear feature of change-related movements at official and civil society levels. The complexities of cross-cultural aspects of collaboration have attracted some attention in the literature but are not deeply studied. For example, Wiest (2010: 50) noted 'building and maintaining transnational coalitions is a difficult process. Cultural heterogeneity, distance and diverse national political systems impose obstacles ...' Coalitions, including groups of people from indigenous and other backgrounds inevitably raise important issues about power, politics, and trust in addition to cultural value differences. For example, Allen (2016: i) in her study of a US cross-cultural coalition to stop a fossil fuel export terminal in the Salish Sea found 'indigenous and non-indigenous coalitions have the potential to both empower communities and affect the policy agenda. These relationships, however, are often complicated by differing worldviews and varying levels of power in legal, social, and political matters'.

The generic strengths of coalitions and partnerships can be seen through different cultural lenses. For example, shared benefits and risks, additional resources, achievement of goals beyond the capacity of one group, and potential for unexpected benefits may be understood differently. Similarly, different perceptions about challenges associated with collaboration can also apply: turf protection and different frames of reference, for example. In all settings, analysis of and efforts to support the quality of the interaction are necessary, in addition to analysis and efforts related to the task at hand. Culturally attuned partnership brokers may offer a great deal to support participants in a collaborative exercise to navigate the complexities.

Multicultural and cross-cultural collaboration is distinguished by its deliberate focus on bringing together groups from different cultural backgrounds to address shared priorities. This can occur within a multicultural context, with migrants from different countries, or between organizations and groups working within different countries. These collaborations are built on the clear assumption that there will be different perspectives, which are celebrated and valued rather than seen as problems or issues to overcome. For example, cultural groups may have differing ideas about how leaders are chosen and exercise power, and about how conflict and disagreement should be managed, but when these groups see these multiple perspectives as strengths which can build greater momentum towards shared goals, rather than challenges, then positive results are possible.

It is inevitable that there will be differences in any collaborative effort, but high-quality facilitation plus goodwill and other factors can help to maximize the benefits of 'healthy disagreement'. Brownlee (n.d.:1) distinguishes a multicultural collaboration from other kinds of collaboration:

> Building a multicultural collaboration entails changing the way people think, perceive, and communicate. There is a difference between recognizing cultural differences and consciously incorporating inclusive and anti-discriminatory attitudes in all aspects of the organization. Embracing cultural differences is ... at the core of the group's perspective on issues, possible solutions, and membership and operating procedures. The organization's structure, leadership, and activities must reflect multiple perspectives, styles, and priorities.

Joint efforts are obviously the most critical element of any change process. Co-creation, co-design and, co-production are widely used in the business world, and related participatory development tools are found in community development and international development. Whether facilitators are working at community, organizational, or sectoral levels, joint efforts are always essential and this book assumes that facilitators share commitment to this aspect of change. Two particular elements are discussed below: co-facilitation and development of shared values.

Co-facilitation, whereby facilitators are from different cultural backgrounds, is a relatively straightforward approach for working cross-culturally and can have multiple benefits. Recognizing that in many contexts two or three heads are better than one, this is especially the case if the facilitators bring different understandings about participants and cultural values. Linguistic skills can be useful to explain new concepts for example, and to interpret questions and issues. Other benefits are that one facilitator can be presenting while another is observing, gauging reactions through a cultural lens, assessing group interactions and energy levels, organizing technology, and preparing materials for activities or for subsequent sessions. Providing a diversity in voices, representation, perspectives, and presentation styles can help participants to stay engaged and to minimize a sense of exclusion or disempowerment associated with external facilitators. From the facilitators' perspective, mutual and respectful support can help with levels of energy, self-care, and balance.

Similarly, approaches which support the development of shared values and norms among participants from different cultures are an obvious response to value differences. When it is acknowledged that participants may hold and express multiple cultural values, and when opportunities are provided for deepening understanding of differences and support given for negotiating shared values, then cross-cultural teams are more able and likely to work effectively on their common interests and goals. Helping participants to understand the views and ideas of others who may have different values is always a useful contribution to collaboration. Practising seeing ideas through another's lens is invariably a valuable contribution towards negotiating the achievement of change which benefits multiple groups of people.

Building trust is an important component of partnership brokering, an emerging body of work which supports collaboration and is being applied in various cultural contexts to achieve change, often in highly complex ways. Multitudes of other global, regional, and cross-sector collaborations take place in every sector imaginable on a daily basis, but the extent to which cultural value differences are actually negotiated varies widely, as does the level of genuine trust.

Facilitators will not have difficulty finding literature on building coalitions (e.g. Landis et al., 1995, Fox, 2010) but most guides include only a short mention about the importance of cross-cultural consideration. One interesting reflection from an Australian military leader involved in multi-country coalitions noted 'cultural differences between coalition partners can be significant and while there may be a political will, coalition military objectives may not be achieved due to cultural frictions' (Leggatt, 2018). He also noted 'what may appear to be a relatively minor issue, if not understood, can quickly lead to frustration and mistrust within the coalition. Understanding of these issues at all levels but particularly among coalition senior leadership to work through cultural differences is important to ensure coalition cohesion'.

The use of translators can be critical in supporting trust-based effective coalitions, and facilitators may wish to consider including them in some or all processes. For example, Fox (2010: 490) noted:

> Given the limitless possibilities for misunderstanding and conflict in coalitions which bring diverse actors together, cross-cultural interlocutors that can bridge the gaps between them are key. They are the "synapses" and "relays" that make communication possible ... They must play the role of translator, both in the linguistic and the conceptual sense – in order to help each actor understand where the others are coming from. These communication skills are also crucial for establishing trust, insofar as by entering into a coalition, actors must trust their new partners to avoid actions that would put them at risk through guilt by association. To play this linking role, these interlocutors require both cultural capital and social capital. In the language of social capital, coalitions embody bridging social capital. In this context, the cross-cultural interlocutors are actors that play this bridging role.

Research and guides for building cross-cultural coalitions, or for building coalitions within cultures other than the facilitator's own, or in non-western cultures are less accessible. The key message found in available material is that the particular context for each collaboration is highly relevant, confirming the need for context-specific analysis and engagement. For example, Okada and Riedl (1999: i), researching a coalition between Austrian and Japanese partners noted: 'our conclusion is that even in environments – like bargaining – where cultural differences may play a prominent role, the show-up of these differences is highly sensitive to the exact context in which people act'. Similarly, Winterford and Laqeretabua (2019: v) noted in an evaluation of funding for a locally initiated coalition in Fiji, that its success to date reflected cultural relevance. They found: 'the coalition model is highly valuable since it leads and sustains Pacific-led feminist action, is culturally appropriate and is effective in achieving gender equality in Pacific Island countries. The We Rise Coalition is able to leverage the experience, expertise, and networks of each coalition partner to achieve project objectives'.

Asking participants in a change-oriented process about their own expectations and preferences can help make the difference between an effective facilitation and a poor one. For example, the following questions could be easily built into a process:

- What values, norms, and behaviours are important to you in the facilitation process?
- How comfortable are you participating in a process facilitated by someone from another cultural background, gender, age group, or religion?

- What can the facilitator do to maximize the benefit of the facilitation process for you and for other groups?
- What works best for facilitating change processes in this cultural context?
- What values, norms, and behaviours can all participants agree upon, for the duration of this collaboration?
- How can trust be developed in this context, given trust is essential for successful collaboration?

Navigating the ups and downs of change processes is a key role for facilitators of change, so the ability to negotiate responses within the context of power and politics, emerging issues, and lessons learned is essential. Determining agreed ways forward, through complex change, is a key role for change-oriented facilitators. Clearly, the ability to understand these processes in complex contexts requires considerable skill and experience, and at minimum a commitment to continuous learning.

Adaptive and flexible ways of working are essential

> Aid programs are increasingly called on to be flexible, adaptive and to 'think and work politically'. (Denney, 2018).

Few could deny that change processes are complex, particularly through a cultural lens. Greater attention has been paid to the need for more adaptive approaches to development practice and political analysis, than the cultural values lens to date, but both provide an opportunity for more attention to be paid to cultural values. This book adds a cultural lens to the concept of adaptation and flexibility, particularly in terms of considering culturally attuned ways to facilitate change.

While there is increasing acceptance that change does not happen in predictable and linear ways, many funding application and grant systems still reflect the opposite, insisting on detailed pre-determined plans. More adaptive and flexible models of engaging on development-related change have been proposed (Andrews et al., 2012), promoted, and variously integrated in recent years (Ramalingam, 2013; Booth et al., 2016; Valters et al., 2016; Olbrecht 2019; Teskey and Tyrrel 2021). Adaptive programming is largely understood as a reaction to critiques of overly rigid, pre-designed, blue-print, and linear project plans, including inflexible logical frameworks and contracts. It has been applied in various ways, often still within pre-designed, contracted, output-focused systems, with mixed assessments to date in various contexts (Christie and Green, 2018). The shift towards more adaptive programming could be seen as a source of increased demand for culturally attuned facilitators, since their role in engaging people in ongoing reflection and constant collective planning processes is critical.

Change-oriented facilitation work must assume that change does not happen in predictable and planned ways. Change processes have a life of their own, given that people and many other complex influences are involved, not least cultural norms, leaders, politics, disasters, relationships, and pandemics. The implications of this are substantial for facilitators involved in change-oriented processes or agendas: they need to be adaptive themselves, able to work in adaptive and flexible ways, and able to support people in change processes to be comfortable with uncertainty and to navigate through to a new place, whether that may be just one or more steps forward.

The practice of adaptive management has been described in different ways but most authors refer to themes related to analysis, reflection, learning, ongoing revision, and continuous improvement of efforts. The aim is to more deliberately seek information (some call for 'evidence') and shared understanding about what happens over time, in order to influence decisions, rather than follow a plan that may no longer be relevant. The approaches incorporate elements of experimentation, innovation, and acknowledging uncertainty, which as noted in Chapter 2 suggest cultural values that are more comfortable with uncertainty and managing risk. Sugden (2016) describes managing adaptively as accepting, working with, and learning from change, and using this learning to be more effective, which may well suit cultures which are more comfortable with uncertainty, but could be quite a challenge with those which are more oriented to stability and certainty.

For facilitators, the ability to work in flexible and adaptable ways is core to their work with participants with various backgrounds. This covers situations where a facilitator is from one cultural background and participants are all from another, or where participants are from disparate backgrounds. A change facilitator's role in supporting people from cultures who may have different degrees of comfort with uncertainty is particularly critical, again whether participants share the same level of comfort as each other (but not the facilitator), or whether participants have various degrees of comfort with uncertainty. The sorts of qualities and attributes described throughout this book are required in all settings.

Cultural understanding is relevant throughout a program cycle

Facilitators commonly work within a programming cycle and related systems. These apply when proposals are called for from funding organizations, such as government departments or service providers, international development agencies, or philanthropic organizations. Program cycles are also used by government, non-government, and commercial organizations as a means to manage multiple activities and the resources required. Facilitators are sometimes able to influence different stages of the cycle, such as encouraging participatory program design processes or shaping evaluation processes. At other times, they may be simply called in at a particular juncture to undertake a one-off or short-term element. Annex 1 includes a table with suggested steps and questions to consider at each stage in order to apply the principles related to cultural value differences discussed in this chapter.

Consideration of cultural value differences in monitoring, evaluation, and learning processes is particularly important. Definitions of good progress and success, as noted earlier, can vary widely through the lens of different cultural values. Conflict may occur when different views are held about what is valued and what is regarded negatively. Facilitators may be called to help resolve differences, navigate different agendas and perspectives, and negotiate agreed ways forward. Chapters 11 and 12 discuss these elements of the principle in more detail.

Implications for practice

The body of research and practice known as 'thinking and working politically' and 'doing development differently' implies that for development partners to facilitate genuine and sustainable changes, they require deep understanding about three aspects of the context in which they are working, one of which is the set of cultural values that underpins societies' preferences (the other two being complexity and politics/power).

Change processes take time and considerable human interaction, effort, and goodwill, even with the most talented facilitation. Inevitably, there are degrees of unpredictability in change process, whether they are simple, complicated, complex, or chaotic (Snowden, 2011). A cultural values lens adds a layer of complexity to even simple change processes, but can substantially challenge standard ways of approaching change. What does this mean for those involved in facilitating change? The author has long grappled with this question, not just in writing this book, but in practising as a development worker and facilitator for the past three decades. Depending on one's worldview or frame of reference, many responses to this critical question are possible. If an organization is grappling with philosophical, existential, and political aspects of the practice of external facilitators of change, certain answers could apply. If you are considering the reality of what to do when an organization, your funder, or your boss asks you to run a workshop to bring about change in the next month, answers could be quite different. This book tries to support both thinking and practice, recognizing that the big issues are important and, in practical reality, that there are often insufficient opportunities to engage at that level.

On one hand, it is reasonable to respond that, ideally, ambitious change facilitators should simply stay in their home country, rather than dabble in culturally complex, contested contexts and risk the potential for practising (or appearing to practise) neo-colonialism or causing harm. This reflects the view that leaders and people in their own countries have their own agency to achieve the change they want to achieve and external people can unknowingly or ignorantly interfere, causing harm and negative consequences. It potentially means that organizations seeking to bring about change in cultures other than their own should cease their efforts and focus on their own context. In this scenario, it follows that donor agencies should stop funding organizations to do so, particularly those who could be seen to be from colonialist powers or 'big brother' dominant political and economic powers. External facilitators can never really fully understand 'other' contexts where cultural values are so different, so maybe they should simply keep away. Their ways of knowing can be so different from indigenous and 'other' ways of knowing (Denzin et al., 2008; Fine et al., 2008), and these may not just clash but cause harm to those they may think they are assisting.

The concepts of decolonizing solidarity (Land, 2015) and protecting indigenous knowledge (Battiste and Henderson, 2000) confirm the challenges associated with the interface between different historical, political, and cultural perspectives. When facilitators are from dominant cultures, in political, racial, or economic terms, the idea that they can be neutral and independent may be unrealistic and simplistic. Facilitators' attitudes, behaviour, and presence can so easily undermine local strengths or cause harm, often without them knowing, in subtle or serious ways. For example, in trying to be inclusive, a facilitator may not show expected levels of respect to community leaders, which may be understood by all participants (not only the leaders) as disrespectful and a sign they cannot be trusted. External facilitators are commonly seen as representatives of those with power over funding decisions (even if they think they are neutral advisors) and thus carry a particular agenda.

On the other hand, it may be possible to argue that facilitators and development organizations can simply continue to do what has always been done – plan interventions, fly in or turn up, run participatory workshops, be confident and inclusive, politely encourage participants to engage in various processes which make them feel they have helped, extract information, and reflect on the level of energy in the room and the sense of achievement – because they are trying to be of benefit and in some cases may actually be assisting positive change. A wide range of principles and tools has already been developed and is readily available for those who wish to use them. Most organizations which work multiculturally have developed values and ideas about how to approach their work, and consulting companies, professional bodies, and researchers have offered suggestions. Reflecting the emphasis placed on individual learning in individualist cultures, there is nothing stopping facilitators learning more and more about others and about ways to interact. However, seen through others' lenses, this idea itself can be challenged. Jones (2008: 471), for example, reflected:

> This chapter critiques desire for collaborative inquiry understood as face-to-face, ongoing dialogue between indigenous and settler colleagues and students. Interrogating the logic of (my own) White/settler enthusiasm for dialogic collaboration, I consider how this desire might be an unwitting imperialist demand – and thereby in danger of strengthening the very impulses it seeks to combat. I do not argue for a **rejection** of collaboration. Rather I unpack its difficulties to suggest a less dialogical and more uneasy, unsettled relationship, based on learning (about difference) **from** the Other, rather than learning about the Other.

Readers are presumed to be looking for ways forward that represent neither of the above options, which are at each end of a simplistic spectrum. They may appreciate the challenges, nuances, and risks and therefore seek to work in more culturally attuned and thoughtful ways, to reduce risks and negative consequences. They may recognize the first option (stay at home) ignores the reality of global challenges and that there are already vast cross-cultural cooperative efforts that exist to address them, some of which can be regarded as positive by all those involved. There is now both unprecedented momentum and imperative to work collaboratively to achieve positive change, despite the challenges of nationalism and poor global leadership.

At the individual level, the stance recommended in this book is akin to finding balance between being bold and humble, between being compassionate and analytical, between being engaged and reflective. It means reflecting deeply on power, values, justice, inequality, history, and complexity as well as developing a suite of skills and qualities to support others. Primarily, the stance encourages ongoing learning about every single context in which facilitators operate, every effort to achieve trust and shared understanding, and every effort to reflect on the intersection between facilitation, change, and cultural values.

At an organizational level, the stance described here suggests revising whole vision and mission statements to reflect an organization's values *within* its national setting but also how it will adjust its values to work collaboratively with people who may have different values, to address shared priorities, to achieve mutually agreed positive change. This may include organizational systems and approaches to research and understanding other cultural values, to engage respectfully with organizations with different cultural values, and to achieve changes that are negotiated within trust and respect-based collaboration and partnerships.

At a sectoral or national level, the stance described here hints at more thoughtful collective action, for example among groups of NGOs from a resource-wealthy country working together to achieve developmental change, or more respectful donor language, which does not portray them as the holders of values that are imposed on others as if they are the 'best' values while others' values are of less importance.

At a systemic level, the proposed approaches suggest that traditional relationships and power hierarchies may need to change significantly, in order to achieve the kinds of positive changes for all that need to be achieved. While this may be just the kind of change sought by some, other authors are better placed to address the achievement of global or major systemic levels of change.

So how do we work together to bring about change, with our varied, complex, and dynamic cultural values? What alternatives do we have? Inevitably, there is no simple answer, but many answers, depending on one's worldview, values, and contexts. Are we talking about changing our system that reflects the dominant cultural values and drivers for change, or operating within the existing system? Are we talking about doing the best quality work, as defined by our system, or working within our system in a way which is the least harmful/most effective for the participants who come from a different system, based on different cultural values? Are we talking about working within our system but flexing it so that it improves in a way which does not harm us as facilitators and does not break the system? Overall, as change facilitators, are we wanting to comply with our system, subvert it, or shape it somehow?

Similarly, are we engaged in ideas about changing someone else's system (governance, power relations at national or local level etc.) or the global system (e.g. Fine et al., 2008)? Or are we explicitly considering change as the process of supporting people in another cultural context to bring about the change that they want to achieve to their own system or to our system? Is this dichotomy between our and others' systems even meaningful, i.e. are we mainly focusing on shared ideas about systemic changes? Or are we really just talking about tweaking at the edges, for a few people here and there, moving around a tiny puzzle piece in a huge jigsaw, the picture of which is not yet defined, clear, or meaningful? These are big questions. The answers are personal, political, philosophical, ecological, global, and dynamic, and they are challenging. Everyone may have a different answer, which could vary over time and depend on who is asking and listening.

Other key questions relate to the type of practice we are talking about. Are we talking about the short-term pragmatics – e.g. we have a partner, we have funding, what do we do next? – or longer-term change – e.g. how do we position our power and influence to change the system, or support those in another cultural context to change their own system or our system or the global system? These questions need to be asked and considered at some stage or another, but readers will be variously open to them at different times.

In the development context, while individuals have long critiqued negative aspects of the power of donors, some national governments also now question the system which subjugates their values and priorities. For example, the Papua New Guinean High Commissioner to Australia expressed clear concerns about the lack of power by Papua New Guinea over the Australian development program to Papua New Guinea (e.g. see Kali, 2019a, 2019b). In Fiji, changing geo-politics at the national, regional, and global levels has also altered perceptions about the relationship with Australia (e.g. O'Keefe, 2015) and similar reactions are being raised at regional levels (e.g. see ABC News, 2019).

This chapter proposed six principles to support change facilitation across cultures, reflecting an analysis of change-related issues through a cultural lens. These interrelated and mutually supportive principles are useful to inform the kinds of reflection necessary for change facilitators to work successfully across cultures. They support the kind of reflective practice and continuous analysis of assumptions and values suggested by double-loop learning (Figure 1.1) (Argyris, 1977).

PART 2

This part of the book is a guide, based on the author's experience and reflections, for how to work successfully as a cross-cultural change facilitator. It reflects a belief that high-quality cross-cultural change facilitation is key to contributing to relevant and feasible change driven by people and organizations seeking change themselves. This is a direct challenge to the idea that technocratic or solution-based and externally imposed development activities will bring about change.

This guide includes a portable and easy-to-remember ABC method, for culturally attuned change facilitation, with three interconnected strategies:

- **A**nalyse the cultural landscape (using Cultural Landscape Analysis).
- **B**uild strengths-based collaboration.
- **C**ollectively choose and use a mix of facilitation methods.

To support 'A for analysis', a cultural landscape analysis framework is offered, complementing and extending other frameworks in development effectiveness such as political economy analysis (Serrat, 2017) and a power and systems approach (Green, 2016).

To support the choice of methods, a range of options is then considered through a cultural values lens. The first set of methods is selected because they emphasize the expression of ideas in cultural ways and have the benefit of enabling people from different cultures to communicate their experiences and ideas about change. They are also considered useful in that they give value to cultural value differences as a source of positive change. In effect, this represents the view that cultural value differences can and should be used positively to create benefits for all. This contrasts with other approaches which seek to 'overcome' differences or barriers, or address 'cultural challenges' or 'bridge gaps' between people, implying that one set of values is being imposed on another or that other values need to be changed.

The second set of methods will look more familiar to 'western'-educated change facilitators: workshops, training, and mentoring, for example. These commonly used methods are considered through a cultural lens, and suggestions made on how facilitators can use them to plan for the sharing of information, participation processes, and how leaders may influence voices of those without relative power, for example.

The list of methods included in Part 2 is not exhaustive. Judgements have been made about what to include through a cultural lens, and not all possible methods were considered. Readers are encouraged to investigate other methods that may not be documented, promoted, and readily accessible and to assess them for their suitability in various cultural contexts, working collaboratively wherever possible with those with deep understanding of values in each place.

Structure of part 2

Chapter 7 offers the ABC of strategies for change facilitation across cultures (Figure 7.1), as well as the elements of a cultural landscape analysis (CLA) (Figure 7.2). Reflecting a combination of contemporary literature and practitioner experience, these are offered as ways to support change facilitation efforts around the world. They seek to contribute to collective efforts to respect and leverage cultural value differences in order to bring about change for all.

Chapter 8 discusses cultural aspects of the selection of methods and offers some criteria for considering which methods might suit various change settings. Consistent with the broader premise that there is no 'best method' for each setting, the discussion encourages collaboration on the selection of methods and continuous attention to understanding appropriateness.

Chapter 9 discusses a range of methods – from art to village-style meetings – which promote the expression of ideas in culturally relevant ways. They may be particularly well suited to cultures which share more collectivist, high-hierarchy, relationship-oriented and high uncertainty avoidance values, and are included in recognition that all cultures have values and express ideas in different ways. For those less familiar, elements of these methods can be included in a variety of ways in more 'regular' change facilitation processes – practice, expanding networks with creative people, and experience all build confidence and expertise.

Chapter 10 applies a cross-cultural lens to commonly used methods which have largely developed in western cultural settings and now dominate most facilitators' work. Methods such as training courses, workshops, coaching, advising, and partnering are the focus. Suggestions are given on how methods can be adapted to suit different cultural settings in collaboration with people who are aware of the particular cultural context and participants.

Chapter 11 responds to the reality that working on change across cultures inevitably leads to differences of opinion and potentially even conflict. It offers a range of approaches for more contested contexts, including conflict situations where cross-cultural negotiations or mediation may be needed. This chapter offers a method to help prevent conflict as well as methods for addressing conflicts and use of contestation methods for bringing about change.

Chapter 12 considers the implications of a cultural lens for evaluating change processes. It discusses methods for assessing progress and the results of change, since facilitators are often engaged in a variety of reflection and review processes, where different frames of reference have a major influence on definitions of success.

Chapter 13 concludes the book and summarizes the key messages and contributions to practice.

CHAPTER 7
Strategies for change facilitation across cultures

> Great tools aren't enough. You need a total change in attitude (front cover of Harvard Business Review, March 2020).
>
> If you really want to change someone's mind on a moral or political matter, you'll need to see things from that person's angle as well as your own. And if you do truly see it the other person's way – deeply and intuitively – you might even find your own mind opening in response. (Haidt, 2012: 49)

A culturally attuned facilitator is one who serves the people in the room in the best ways possible. This means maximizing benefits for all, recognizing that the complexity inherent in each context and within each group makes this challenging. A facilitator can support the development of more nuanced strategies than could be found within a single cultural context. They can engage respectfully and effectively with people from different backgrounds and contribute to translating between different worldviews. They can stimulate and extend complex conversations, generate shared understanding, and support participants to find pathways that they are willing to take towards a better future. This can apply regardless of the 'source' culture or resource context of the facilitator or the participants.

A set of strategies for culturally attuned change facilitation is introduced in this chapter, based on discussion in Part 1. This set of strategies will enable those involved in facilitating change to consider the cultural context of their work and apply their reflections before they jump into the facilitation task itself. The three strategies, as simple as ABC, are included in Figure 7.1.

These three strategies combined aim to surface and explore cultural value differences, generate trust, respect and shared values across cultures, and enable facilitators to mobilize groups from different cultures in order to bring about changes that may not have been possible otherwise. This is consistent with Figure 3.1 in Chapter 3, which links understanding cultural contexts with the process of building collaboration and trust as means for bringing about any kind of positive change. The elements included in the ABC above are not necessarily required to be undertaken in that specific order, but imply a sequential movement and interactive relationship between them.

Each of the strategies is described in this chapter, with most attention paid to the first and second strategies. The third strategy, the process of determining a culturally appropriate mix of methods, is expanded in Chapter 9.

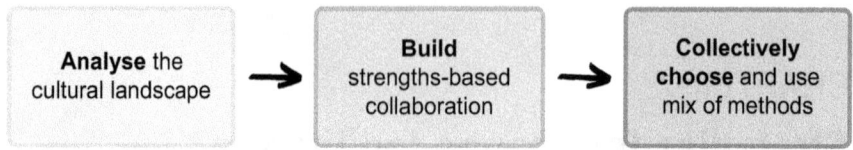

Figure 7.1 Elements of cross-cultural change facilitation

A Cultural landscape analysis

> Curiosity about the system needs to be laced with humility and self-knowledge. We don't – can't – have all the answers; we can't predict events; what works in one place won't work in another. We need to become uncomfortable with (maybe even enjoy) messiness and uncertainty, and give weight to local knowledge and feedback. (Green, 2016: 240)

Inevitably, an analysis is required of the context in which change is sought. A cultural landscape analysis (CLA) comprises four elements:

- Understanding of **cultural values**, both of the facilitator and those who will be 'facilitated', within a change context.
- Analysis of the **nature of power and leadership** related to the change context and the partnership with the facilitating entity/organisation/country.
- Assessment of the **scope for inclusive collaboration**.
- Reflection on the **assumptions about and scope for change**, and any otherwise unspoken issues that may influence the likelihood of positive benefits.

These elements are summarized in Figure 7.2, illustrating the suggested order in which they can be considered when planning a change facilitation process. The depth and nature of analysis will depend on the nature of the facilitation role, scope of the facilitation task, and the source of the facilitator and participants in each context. An independent, authoritative, or rigorous piece of research is not likely to be required, but rather a collaborative reflection and discussion process. Even a 'light touch' facilitation role should at least consider each of the elements during the design of a process. Large-scale, longer-term, or more complex facilitation may involve dedicated study and maybe even some training as well as deeper efforts on collaboration and reflection.

The CLA situates change facilitation processes within an understanding of the cultural values that influence participants and relationships in each context. A CLA is appropriate for applying a cultural lens to a change context, just as political economy analysis (PEA) is now used widely in international development and other contexts to situate development interventions within an understanding of the prevailing political and economic processes in society (Leftwich, 1995, 2009, 2011; Serrat, 2017). A CLA also complements

Cultural landscape analysis

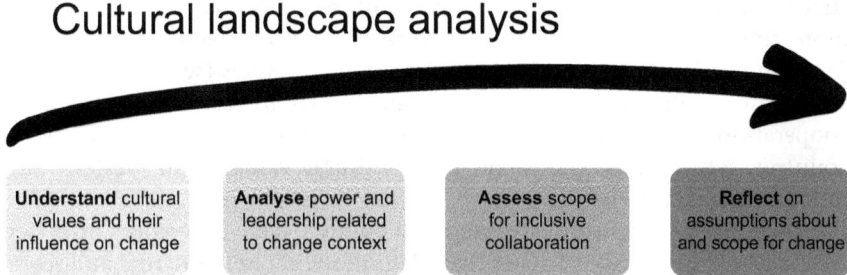

Figure 7.2 Cultural Landscape Analysis

and expands a framework that Green (2016: 240) suggested for activists – a power and systems approach (PSA) – which encourages them 'to cultivate curiosity, humility, self-awareness, and openness to a diversity of viewpoints'. Some of the elements in a PEA, PSA, and CLA are related – they recognize and share interest in power, incentives, and influences on how change happens in different contexts. The CLA focuses a spotlight on the cultural values dimension, not given sufficient weight in previous approaches.

Importantly, a CLA is not proposed as a means for change facilitators to understand another context. It is proposed as a framework for the stimulation of **joint** conversations to generate **shared** understanding for all those involved in change, so that any changes sought are appropriately located. Any one-way analysis is limited by the cultural lens of the analyst. The purpose of the analysis is to maximize shared understanding among all those involved in a change process.

Also, a CLA is not proposed as a one-off tick-a-box step, and not recommended to be applied in a technocratic way. Rather, it is envisaged as a continual process of analysing and re-analysing, discussing and revising understanding of the context and the changes envisaged. It captures the idea of continual reflection, deepening shared understanding over time, trying new ways, more learning, and being open to the idea that change processes are messy and, collectively, we can never really expect to know what is going on. It applies double-loop learning (Chapter 1), providing language for questioning core assumptions and values, and applying this to the relevance of cultural value differences where changes are sought.

The four stages in CLA are discussed below.

Understand cultural values

In the international development context, dominant program management systems are largely driven by donor-country values (Elgstrom, 1990), but there is increasing awareness of different perspectives and recognition of 'southern voices' (e.g. Wright, 2018). Rapidly increasing access to knowledge facilitated by the internet and other factors has led to considerably more sharing of development ideas between countries which may have potentially more similar values. An online network of 'southern voice' think tanks, for example, is sharing analyses on development issues (see <https://www.southernvoice.org> [accessed 28 September 2021]). Increases in south–south cooperation in the development sector reflect the interaction between countries which may also share more cultural values than western and non-western countries.

While it may be broadly accepted that cultural value differences exist (see Chapter 2), it is difficult to apply tight definitions about the nature and scope of these differences. While Hofstede, GLOBE Study, and other researchers try hard to analyse and quantify variations, vastly different philosophical views challenge the validity of their efforts. While it is possible to study the concept of culture in many disciplines, in practice, any frame of reference is probably best kept in one's back pocket, rather than applied in a definitive way. Categorizing cultures too definitively is particularly best kept away from technocratic approaches to change, which seek to box people and cultures, and neatly categorize plans and systems. The most significant key message is that 'people see things differently': most would find this hard to challenge. For change facilitators, it is therefore suggested that efforts are best focused on how to facilitate respectful and power-sensitive conversations about how we all see the world differently and what that means for collaboration.

Values have a significant, even if unmeasurable, influence on people, communities, organizations, and societies. There is also no doubt that values can be used for positive and negative purposes, even though defining the line can be challenging, given that one person's or culture's positive can be another's negative. Values can be used productively, respectfully, and positively to generate the kinds of change which are desired by those involved in the facilitation process. Since this book is focused on ways that the differences in values can actually be used positively, this is the emphasis here.

The key is to stimulate reflection, collaborative analysis, and deeper understanding about the connection between values and the way that people see the world, behave, and prioritize things in their lives. While it could be straightforward to provide a simple framework for those involved in facilitating change to analyse others' cultural values, this is not what is being proposed here. The priority is on understanding **how cultural values influence everyone in the change context**. This includes the facilitator and their organization, the source of policy direction, and/or funding for the change-oriented program, as well as the nature of the relationship between people from different cultures, for example. Many change facilitators may find the Hofstede and GLOBE Study dimensions useful and relevant to working with leaders and in organizations, especially since the language can be helpful for translating between people with different worldviews. Others may prefer to stimulate blank-slate discussions about values in each context without such a framework.

The most obvious way for facilitators of change to maximize the quality of intercultural interactions is to contribute to deepening understanding about the link between cultural values and change. Critically, this involves ensuring they and their organizations continuously consider the links themselves, not just consider that this is about 'others'. Encouraging participants in cross-cultural change processes to deepen understanding about connections between values and how change happens as well as increasing skills to support this understanding and practice will support everyone to consider the future in a more informed way and to potentially address many other challenges in unpredictable ways. For example, in many cultural contexts, raising men's awareness about the connection between their values related to gender inequality and the high rates of gender-based violence may not only contribute to changed behaviour in relation to violence, but may also contribute to other social changes related to gender roles at work or in the home.

Drawing on the highest level of cultural understanding possible (see Chapter 4), those involved in change facilitation can contribute in many ways to make sense of the context by using a cultural lens. This may include asking and collaboratively answering some or all of the following questions:

For ourselves:

- What are the dominant cultural values in our society and organization, using the GLOBE Study dimensions?
- What cultural values are shaping our engagement in this change?
- How do these cultural values influence our interests?
- How might our cultural values be understood from a different cultural perspective?
- How flexible and dynamic are these cultural values?
- How might our values have changed through interaction with other cultures?
- What is the potential interest in and scope for changing our values?
- Are we more individualist or more collectivist and how does this shape us and our views of change?
- Are we more task or relationship oriented and how does this shape the way we engage with people and work?

For the people and organizations we are collaborating with:

- What are the dominant cultural values in the society and organization with whom we are working, using the GLOBE Study dimensions?
- What cultural values are shaping their engagement in this change?
- How do these cultural values influence their interests?
- How might their cultural values be understood from a different cultural perspective?
- How flexible and dynamic are these cultural values?

- How might their values have changed through interaction with other cultures?
- What is the potential interest in and scope for changing their values?
- Are they more individualist or more collectivist and how does this shape them and their views of change?
- Are they more task or relationship oriented and how does this shape the way they engage with people and work?

Power and leadership

> Leaders never have full autonomy. They are always situated in a particular context of rules, resources and ideas. They can, however, make choices about how they see this context, and act in it. Leadership is practiced differently in different parts of the world. (Corbett, 2019)

> Leadership certainly plays a key role in encouraging the shared vision, mutual understanding, and respect for difference that are all required to keep disparate actors working together. Deep down, however, where one stands depends on where one sits. (Fox, 2010)

Just as a political economy analysis considers the incentives, relationships, and distribution and contestation of power between different groups and individuals, a CLA considers these and other issues through a cultural values lens. It seeks to deepen shared understanding about the connections between power and values. Given the centrality of power and leadership in any change process and in any intercultural collaboration, this element is separate from the broader analysis of cultural values.

The influence of leaders on the nature, pace, and scale of change is undisputed. Leaders include people in authority roles in all contexts (government, private sector, civil society, community) as well as potential leaders or people who simply practise leadership in their daily lives. A useful strategy for supporting change is to include young people, emerging leaders, and leaders from informal settings in leadership development opportunities. In high power distance settings, leadership is almost always considered in terms of formal status positions, so respectful ways to broaden definitions and encourage engagement with other leaders are often necessary.

The vast literature on the topic of leadership includes substantial research findings about leadership across cultures. Leadership practice is significantly influenced by cultural values, so understanding the values which are prioritized in each cultural context is relevant for every level of engagement. A good leader in one context can be seen as a bad leader in another. The GLOBE Study sheds light on expressions of leadership in different cultures, qualities of leaders that are universal and different in each context, and links between leadership and organizational success (House et al., 2004). The most recent iteration of the GLOBE Study will focus on the role of gender and gender differences in leadership behaviour and effectiveness across cultures to determine if perceptions of outstanding leaders differ across genders and whether these perceived gender differences vary cross-culturally (GLOBE Project, 2020). The relevance of different cultural contexts for leadership is also of increasing interest to the Developmental Leadership Program (DLP), a joint research program of Birmingham (UK) and La Trobe (Australia) Universities, supported by a range of government development donor agencies (DLP, 2020b).

While it may seem efficient to consider using a familiar leadership assessment framework to analyse another context, a culturally attuned facilitator may prefer to avoid this approach. Familiar frameworks are usually drawn from the facilitator's own type of culture and are not necessarily relevant to another. A culturally attuned facilitator could ask various people 'what makes a good leader here?' thus stimulating discussion about the link between values and leadership. Analysing leadership and determining what makes a good leader in different cultures is challenging, especially in a short period of time. Methods generated under the umbrella of PEA and Green's PSA (Green, 2016) are helpful to inform collaboration. However, since leaders' personalities are involved, leaders' relationships with each other and their followers are often complex and dynamic: deep historical matters may be impossible for outsiders to understand in depth. There are clear risks associated with trying to generate a clear picture of leadership in another's context.

To bring about change, one needs to work with all sorts of leaders, not just those in positions of authority, but critics and civil society (Denney and McLaren, 2016). Complexities associated with identifying 'good' leaders (according to which measures?) and then assuming they can stay 'good' for the duration of a partnership are myriad. Many development programs have encountered challenges as their own influence has distorted the power of selected leaders to influence policies or other changes, for example. They may select 'champions for change' and then find their association with a foreign-funded entity reduces their credibility in relationships with followers, or their externally proposed approaches are culturally impossible to navigate. Lessons about external support for leadership in varied cultural contexts are summarized well in two examples: Pacific Leadership Program (Denney and McLaren, 2016) and the Pacific Green Growth Leaders' Coalition (Craney and Hudson, 2020).

Leaders inevitably rely on a coalition of people to remain in power, in the form of a social contract, based on historical factors and perceptions of loyalty. Relationships between leaders and followers are heavily culturally influenced – the social contract has many aspects, which reflect beliefs, family links, allegiances, past events, and other factors that change over time. When facilitators do not understand the relative power of individuals and their followers, assuming less or greater influence than may be the case in reality, change processes can be significantly affected. Social contracts can be seen differently through different cultural lenses. Social contracts can also be broken, or strengthened for all sorts of predictable or unpredictable reasons, both positively and negatively, across various timeframes: complexities are boundless.

The nature of leadership and power within communities, by movements or by facilitators working within their own cultural contexts, are important parts of this analysis: there will be wide variations between contexts. For example, Latin American solidarity movements have been led and facilitated by local communities and leaders for decades: Latin American facilitators have developed philosophies and methods accordingly. Indigenous communities in many parts of the world are also facilitating change, where the processes and changes are defined and achieved by themselves. External partner organizations and facilitators need to consider existing community-led change processes and their implications for their own approaches.

Facilitation approaches are more likely to succeed if they acknowledge different leadership traits and how they are seen across cultures, rather than undermine leaders. For example, research undertaken by Stephan and Pathak (2016: 521) on the uptake of entrepreneurship found that 'charismatic leadership is widely endorsed across cultures, [so] entrepreneurship training could incorporate role modelling charismatic behaviors' but 'self-protective leadership behaviours, … which are important for competitiveness, are often viewed negatively by others.' This confirms that different approaches are necessary in different cultures to promote entrepreneurial success. An analysis of leadership could include consideration of the scope for inclusive leadership (see Chapter 5), depending on the context.

Based on these considerations, CLA encourages discussions and reflections about the following types of questions.

For ourselves:

- What are our assumptions about what makes a good leader in our context and in other contexts?
- How might we be seen as facilitators through a leadership lens?
- Is it feasible to practise neutrally, if we are seen as leaders through another's lens?
- How might our values be understood in terms of power over, power with, power to, and power within?
- How might our behaviour be understood in terms of status, vis-à-vis others?

For the people and organizations we are collaborating with:

- What makes a good leader in this context? E.g. characteristics, qualities, behaviour?
- How do leaders practise leadership here?
- How do leaders make change happen here? E.g. What do they do to achieve change?
- What is the quality of the relationship between leaders and followers?
- How do people view and treat leaders in this context?

- How is it best to involve leaders in change processes here?
- Do or can leaders work in inclusive ways or are they more likely to lead for their own particular group?

Scope for inclusive collaboration

This element of the CLA covers both existing and potential levels of inclusion as well as scope for effective collaboration between participating entities. Since all these elements are complex in themselves and can be understood differently in each context, there is value in considering how such an analysis could be framed. As is clear from discussion of the first two elements above, understanding cultural values and power and leadership, joint discussions and reflections are essential.

Inclusion

Analysis of the existing nature and scope of inclusion is an important element of CLA, given that change agendas are often focused on inequality and seek to reduce gaps between those with and without power and resources, i.e. those who dominate and those who are marginalized or excluded by nature of their status or group membership. Such analysis is consistent with and confirms the importance of other analyses about levels of inequality, the rights of minority groups, and marginalized communities. An analysis of the potential scope for increasing inclusion over time is also useful for informing the nature of collaboration and its likelihood for bringing about inclusive change. A strengths-based approach is highly recommended here: no cultures are actually fully inclusive or equal, so movement towards equality, necessary in all cultures, requires shared commitment, energy, and motivation, which a strengths-based approach will help generate (see below).

Analysis of the nature and scope of inclusion within organizations and participants involved in a change process is recommended for several reasons. First, it raises collective understanding about the link between diversity of ideas and definitions and achievement of change. Second, it may lead to different ways of collaborating, including efforts to diversify and include participants who otherwise may not be included. Third, it may stimulate different approaches for considering the nature of change that is appropriate in each context. Importantly, there is value in looking at both the nature and the extent of diversity and inclusion in commissioning organizations and in the context where change is expected to take place.

While advice and tools for working in inclusive ways are readily accessible, being cognisant of the cultural values which underpin those tools and how they may be seen differently in other cultural contexts is useful (see Chapter 2). While low power distance cultures tend to seek to reduce the gap between those with and without power, people in high power distance cultures tend to place high value on systems and symbols which affirm the gap, demonstrate respect for those in power, and accord lower value to those with low power. The latter are usually defined as 'marginalized' or 'disadvantaged' from the perspective of low power distance cultures. Challenging these values is the intention of inclusion strategies, but doing so in a way which is more likely to succeed, and more likely to avoid risks to those who have low levels of power is crucial. Imposing inclusion values on another culture can be as ineffective as imposing any other values.

Assessing the nature of inclusion and its potential requires a sophisticated and context-specific understanding of inclusion. In the US, where many of the frameworks and strategies emerged, emphasis is largely related to race, skin colour, and gender, reflecting US political and social history. In Vietnam, inclusion may be more related to ethnic identity and disability inclusion, for example. In Malaysia, inclusion might be more related to religious identity and race. In Australia, depending on who is answering the questions, inclusion may be most relevant to Indigenous communities, LGBTQI+ communities, or other groups. Applying a framework from one place to another is risky and may set up inappropriate comparisons. Thus, once again, analysis of the nature and extent of inclusion requires collaboration, respectful conversations, and frameworks that are context specific.

The biggest risk to using inclusive approaches in high power distance cultural contexts is that people who are deemed to hold low levels of power (by themselves and others in their context) may feel uncomfortable expressing their views, which may be at odds with people in power. Further, they may suffer negative consequences of 'speaking up' or 'speaking against those in power' after the facilitation process occurs and external facilitators have left. In contexts with a history of development program implementation, participants are more used to the concept of inclusive facilitation, and the consequences of speaking up may be minor, but in others, harm may be caused. The need for methods which keep people safe from this risk is obvious, and a cultural guide may be necessary to give proper consideration.

The kinds of questions that help generate a meaningful analysis of current and potential inclusion include the following:

For ourselves:

- What are our assumptions about inclusion?
- How is inclusion understood in our context and in the contexts where we are expecting to see change? What do the differences tell us about values related to inclusion?
- What does inclusion look like in both contexts?

For the people and organizations we are collaborating with:

- How is inclusion understood here?
- What differences are there between this context and the context where partners are from? What does this tell us about values related to inclusion?
- What does inclusion look like here?

STRATEGIES FOR CHANGE FACILITATION ACROSS CULTURES   113

- How are marginalized groups considered in the culture and how do marginalized groups see themselves in the culture?
- What laws and policies influence the nature and extent of inclusion in public life?
- What social norms influence the inclusion of people from various groups in public life?
- What evidence is there of successful efforts to achieve inclusion to date? What strategies worked well in this context? How long did it take?

Collaboration

Deliberate efforts to build respectful and trust-based cross-cultural collaboration are both a broad and specific way of working to facilitate change. Broadly, collaboration can contribute to unexpected and unpredictable changes for all involved, and, specifically, it can achieve particular planned changes. Therefore, the nature and quality of collaboration and its potential, considered through a cultural and power analysis, is an important aspect of CLA. Such analysis helps strengthen mutual understanding about the features, strengths, and possible limitations of the collaboration and its potential. The potential could be defined against a particular change or a broader sense of what collaboration could achieve beyond current priorities. The elements that make up a good partnership in one culture may be different from those defined through another cultural lens. However, there are likely to be some common themes, such as trust, a sense of common purpose, effective communications (not necessarily direct), safety, and commitment.

Analysis of the existing nature of collaboration and its potential is not necessarily about finding completely common approaches, but also understanding differences since these have the potential to generate and fuel new goals and new ways of working. Analysis needs to go beyond 'bridging differences' to focus on the benefits gained from cultural value differences.

The types of questions that help generate a meaningful analysis of current and potential collaboration include:

- What is the nature and quality of current collaboration through a cultural lens?
- What is the nature of power between partners and their respective contexts: what steps can be taken to manage inequalities?
- What is the scope for extending current levels of collaboration, with available resources?
- Might a neutral partnership broker help to extend the quality and benefits of collaboration?

Assumptions about and scope for change

Analysis of the scope for change through a cultural lens may alter perceptions about what is deemed possible and appropriate through other lenses, as suggested in double-loop learning (Argyris, 1977). This analysis involves not just the context in which change is expected to occur, but also the collaboration itself. Are facilitators and commissioning organizations open to being changed through their experience of working cross-culturally or are their own values fixed? What are the unspoken assumptions related to expected changes in a particular context? Change facilitators themselves need to answer these questions and engage others in conversations about the second question in particular.

Bringing people together and focusing explicitly on cultural value differences to bring about change is an opportunity in itself. The process can: define shared goals; raise awareness about the influence of values on change; raise awareness about shared humanity and similarities; and exchange the benefits of other values. Even if planned developmental changes are not achieved, a process which helps to break down ideas that lead to 'othering' and distance between people may well be an excellent result. The well-founded premise that the experience of negotiating and articulating shared ideas leads to greater success (e.g. see Pettigrew and Tropp, 2006) is relevant to this analysis. New understanding about those who are different has the potential to lead to both broadening views of the world and the opportunity to reflect on ourselves through different perspectives.

An analysis of the assumptions related to opportunities for change may need to consider what are colloquially called 'elephants in the room' – the unspoken issues that can influence the likelihood of collaborative processes and effective achievement of positive change. For those unfamiliar with the concept of 'elephants in the room', it is an English expression, a metaphor, to explain the idea that there can be an obvious, large, important issue or question that everyone in that context knows about, but is reluctant to discuss because it could be seen as threatening, embarrassing, controversial, or inflammatory either for one person or the group. The term implies that this enormous issue can be overlooked while a group focuses on 'safer' topics to an extent that recognition of the issue can be repressed. Cultural value differences can influence the definition and portrayal of 'elephants' and how they may be addressed. Elephants in the room inevitably need to be understood and addressed, particularly if they are related to the particular changes sought. Change facilitators from different cultures may be involved in processes to name and address these issues, but will always need to do so with great care, ensuring safety for participants.

It is easy to challenge the idea that shared agreement can actually be found on the nature and number of elephants associated with change facilitation across cultures. In highly individualist cultures, people are expected to express their individuality and thus to have different perspectives on what is important. In many ways, individualist cultures encourage and support original thinking – innovative, out of the box, blue-sky thinking, for example – rather than shared thinking. A wide variety of factors will shape people's selection and definition of 'the big obvious issues'. One's frame of reference is shaped by education, life experience, upbringing, and many psychological, social, cultural, and other influences. One's status and one's perception of one's own status and others' status, for example, can influence perceptions of what is most important, and this can vary at different times in one's life.

In cultural contexts which place relatively more value on shared thinking, collectivist practice, and harmonious relationships within mutual-obligation-based groups, the idea that everyone in a room could agree on the most important issues is more ingrained. For example, in Samoan culture, behaviour which complies with dominant ideas held in a village is strongly emphasized, so people place high value on agreements with the dominant ideas about behaviour, religious beliefs, and norms. In this setting, the chances that there will be agreement about 'the big obvious issues' are much higher than in more individualist cultural settings. If a facilitator from an individualist culture comes to a meeting in a Samoan village, they would need to understand the ways in which agreements are reached in that context to be able to understand the likelihood that metaphorical elephants, or another cultural equivalent, could be mentioned.

The questions that could be discussed by those involved in a change process include:

- How is change understood in the culture in which change is expected to happen? Does this view of change differ in the culture of the facilitator? If so, will the differences be explored explicitly and how will they be navigated?
- Is the expected change related to people's or organizational behaviour, norms, or values?
- Who is expected to change?
- Is the change expected to be incremental or transformative?
- Is the change expected to be short term or long term?

B Build strengths-based collaboration

This second strategy encompasses a selection of interconnected and mutually supportive approaches to support the **quality of collaboration**, in any cultural context, regardless of the source of the facilitator and participants. The collection of approaches is intended primarily to **build trust**, since this is the most important factor for meaningful and enduring collaboration on change-related processes and outcomes. Selected approaches include:

- a strengths-based approach;
- a partnership approach;
- building shared culture;
- promotion of high-quality cross-cultural communications;
- co-selection of change facilitators.

Contributing to understanding about connections between cultural values and change is a key element in this strategy. An array of activities which raise awareness can be incorporated into any change facilitation process. Many guides and books of cross-cultural activities have been produced: selecting one or two to suit each context can help stimulate the kinds of conversations to deepen understanding over time, from basic awareness to more sophisticated levels. Examples include:

- Fowler, S. and Mumford, M. (1995) *Intercultural Sourcebook: Cross-Cultural Training Methods*, Vol. 1, Intercultural Press Inc.
- Hansen, E., Torkler, A-K., Covarrubias Venegas, B. (eds) (2018), *Intercultural Training Tool Kit: Activities for Developing Intercultural Competence for Virtual and Face-to-face Teams*, SIETAR Europa Intercultural Book Series.
- Hofstede, G. J., Pedersen, P. and Hofstede, G. (2002) *Exploring culture: Exercises, Stories and Synthetic Cultures*, Intercultural Press Inc.
- Kohls, L. R. and Knight, J. M. (1994), *Developing Intercultural Awareness: A Cross-Cultural Training Handbook*, Intercultural Press Inc.
- Seelye, H. N. (editor) (1996), *Experiential Activities for Intercultural Learning*, Intercultural Press Inc.

Free online sources are another source of activities for change facilitation processes, including:

- <https://culturalatlas.sbs.com.au/training-and-resources>
- <https://cultural-competence.com.au/>
- <https://clearlycultural.com/games-simulations/>
- <https://www.ambitia.eu/wp-content/uploads/2019/02/2%20Intercultural%20Trainig%20Exercise%20Pack.pdf> [All accessed on 29 September 2021]

In effect, this strategy confirms the benefits of increasing cross-cultural understanding for everyone. It reflects evidence that the more people understand why others think differently, the more respectful collaboration is possible. Even if collaboration is about seeking to change others' thinking, an awareness of one's own values and an understanding of the processes associated with change through a cultural lens will help influence expectations about what is possible.

Strengths-based approach

A strengths-based approach benefits cross-cultural interactions generally, and change-oriented facilitation processes in particular, for many powerful reasons (Winterford et al., (forthcoming). Primarily, a strengths-based approach is culturally respectful, because it seeks to uncover and value the strengths that exist in each context, as the basis for determining change. Giving voice to perceptions about what is valued in each context creates opportunities to discuss connections between cultural values and what is deemed to be 'good' and 'the way things are done around here'. This contrasts with many facilitation approaches that start by identifying the 'problem' or the 'gap' or the 'need' as a means for defining what change is sought. Problem-based or deficit-discourse approaches by definition allocate a negative status or liability to the participants or issue in the respective context by considering them as somehow lesser, lacking, problematic, or weak. Problem-based approaches ignore the reality that there are equally challenging problems in the context of those facilitating change, creating an uneven emphasis on the problems of the 'other'.

A strengths-based approach helps to mitigate against perceptions that the change facilitator is the expert. It places the power of analysis and planning in the hands of the people who know their own context best. If participants in a context hold different cultural values from the change facilitator or partner organization, a commonly assumed implication is that the change facilitator (organization, country, or 'foreign expert') has the solutions, assets, strengths or 'fix,' by nature of their values. An easily understood extension of that assumption is that one culture is better or stronger than the other, thereby creating an unequal relationship and a flawed foundation for cross-cultural collaboration. In reality, the proposition that one culture has the answers to another culture's issues is almost never the case. All cultures and contexts have strengths and challenges. In an increasingly globalized world, most major challenges are shared and it is the degree of or particular manifestations of strengths and challenges that vary. This underpins the demand for cross-cultural collaboration: pooling strengths of several partners to address a shared priority.

A second reason why a strengths-based approach is useful in change facilitation is its focus on generative change. This means it can encourage and lead to participants achieving more than they expected was possible (Bushe, 2013), i.e. they can achieve more than simply fixing the initially identified problem. Once people and groups recognize their own assets, strengths, and abilities, and that they are able to, and have the power to, make positive changes not only themselves, but also in their own lives, then they can build on this to achieve more and more, with the sky as the limit.

Thirdly, a strengths-based approach enables more context-specific goals to be negotiated. Many facilitation processes assume a shared understanding about the particular results of a collaboration, a program, or a policy. However, it cannot be assumed that a specific change agenda is shared when different values accord priority to different results. A strengths-based approach supports collaboration based on knowledge of what has worked well in the past in each setting, thereby giving respect to what is valued and what is possible in that context.

Finally, a strengths-based approach contributes to culturally relevant motivation. People in different cultures are motivated in different ways, reflecting values about priorities and definitions of good and bad. A strengths-based approach generates information about a particular context or plan, as well as contributes to the mobilization of energy, based on psychological aspects of positive thinking. Motivation in relation to change is essential, as change inherently requires people to move towards a new idea or new 'place' either in ideas or practices. If motivation is based on knowledge or experience of what is possible in a particular cultural context, then it is well-founded and more realistic than motivation based on what might work or what has worked in other cultural contexts.

Change facilitators can consider the following steps:

- Selection and use of a strengths-based approach to all change facilitation processes, e.g.
  - Appreciative Inquiry for planning (see Chapter 9);
  - Strengths, Opportunities, Actions and Results (SOAR) for planning (explained below);
  - Asset-based community development (ABCD) for community development (explained below);
  - Appreciative Inquiry for management and monitoring (see Chapter 9);
  - Positive Deviance and Success Case Method for evaluation (see Chapter 12).
- Encouragement for organizations and communities to use strengths-based thinking in all aspects of their work, planning, and life.
- Participation in a global strengths-based movement.

Appreciative Inquiry is highly suited for most facilitation, management, and monitoring tasks, given its multiple benefits, particularly for cross-cultural interaction (see Appreciative Inquiry section in Chapter 9). It is one of many ways to apply a strengths-based philosophy. For example, in regular planning cycles within organizations, SOAR can be used in place of 'strengths, weaknesses, opportunities and threats' (SWOT) analysis. SOAR contributes to better levels of motivation and enthusiasm for positive change. In community development contexts, ABCD is a means to: focus attention on assets and highlights (rather than deficiencies and problems); identify and mobilize existing community strengths; identify and support natural leaders to bring about change; discover the latent skills of people in the community and in existing networks; and contribute to a sense of momentum and potential (rather than waiting for an external wealthy saviour). A wide range of resources on ABCD is found at <https://resources.depaul.edu/abcd-institute/Pages/default.aspx> [accessed 29 September 2021].

Partnership approach

Change facilitation inevitably benefits from collaborative partnership rather than master-servant or other forms of unequal relationships. Contemporary approaches to brokering partnerships incorporate elements which support high-quality change-oriented facilitation (see Chapter 5). In particular, processes for considering the interests and priorities of partners, the negotiation of principles for interaction, decision-making and reflection, as well as the emphasis on trust are highly relevant. Linked to the first strategy – a cultural landscape analysis that considers power within the partnership and change contexts – this element emphasizes attention on the quality of partnerships, not just on the change-oriented work undertaken by partnerships.

If joint CLA has been undertaken as described above, then some key foundations for a successful partnership have been laid. A culturally attuned partnership broker could be engaged to support the navigation of different frames of reference, if all parties are interested. The benefits can far exceed the achievement of a particular change, since parties become more experienced in expressing their interests, negotiating with others, attracting resources, and reflecting on change processes over time.

The case for dedicated effort to support effective partnerships is well expressed by the Partnership Brokers Association (2019):

> There are reasons why partnering has become the leading delivery mechanism for social, economic, cultural, environmental, crisis management and/or conflict prevention programmes across the globe. It is clear that single entity interventions have failed to achieve the hoped-for results – they have been too narrow in their approach and too restricted in their reach. It is also the case that many issues are more unpredictable, complex and interconnected than they were before – requiring far more layered and flexible responses. And there is the additional issue of the increased speed, scale and impact when crises occur that make containment increasingly challenging. If the issues we face were easy to address, partnerships would not be necessary. But it isn't (easy) and therefore they are (necessary). Partnerships, at their best, offer a model of working that draws on the unique competencies and expertise of what different communities, organizations and sectors have to offer in ways that are intentionally designed to be inclusive and that are dedicated to building sustainable solutions. It is painful to imagine the kind of world that awaits future generations should we fail to collaborate effectively.

Particular elements of successful partnership may vary across cultures, but the principles are likely to apply more broadly. The Partnership Brokers Association (2019) identified 10 key attributes for effective partnering:

1. A clear understanding between the partners of the word 'partnership'.
2. Agreement to a shared vision and common purpose.
3. Account and allowance being made for individual partners' interests.
4. The co-creation of design, decisions, and solutions.
5. Commitment to sharing risks as well as benefits.
6. Every partner contributes resources (whether tangible or intangible).
7. Partners share decision-making and leadership responsibilities.
8. Partners commit to mutual/horizontal accountability.

9. Partners work together to develop a principled approach to their partnering endeavours.
10. Attention is paid to the partnering process as well as the partnership's projects.

In the context of multicultural collaboration, Brownlee (n.d.) suggests another six components which overlap with the above list and add a cultural lens. While likely contexts for this list are multicultural communities within low power distance cultures, they may be useful for other contexts and international collaboration. Brownlee's components are:

1. Formulate and state the vision and mission of the collaboration to model the multicultural relationships.
2. Conduct strategic outreach and membership development.
3. Establish structures and operating procedures that reinforce equity.
4. Practice new and various modes of communication and special support.
5. Create leadership opportunities for everyone.
6. Engage in activities that are culturally sensitive or that directly fight oppression.

Shared culture

Building effective collaboration includes the negotiation of shared values, norms, and behaviour. Unless these are discussed and resolved, many assumptions about and different perspectives on values, norms, and behaviour can lead to misunderstanding and conflict. Formal partnerships generally prioritize discussion of agreed principles and regular checks to ensure these are followed and to find ways to deepen the quality of the partnership. Adding discussion about cultural value differences that underpin cross-cultural partnerships is recommended.

Change facilitators working across cultures recognize the importance of valuing different perspectives 'in the room' and could use various methods to draw out and negotiate shared values. Methods described in Chapters 9 and 10 can be included in a change facilitator's toolkit.

Once a decision has been made for groups of people from different cultures to work together, a means to negotiate shared values is useful. Map Bridge Integrate (MBI) is an example of a tool for negotiating shared values among teams of people from different cultural backgrounds (Lane et al., 2010) (see Chapter 12). Tools which deliberately surface different perspectives that exist in multicultural or cross-cultural teams for the purpose of generating a variety of potential ways of proceeding inevitably focus on the potential for synergy or cooperation.

Maximize the quality of cross-cultural communications

Paying continuous attention to effective communications across cultures is one of the most critical strategies associated with facilitating change.

This requires personal sensitivities, professional skills, culturally attuned systems, and leaders, as well as a suite of methods. Change-makers often assume their shared focus on a particular outcome is sufficient to link people from different backgrounds, and at many levels this can be true. However, greater consideration of the values, communications styles, and ways of working that influence collaboration will significantly strengthen the quality of engagement and thus the likelihood of success. This effort can at minimum help reduce or manage clashes along the way towards achieving expected results, but primarily is intended to build the levels of trust and mutual understanding that are essential for effective collaboration.

The quality of communications across cultures is influenced by levels of cultural understanding among participants in each context, from 'awareness' to 'mindfulness' (see Chapter 4). The higher the level of understanding, the more nuanced and rich communications can be for all those involved. When facilitators can respond to group dynamics across cultures, identify and draw out otherwise hidden ideas, motivations, and interests, they can support successful change processes. When facilitators are deeply aware of the influence of different values, they can ask the right questions, interpret responses through a cultural lens, dig deeper where appropriate, encourage shared understanding with those with different values, as well as mediate conflict (see Chapter 11). The intention is to give value to and benefit from the richness, complexity, and depth that can be found in a room of people with different cultural values and perspectives to identify a new future, plan for its achievement, and motivate action.

Cross-cultural communication has been researched for decades, particularly in the business world. While objectives may differ, some of this research is useful for change facilitators focused on social or governance benefits. The way messages are spoken, heard, and read between the lines differs widely between cultures. In many cultures, direct language is preferred and promoted, while in others, messages are preferably implied, nuanced, and deliberately ambiguous. Body language is a critical aspect of communication and also differs widely between cultures. A common issue arising in change-oriented cross-cultural communications relates to the management of silence and voice (Brear, 2020). Selecting methods which reflect an understanding of the degree of comfort within each context for speaking up or holding back is therefore important. When people come together from different cultures to discuss change processes or set shared goals, effective communications is obviously crucial.

Collectively select facilitators, increase number of facilitators, and determine roles

This element confirms the importance of reflecting on different cultural perceptions about the source and power of the facilitator as a person. In an individualist society, change facilitators may be seen and may see themselves as 'neutral', with the power to shape the nature and style of conversations, but not the content. However, in collectivist societies, this perspective may not be shared. Reflection on the selection and role of facilitators, particularly through the lens of cultural values about power, is recommended.

Change facilitation and therefore facilitators are found in most contexts around the world. Changes can be initiated by communities themselves or by participation in broader networks and movements. They can also be variously supported by governments and development partners, just as often as they can be thwarted by them. Communities can drive and facilitate locally important priorities through to global change agendas using available resources and networks, including their own facilitators. Communities are significant potential sources of guidance, ideas, and methods for change-oriented collaboration, as well as highly culturally attuned and experienced facilitators. In some contexts, analysis which finds effective existing facilitation capacity could well result in a decision to further support this capacity rather than bring in external facilitation resources.

Change facilitators are also found in many disciplines – from air safety to social justice, biosecurity to infrastructure, community development to governance – each with their own perceptions and experiences of appropriate ways of facilitating change. They also can originate and operate in any country and organization, not only high-resource settings. Many individual facilitators stumble into facilitation roles by accident after building confidence or expertise in their area of technical proficiency. Others seek the role more deliberately, based on interest or natural ability, for example. Some may be formally trained, e.g. in adult and workplace learning, organizational psychology, facilitation skills, or cross-cultural understanding. Others pick up methods and tools from their own experience or research. Organizations involved in facilitating change processes also develop their own methods and tools, depending on their values and experience. No formal courses have been found to date on 'how to facilitate change across cultures', so there is an opportunity!

Selection of facilitators

The selection of facilitators involves aspects of power. Who decides what qualities and features are prioritized? Does a change facilitator need to come from a culture different from those involved in the change? Which partner determines the types of skills sought in a partnership? Who decides what language is going to be used in an event? Who decides on the agenda, the selection of methods, the venue, and the level of comfort (food, facilities etc.)? Considering these questions through a cultural lens is rarely in the control of individual change facilitators themselves.

Broadly, the more culturally attuned facilitators of change that there are, the better that interactions will be. Specifically, selecting multiple facilitators may be a useful way to draw in multiple perspectives, operate in several languages, and use a mix of methods. This will take additional efforts, negotiations, and resources, and may raise other issues, but is worthy of consideration through a cultural lens (see 'increasing the pool' below). There is likely value in facilitators from different cultures seeking to work together (as co-facilitators) wherever possible. From an individualist culture, more likely to be competitive than collaborative, this may appear counter-intuitive, but promoting the practice of culturally attuned facilitation worldwide is recommended – building the demand, sharing stories of success, and communicating benefits. Supporting both existing facilitators and people who have the potential to become facilitators is also worthwhile. The concepts and practices associated with co-creation, co-design, and co-facilitation of change are obviously interlinked and consistent with the types of collaboration inherent in positive change mooted in this book

In reality, the types of training available for facilitators are more likely to be prioritized and available in high-resource settings. The kinds of facilitation which are learned in countries where development programs are implemented, or in the communities where migrants originate, are less likely to be valued by those doing the selection. Religious leaders or traditional leaders may use complex processes for engaging with communities in ways which match cultural values, but these are not necessarily recognized by secular government, donor agencies, or contracting businesses.

Apart from personal qualities that make a facilitator a good listener or interpreter across cultures, some specific skills can be learned. People can learn to read between the lines, and understand metaphors and body language across cultures, for example. Learning how to frame questions and interpret answers that may be expressed in different ways takes practice, but makes a difference to the quality of engagement. Learning how to cope with silence or pauses is particularly useful.

Increasing the pool of culturally attuned facilitators

As the world needs more culturally attuned facilitators, and change is largely inevitable, a reasonable goal is to increase the number, quality, and coverage of skilled practitioners in this area. Responding to ideas described in Chapters 3 and 4 about different cultures prioritizing different ways of working, generating more facilitation capacity needs to be considered through a cultural lens. Supporting a Fijian or Indonesian or Nigerian facilitator to only use methods that have been generated in an Australian cultural context, for example, unless they are culturally relevant, may not be the best way of achieving the goal. Blending a mix of 'local' and 'foreign' methods may achieve a shared goal, recognizing that reliance on one method may not be successful or effective for everyone. Promoting Indigenous ways of facilitating change will benefit not only Indigenous communities but also collaborations across cultures and other communities too.

Three approaches which contribute to capacity include: co-facilitating with people drawn from different cultures; support for the promotion and use of culturally attuned methods; and the use of cultural guides to participate in all processes. Co-facilitation with people from the cultural context of participants, particularly if undertaken from the outset of any planning, can significantly improve the cultural relevance of facilitation processes. Planning which takes account of the context (culturally and politically) and of the participants' values is more likely to be effective in engaging people and achieving the intended benefits, particularly from the perspective of the participants.

If it is not possible to find co-facilitators from the same cultural context of participants, another means to maximize relevance is to use 'cultural guides' or 'cultural mentors'. They can help translate cross-cultural conversations, identifying and explaining spoken or unspoken messages or conflicts, supporting shared understanding, and contributing to smooth engagement. Of course, cultural guides have cultural values themselves and may come from particular sub-groups or elites (for example, if they are educated internationally to the extent they can interpret foreign languages), which will need to be considered and accounted for, as appropriate.

Change facilitators' roles

Culturally attuned change facilitators have many roles, including:

- Negotiating with as many of the participants in the change process as possible about the purpose, desired process, and expected outcomes to reflect the context's values, power and leadership issues and scope for inclusive collaboration and change.
- Considering in advance how to serve all the people in the room in the best ways possible and in ways which maximize benefits for all that do not cause harm to any particular group.
- Planning the selection of methods (see C below and Chapter 9) which support participants to respectfully and effectively collaborate to generate shared understanding, determine the kinds of change sought, and the pathways and steps to achieve the change.
- Designing processes which value nuanced, respectful, rich discussions and negotiations.
- Undertaking facilitated processes which maximize the quality of participation, safety, and engagement of participants, respect for different perspectives, a sense of self- and group-empowerment related to individual and collective motivation.
- Reflecting on the processes and outcomes of their work, through a cultural lens.

Change facilitators need to consider their own role in the context of power and leadership issues within their own context and the context where the change is expected to occur. Beyond understanding the cultural value influences on leadership in each context, building links with leaders is essential for facilitators of change. As leaders are critical drivers of change, facilitators are likely to need to support good leadership practice.

Change facilitators can potentially find themselves supporting or challenging poor leaders or inequality or both, either deliberately or accidentally. They need to be able to understand leadership as expressed in each cultural context, mix with and potentially engage leaders in change processes, and have a suite of methods which help navigate the complexities of leadership, power, inequality, and change. As noted above, being aware that race, power, and cultural values are interconnected and critical to the way the world works brings with it a responsibility to work respectfully, humbly, and in a constant state of listening and learning.

A facilitator may play a role in enabling participants to engage with 'elephants in the room' (see 'Assumptions about and scope for change' above) or 'difficult conversations' if that is appropriate. One example is described in an organizational cultural change setting by McKinsey (Cohen et al., 2019), whereby staff and leaders used model elephants as a symbolic means to engage in difficult conversations. Participants in workshops may raise the issue themselves. For example, a participant in the first of a series of repeated training workshops for a large multinational organization raised their hand and said 'this is all very well and good, but what about the elephant in the room?' When the participant was asked to define the elephant, they did so, only to find other participants did not agree this was an important issue. In subsequent workshops, other participants raised different elephants. For facilitation purposes, time was provided for discussion of the elephants, and the fact that there were different elephants across the organization featured in future discussions and resulted in subsequent efforts to address some of the key issues.

In practice, facilitators can use a range of processes and methods to provide opportunities for participants to consider or deepen understanding of their context, define their agendas, raise and consider key issues and change agendas, as well as make plans. Ensuring the context is safe and appropriate for participants to engage in these discussions is crucial. Participants should not be expected to simply comply with external agendas, norms, and values: efforts should be made so they have control over the way in which information is used, responded to, and communicated with others.

Change facilitators could consider the following questions:

- What is my key role as a facilitator of change?
- Who am I facilitating for?
- What cultural values underpin my role, my presence in this context, and the expectations of my work?
- How might these values differ from the perspective of the cultural values in the context where I am facilitating change?
- How can I approach the task of facilitating change in a culturally attuned and respectful way?

- What methods could be used to support facilitation which benefits from the diversity of different cultural values?
- What mix of methods could be used which are well suited to multicultural or cross-cultural participants?
- How can standard facilitation methods be adjusted to make them as culturally attuned as possible?
- How can the facilitation process navigate the particular complexities of conflict, safety, and security?
- How can change facilitation processes be monitored in a way which acknowledges cultural value differences?
- How can the success of change processes be judged or evaluated in a way which acknowledges cultural value differences?

C Collectively choose and use a mix of facilitation methods

> What actual strategies are you going to try? This is where most manuals and toolkits start generating lists of options. I'm not even going to try, because the list of potential strategies is as great as your imagination. (Green, 2016: 245)

Steps A and B above confirm that consideration of the 'location' of facilitation within a change process is essential before methods are chosen. Understanding the location is not a geographical question: it is a broader one which contextualises the particular change process in an understanding of factors that shape and influence change and the potential for collaboration and change within a particular collaborative setting. Potentially, all people and organizations involved in a change context could be involved in the selection of methods, including the participants, but rarely is this opportunity available. Joint efforts, rather than unilateral decision-making, are recommended.

In culturally attuned change facilitation, the intention of methods is **to deliberately harness or mobilize cultural value differences for the purpose of benefitting all**. Whether they are individuals, teams, or organizations, facilitators can contribute to change which exceeds that which one culture could achieve on its own. A process which reflects joint understanding of these elements will benefit from the selection of methods which are culturally relevant. A culturally attuned mix of methods will apply and extend cultural understanding across the processes so all participants will benefit, not just one group or another, and further generative change is possible.

At a strategic level, selecting an appropriate mix of methods, should respond to understanding of the purpose, context, and drivers for change. Methods which can surface and leverage cultural diversity in the process of defining, planning for, and supporting change are recommended. Methods which recognize and give value to the expression of ideas in culturally familiar ways are also endorsed, since they will promote greater inclusion, familiarity, and confidence. This includes methods which contribute to and maximize collaboration and accord value to cultural value differences, as well as maximize the benefits of different perspectives.

This chapter introduced a framework for enabling change facilitators to proceed, as a means to recognize that cultural values in each context are significant influences on the nature and scope of change, and a means to maximize this understanding in order to bring about change. The ABC elements remind change facilitators of the importance of generating shared understanding of values and power, and in particular of building respectful collaboration and of joint selection of methods. The selection of methods is further detailed in Chapter 8.

CHAPTER 8
Selection of methods

The diversity of methods to support groups of people to come together and envision a different future is substantial. This chapter emphasizes the importance of selecting a mix of methods, rather than reliance on a single method, and the value of using both familiar and unfamiliar methods, adjusted to suit each context. Methods that enable people to express their views comfortably and creatively, consider ideas from others' perspectives, and use different perspectives to imagine new futures and mobilize action towards positive change are prioritized. Critically, a selection of methods which prioritizes recognition of different cultural values and the benefits that these can bring to change is key.

Like the author, many facilitators pick up their first methods from watching others, or from participation in processes themselves. Some use similar methods every time they facilitate. This chapter encourages more experimentation, for the sake of strengthening cultural relevance, and gives priority to methods which promote cultural expression using the more objective aspects of culture – art, symbols, music, and theatre, for example.

Most accessible resources on facilitation have been generated within or by people from western cultures. A well-regarded collection, *The Change Handbook* (Holman et al., 2007) includes over 60 facilitation methods and tools contributed by 95 authors: some describe their application across the globe. Other toolkits developed in western contexts have considered applications with people from different cultures within their own setting. For example, in Canada, the Righting Relations network has developed and brought together a range of facilitation toolkits related to social justice for groups of people from cultures other than the dominant majority <http://www.catherinedonnellyfoundation.org/righting/rrabout.html> [accessed 8 October 2021].

New Zealand's Will Allen has compiled a set of resources under the heading 'Learning for Sustainability' which includes methods and tools which can be adapted to working in different cultures <https://learningforsustainability.net/facilitation/> [accessed 8 October 2021]. The Community Development Journal regularly includes new methods, as well as research about their application in various contexts.

Resources are increasingly being developed for facilitation within indigenous groups. For example, the International Association of Facilitators has members in many countries who share methods used in different contexts (see, for example: <https://www.iaf-world.org/site/global-flipchart/4/good-way-facilitation> [accessed 8 October 2021].

In Australia, a 2017 conference of the Australasian Facilitators Network included an 'Indigenous-informed facilitation practice' <http://www.markbutz.com/afn/3219_AFN_brochure_fin.pdf> [accessed 8 October 2021].

In Canada, a number of organizations and First Nations facilitators are documenting facilitation methods (for example, see <http://www.fngovernance.org/resources_docs/A_Model_For_Aboriginal_Facilitation.pdf and https://www.kairoscanada.org/what-we-do/indigenous-rights/blanket-exercise>) [both accessed 8 October 2021].

In New Zealand, a wide range of organizations promote inclusive facilitation that reflects the cultures of Pacific communities (for example, Pipi, 2016). In Pacific countries, the concept of *talanoa* is increasingly used by and with non-Pacific facilitators to address change-related processes, for example in relation to climate change (e.g. Climate Action Network, 2017; Sauer, 2018; Basu, 2018) (also Chapter 10 on village meeting style). A broader range of methods for achieving social change in relation to climate change in Pacific countries was offered by Dilling and Moser (2007).

Some facilitation methods will work better than others, depending on both cultural context and other factors. Striving to identify methods to best suit a specific purpose and cultural setting requires analysis and understanding, skills, judgement, experience, courage, and an interest in learning, as well as the ability to negotiate suggestions from others. It also requires the ability to maximize the benefits and strengths of each method and manage the limitations, since every method has both strengths and limitations. The selection process itself can be culturally influenced. For example, facilitators in collectivist cultures may select methods according to their own group's sense of the 'right answer', whereas in individualist cultures, facilitators may use methods they prefer personally or are most familiar with. Facilitators with a suite of methods 'up their sleeve' and the ability to know which one to use and apply at short notice are more likely to make a useful contribution than those who stick to one method, regardless of the context. Having the skill to either persist or change method if issues arise takes particular courage and adaptability.

Since facilitation methods are not sufficient on their own to bring about change, discussion of methods in this book is framed within a context in which respect between people, communities, organizations, and nations of different cultural values is foundational. If there is a lack of respect and no intention to build trust in collaborative effort, no facilitation methods are going to overcome such a situation. Facilitation methods are used within broader contexts of partnership, mutual respect, and shared commitment to improving the lives of people across the world in complex settings. Outside these contexts, facilitation methods are just tools without a project, or a paintbrush without paint or a canvas.

Facilitation methods must never be used to disempower, threaten, or cajole people into compliance with agendas from outside. Deliberately raising expectations that cannot be met or placing people in stressful, harmful or insecure situations must also be avoided. There is much written about 'do no harm' and increasing awareness of the negative aspects of racist, disempowering, and neo-colonial behaviour, which applies to facilitation methods. Ongoing efforts to seek a deeper level of understanding of cultural values and applying double-loop learning will assist in practice.

It is relatively easy to access lists of and information about many methods developed in (and arguably for) English-speaking and western countries. Thousands of companies and consultants offer them – 12 great toolkits or 5 essential techniques or 10 critical methods to make your facilitation processes succeed – and apply them to and with their clients around the world. Some methods have been adapted for online communications in recent years, with increasing access to technology and the development of facilitation software packages.

Through a cultural lens, most documented and readily accessible methods largely reflect low power distance, individualist, task-oriented, and low uncertainty avoidance values. They tend to emphasize participation of task-oriented individuals on the assumption that, given an appropriate opportunity, they will freely express their individual views and engage with others for the 'greater' good. This 'good' might be a business bottom line, an organization's goals, a program's objectives, or a community-driven change agenda. In multiple sources, thousands of warm-ups, energizers, and reflection exercises developed for all kinds of groups and sectors can be found. These can be incorporated into facilitation processes, with varying degrees of expertise needed. Whole organizations exist, for example, to provide outdoor team-building exercises, playback theatre, or adventure-based challenges.

Consideration of the source of methods is worthwhile before they are applied or deemed relevant for other cultural contexts or for people from mixed cultural backgrounds. In multicultural settings, the context in which the facilitation takes place is likely to have an influence on the selection of facilitators and the methods they are familiar with. For example, a youth program in inner-city Sydney or Vancouver, seeking to strengthen members' resilience, will likely approach the task in ways consistent with white Australian or Canadian cultural values (e.g. more egalitarian, individualist etc.). Similar methods may not work well in a rural Indigenous community setting. In the city, 'merit-based' recruitment approaches will likely be used to select facilitators, and individualist thinking applied to preparing for individual agency of young people when selecting methods. Participants holding different cultural values (e.g. hierarchical and collectivist) who are new to Australian or Canadian culture may struggle to take advice from people of the same age or to engage comfortably with people outside their cultural group. Some argue 'when in Australia, this is the way we do it' and expect the participants to adjust, but if the purpose is to engage participants in a way which brings about a change in behaviour, for example, then at least demonstrating an understanding of their existing values is relevant to the purpose. When working with participants from multiple cultures, considered attention is necessary to select and use effective and relevant methods. In an Indigenous community setting, the selection of facilitators may reflect cultural values about connection or language group, and collectivist values may be applied to determining the selection of methods.

Identification and use of methods suitable for high power distance, collectivist, relationship-oriented, and high uncertainty avoidance cultural value contexts is more difficult for those from different cultures. Some facilitation methods from other cultural contexts may be documented in other languages or not documented at all: for example in cultures which place more priority on oral than written communication. They may be unique to one community or culture or country. They may be seen as exclusive rather than inclusive from different cultural perspectives. They may be secret or taboo or considered sensitive to misinterpretation or abuse, so not shared with others from outside the group. In many hierarchical cultures, there may not be established means for engaging community members in change processes, since emphasis is on how leaders communicate changes, for example. Other hierarchical cultures may have developed complex systems for leaders to listen to and engage with their own group members, but these may be difficult for outsiders to understand, apply, or adapt. While the rapidly globalizing world is breaking down many differences and potentially contributing to more shared values (and/or more division on racial, political, or nationalist lines, depending on your frame of reference), there is value in considering approaches which might be most suitable with various cultures.

It is possible to argue that, in theory, all facilitation methods could be potentially suitable for all communities and contexts. Authors of different methods usually consider how their method could best be used, according to their own experience and judgements. Some facilitators may relish the opportunity to test or challenge participants by using methods that may directly contradict predominant values, for a particular purpose or at a particular time. For example, using highly creative methods with groups that could be perceived to be low on creativity or very formal could be effective or ineffective, fun or disastrous, depending on the skills and personalities of those involved. Similarly, using highly participatory methods for hierarchical participants could be successful or unsuccessful, challenging or dangerous, depending on many factors.

Criteria for selection of methods

Some change facilitators may seek criteria to inform the selection of methods based on understanding of cultural value differences, while others may consider that any method could and should be considered. Box 8.1 includes suggested criteria for those who like to see such a list: other questions could also be asked. Table 8.1 offers some considerations for the selection of methods and possible implications of different cultural values using the GLOBE Study categories.

Box 8.1 Criteria for selecting facilitation methods

- Will methods enable participants **to engage and share information about change** in ways that are consistent with cultural values in this context? (see Table 8.1)
- Will the **purpose of facilitation** be understood differently through cultural lenses and how might this influence engagement and thus the selection of methods?
- Given an analysis of power in the context, will methods help participants **to uncover, address, or overcome power imbalances** (if appropriate) without undermining social contracts in a way which creates risks for participants?
- Will methods be **inclusive** of all who will participate, i.e. for people from different linguistic, educational, and cultural backgrounds as well as gender identities and disability? What efforts will be made to ensure that people who wish to participate are able to?
- Who is available and suitable to **co-facilitate** and generate shared cultural values within the facilitation process? How can potential new culturally attuned facilitators be involved in the planning and delivery of events and processes?
- Will methods apply a **strengths-based approach** to demonstrate respect for the existing context and to help generate motivation towards the desired changes?
- Will methods **generate plans** which can be adapted and flexibly implemented over time, rather than fixed and limiting goals?
- What measures will be used, from different cultural perspectives, to understand the quality, relevance, and effectiveness of the facilitation process and outcomes?

Table 8.1 Considerations and possible implications of different cultural values

Considerations	Implications	Comments
If the culture is predominantly hierarchical	Participants may be more comfortable with expert and leaders' presentations rather than participant-generated processes	Pushing people who have low power to speak up and challenge leaders in these contexts should be avoided, unless in exceptional and well-supported circumstances
If the culture is predominantly egalitarian	Participants may prefer more participant-generated processes	Acknowledging individuals' agency to make their own choices and express their viewpoint is valued in these contexts
If there is a mix of cultural preferences	Include a coherent mix of methods to suit various ways of expressing information	Participants should be encouraged to 'experiment safely' with various methods, acknowledging diversity of preferences
If a cultural context is predominantly collectivist	Use methods to maximize the benefits of participation within existing groups (e.g. ethnic, linguistic, religious, or other self-identified groups) Where appropriate, support processes which generate collaboration across groups, safely and respectfully	Facilitators should avoid asking individuals to answer a question or be a spokesperson for a group, without allowing adequate time for collective reflection, determination of responses, and group selection of the spokesperson

(Continued)

Table 8.1 Continued

Considerations	Implications	Comments
If the culture is predominantly individualist	Use methods which maximize active participation for all involved, promote diversity of ideas, and stimulate rich discussions	Participants in individualist cultures are well-used to participatory methods, but consideration of power dynamics is still appropriate
If there is a mix of collectivist and individualist cultures	Use a coherent mix of methods which engage all participants and avoid pushing people into participation	Co-facilitation by people with different cultural backgrounds may assist in setting an appropriate context for participation
If the culture is predominantly task- or performance-oriented	Use methods that will give participants a sense of satisfaction related to the completion of tasks and meeting standards	There are many guides on these methods, ranging from the simple to the more nuanced and sophisticated
If the culture is predominantly relationship-oriented	Use methods that will encourage participation without causing participants to lose face, to feel critiqued, to be undermined by others, or to risk offence	Facilitators who have a wide range of collaboration-building methods and particular sensitivity to group dynamics will succeed in these contexts
If there is a mix of task- and relationship-oriented cultural values	Use a coherent mix of methods that will respectfully engage all participants	Co-facilitation is recommended in these contexts
If the culture is low on uncertainty avoidance	Use methods that will promote innovative and highly creative thinking, blue-sky planning, transformational change agendas, and big picture design	These methods are increasingly common in western contexts but can sometimes be seen as threatening in other settings
If the culture is high on uncertainty avoidance	Use methods that will support the generation of consensus, achievable objectives, and shared commitment to changes that are deemed feasible within short-term timeframes	Use of these methods requires good understanding of high-context communications as well as sensitivity to group dynamics
If there is a mix of low and high uncertainty avoidance cultural values	Use a mix of methods that will provide a comfortable context for participation for those with different levels of perceptions about change	Co-facilitation is recommended in these contexts

If the intention is to challenge dominant cultural values, rather than engage with and respond to them in a respectful and inclusive way, then which methods will be suitable to enable challenging but respectful conversations to take place? Which methods encourage robust exchange between different groups to promote shared values and realistic and relevant outcomes? Before introducing methods, it is important to reiterate the sensitivities involved. The politics and intricacies associated with the process of engagement between people from different cultures – identified by Fine (1994) as the hyphen representing the complex gap between Self-Other – cannot be underestimated. Aspects of power and leadership are fundamental to all relationships and particularly change facilitation processes. The significance of issues emerging when those from invader/settler communities seek to facilitate change with or by those from Indigenous communities, without understanding cultural values, cannot be ignored. There is no shortage of evidence about how hard it is to address issues without recognizing power imbalances and cultural values. Similar issues apply in less direct colonial relationships and where there are power imbalances, between dominant and smaller parties to an agreement, based on political, economic, or demographic factors. The selection of methods, like all other aspects of facilitating change, is therefore best undertaken within a context of joint analysis and with people who deeply understand the context in which change processes are expected.

This chapter described sources of facilitation methods and issues involved in selection. It offered criteria for culturally informed selection of methods which can be used when working with groups of people and organizations to bring about change. This does not obviate the need for other criteria, but adds a cultural lens to the selection process. The following two chapters describe a range of methods for facilitators to consider. The first set has been selected for their capacity to promote the expression of ideas in cultural ways. The second set comprises more commonly used methods across the world, considered through a cross-cultural lens.

CHAPTER 9
Culturally attuned change facilitation methods

As a facilitator, it is easy to find means for engaging people across the world in change processes because people and organizations across the world share many characteristics. Lines that have distinguished societies across the planet for thousands of years have softened in many cases, resulting in increased awareness of the shared nature of contemporary challenges. On the other hand, the ways in which information is expressed and understood vary across cultures. The differences between Italian and Chinese opera, between Cook Islander and Spanish dancing, or between Russian and Indigenous Australian music illustrate the different ways that ideas are expressed culturally.

This chapter compiles a set of methods that can be incorporated into change facilitation processes, which give value to the varied cultural expression of ideas across the world. Methods which enable participants to express their perspectives in ways which are culturally familiar to them inevitably promote culturally relevant communication. Methods which maximize communication between people with different values are the focus. These methods may be used in a stand-alone way or incorporated into a workshop, event, or change-oriented process. For example, community theatre could be used as a means on its own to bring about a particular change, or as one component in a participatory process to identify a change. A training course which introduces a new governance approach to school management, for example, could include an element of story-telling to engage participants. A planning workshop could include an artistic activity or symbol element to enable groups to express their ideas visually rather than or to complement written or spoken words.

These methods work for people from all walks of life, including government officials, leaders, and community members. Some could be suitable in almost all contexts while others are more suitable in a limited range of contexts. Through a cultural lens, the methods included in this chapter may be more oriented to collectivist cultures but they do not ignore the agency of people in more individualist contexts. The methods assume a higher degree of comfort with activities which enable participants to express harmony with each other, rather than competition and task completion: this does not mean that elements of competition and task completion cannot be incorporated. They could be suitable in contexts with varied degrees of comfort with change, from those who seek measured, small-scale, or iterative change, or those who are seeking more transformational change.

The methods included in this chapter are a mix of those used by the author and those found in guides and other literature. They have been selected as they are designed in ways which are more likely to support participants as people from societies, and as citizens of countries, to participate in change processes. As noted in Chapter 7, the selection of methods is only one part of the picture when facilitation takes place, in terms of success. While a 'good fit' method can make a major contribution, the quality of the use of the method; the interpersonal chemistry between facilitator and participants; perceptions of the relative power of the facilitator; the historical, political, and social contexts; and many other factors can influence the nature of that contribution. Using a blend of methods takes skill, preparation, respect, and humility (Holman, 2007: 44). All these can be deepened with practice, maturity, and openness to learning.

Methods that engage participants at a human or personal level recognize that people are always at the centre of any change process, whether the change is high level, systemic and global, or at a village, household, or micro-scale.

The methods included in this chapter are:

- narratives and story-telling;
- theatre;
- music and dance;
- Appreciative Inquiry;
- art and visual methods;
- action learning and research;
- symbols;
- village-meeting style;
- networks and movements.

Narratives and story-telling

> Stories make, prop up, and bring down systems. Stories shape how we understand the world, our place in it, and our ability to change it.
> (Saltmarshe, 2018)

This method is one of the most powerful means to engage people across the world in change processes. Change facilitators will find an array of narrative and story-telling methods to support participants to imagine, design, and reflect on change. Stories or narratives comprise a set of elements which are causally connected in some way. They can be true or fictional and are usually constructed and communicated with sufficient detail and feeling to stimulate the imagination and emotions of the listener or reader. Stories for engaging with change may or may not have the same features of stories more broadly (e.g. a plot and a structure (beginning, middle, and end) and characters), as well as some kind of metaphor, symbol, message, or moral relevant to the context or familiar to the people in that context. Story-telling is a core element of strengths-based approaches, such as Asset-Based Community Development, and others.

Cultures are often defined and distinguished by the stories that have been passed down from previous generations. The uniqueness of each culture is reflected in these narratives, which may be written, verbal, or communicated through art or symbols. Connections to and the power of stories, tales, fables, metaphors, and narratives form a particularly strong feature of communities across the world. Stories often reflect a history of momentous change or great leaders' efforts to bring about or resist change. Narratives and story-telling have a powerful role to play in describing, defining, and contributing to change processes in the modern world.

Story-based methods are useful to generate shared understanding of issues and events that underpin change-related ideas within organizations or communities. They are also described by some as a long-used means to bring about change, including at systemic levels. For example, Saltmarshe (2018) wrote 'the work of systems change involves *seeing* systemically—looking at the elements, interconnections, and wider purposes of systems—and *acting* systemically. Story plays a vital role in helping us do both of these things'.

In Melanesian cultures, such as Vanuatu, Solomon Islands, and Papua New Guinea in the Pacific region, *tok stori* and *storians* are examples of indigenous means of sharing views, generating shared understanding, and potentially negotiating agreements (Walker, 2013; Sanga and Reynolds, 2018). These have been used in a small number of contemporary development collaboration activities as a familiar context for discussion on issues such as governance, leadership, and climate change adaptation.

Story-telling methods include a wide range of activities from formal or informal facilitated dialogues on specific topics to organization-wide reflections and public story-telling. They generally require particular skills and expertise, and can be highly effective when there is collaboration between creative specialists (script-writers, actors, story-tellers) and change facilitators. The emphasis is on the use of engaging and motivating processes which stimulate emotional engagement, reflection, the identification of patterns, and the development of shared understanding and shared language. When used well, these methods lead to the development of shared commitments and messages, plans, and strategies at all kinds of levels. They can be used for a wide variety of topics and changes, for example in relation to raising awareness about human rights, addressing new health challenges, or achieving a shift in attitudes. Sources of techniques include the work of Changemakers <https://www.changemakers.com/storytelling> [accessed 8 November 2021] and a comprehensive guide by Boje (2014).

Culture influences how people react to a story, not just the content of a plot but also the style of the narrative story-telling: when we watch movies from different cultures, we witness diverse styles of story-telling which reflect different values.

Why are stories useful for facilitating change across cultures?

Narrative and story-telling methods engage people in all cultures, and they can be used in various ways to support widespread change or to engage people and groups in determining their own change objectives (Prasetyo 2017). Since all cultures have developed their own styles of story-telling and engaging communities, there will always be local specialists to work with to generate relevant processes.

Story-telling primarily involves **listening** for understanding, historicizing, and futuring, as well as **interpreting** for knowing, producing, and entrepreneuring, in addition to other elements (Boje 2014). Given the importance of cultural values in shaping how people and groups interpret information, the use of story-telling techniques is particularly powerful for both generating shared understanding across different cultures and supporting collective action within particular cultures.

Story-telling methods can engage stakeholders to reflect or challenge existing power structures, include or exclude particular groups, and generate a variety of outcomes, so consideration needs to be given in advance to determine how they will be applied and how values will be discussed, negotiated, and navigated where appropriate.

Depending on the purpose of the story-telling, for example, to generate change, to convince people of the value of change, to shape reactions to a pre-determined change, or to help people cope with change, different methods may be used. Distinctions need to be made between different purposes of story-telling, for example between people telling their own personal stories in order to bring about systemic change or people creating collective stories to articulate a shared vision for change. In the case of the former, Zingaro (2009) describes some of the challenges inherent in efforts to 'empower' people by enabling them to speak out, using their own personal stories to address change, confirming that care must be taken in any context in this regard. In the case of the creation of collective stories, the same safeguards need to be considered as apply to all methods: ensuring participants both feel and actually are safe to create visions for the future that differ from current power systems. For example, Parkin (2015) proposes a relatively simple method for using story-telling to develop people and organizations, whereby a context-specific story is communicated and participants are encouraged, through a set of questions, to reflect on the story, the story behind the story, the message, how the reader responds, and the relevance to their situation. Drawing from locally relevant stories, a similar method could be used anywhere, especially if facilitators are familiar with the stories. Wright and Neimand (2018) also describe key ingredients for using storytelling to activate people for social change.

Key elements

Each technique has its own elements, which will reflect particular frames of reference or local ways of engaging teams, organizations, or communities. Most narrative and story-telling methods use or include the following elements:

- Identification or development of culturally relevant stories which are expected to help participants to understand or interpret lived experiences or be stimulated to imagine the future.
  OR processes for enabling participants in change processes to develop their own stories.
- Activities for sharing and listening to the stories in engaging ways.
- Activities which enable participants to interpret stories and discuss their relevance for understanding, sharing, or future planning.

Examples of use

In a leadership development program in Indonesia, facilitators asked participants to tell a story about a leader who inspired them and the reasons why their leadership resonated. The intention was to enable participants to anchor their own leadership practice to actual events and people who have shaped their lives and their practice. The story-telling activity enabled participants to share personal information about their journey as well as express vulnerability, courage, and trust. This is based on evidence that leaders who can connect with others and express their vulnerability are more likely to achieve the kinds of change they seek.

In an organizational development program in Nepal, facilitators supported staff to tell a story about their history using a river as a metaphor. Staff identified waterfalls, rocks, twists, and ravines to illustrate events and experiences, and then reflected overall on their journey to date. The process brought together staff who had started at different times, and generated a strong sense of identity and a solid foundation for organizational and strategic planning, which lasted years after the workshop.

Further reading

Boje, D. J. (2014) *Storytelling Organizational Practices*, Routledge.

Prasetyo, Y.E. (2017) 'From storytelling to social change: the power of story in the community building', *SSRN Electronic Journal*, Community Development Academy III <https://www.bvsc.org/from-storytelling-to-social-change-the-power-of-story-in-the-community-building> [accessed 8 October 2021].

Wright, S. and Neimand, A. (2018) 'The secret to better storytelling for social change', *Stanford Socal Innovation Review* <https://ssir.org/articles/entry/the_secret_to_better_storytelling_for_social_change_better_partnerships#> [accessed 8 October 2021].

Theatre

> Sometimes the plays speak what everybody knows; sometimes they speak what nobody says. Sometimes they open paths or unveil truths; sometimes they challenge the way things are done or understood. (Leonard et al., 2006)

Change facilitators can use a variety of theatrical activities as means to engage participants in change processes, both as actors and audiences (Pataranutaporn, 2017). Theatre is often distinguished from other forms of change-related interaction by the way it can connect with the full body – the emotional, intellectual, physical, and spiritual aspects of human life. Theatre can be used within workshops as a complement to broader change-related processes or as free-standing events. Facilitators and community development practitioners can develop skills in theatrical techniques themselves, seek theatrical groups to co-design and co-facilitate activities, or commission them to undertake stand-alone events. The proliferation of globalized communications and online platforms means there is much greater access to skits, plays, and other theatrical resources for change-related purposes.

The potential value of theatre for social change is understood across both formal and informal contexts and is used to contribute to and support a wide range of processes, from developing an organizational vision to changing deeply held values. In international community development, Sloman (2012) identified that theatre has been used since the 1960s and 1970s as a manifestation of the idea that visual, collective, community-based ways of working contribute to strengthening poor people's participation in policymaking and implementation of development. Augosto Boal, founder of Theatre of the Oppressed in Brazil, was regarded as a key figure in the use of theatre for developmental change and has influenced the formation of other theatres around the world. He famously said 'the theatre itself is not revolutionary: it is a rehearsal for the revolution' (Boal, 1974).

In organizational change contexts, theatre is used to promote dialogue, connections, and understanding, and thus can contribute to surfacing critical issues, changing norms, and building team cohesion, for example. Playback theatre is a specific method to support change management in organizations, using improvisation related to stories told by participants relevant to the topic of focus. It generally applies inclusive principles, enabling all stories to be heard and all story-tellers to participate. It seeks to draw on the aesthetic and creative capacities of participants. Playback theatre does not use scripts but engages with and responds to participants' inputs and combines both educational and entertainment elements (Halley and Fox, 2007).

Community theatre groups are involved in social change agendas in many countries. Sometimes labelled participatory theatre or theatre for social change, these groups directly link participant engagement with specific social or developmental issues. They can be undertaken by community members or in collaboration with professional theatre artists, drawing on various popular theatrical forms, such as circus, carnival, music, and methods used in commercial theatre. Professional change-related theatre groups have also emerged in some countries (see example below).

Why is theatre useful for facilitating change across cultures?

Theatre can be highly inclusive, accessible, and effective in addressing change-related issues. Community theatre, developed and offered in culturally specific ways, can reach and engage audiences on a variety of complex issues (Ferreira 2018). Playback theatre is regarded by its proponents as culturally respectful and adaptable (Halley and Fox, 2007).

Theatre engages people in physical, emotional, and intellectual ways, and draws from ancient traditions and practices, which are either specific to particular cultures or widely understood across borders. Its potential to contribute to social change is being exploited in various contexts, from villages to boardrooms. It is interactive, involves collective experience, and has the opportunity for shared understanding of issues, opportunities, and potential actions associated with social, political, organizational, and other changes. Theatre's potential for inclusion enables people from all backgrounds to experience opportunities to convert sometimes abstract ideas into something tangible, or to relate their own experience, including a new vision or image of the future.

Theatre also has the potential to engage people who otherwise do not access information, for example because of reasons of literacy, education, or disability. It can also tackle issues that are otherwise considered taboo or challenging in metaphorical ways, reducing the confrontation that is inherent in many change agendas, but communicating complexities in accessible ways.

Key elements

Using theatre for social change can involve the elements from theatre – selection of topics, scripts, actors, stagecraft, rehearsals – centred around specific change themes, plus the use of activities in which the themes can be discussed and considered. Playback theatre, in contrast, does not use scripts or rehearsals but draws stories from the audience or participants in a change process. In some cases, there may be more explicit activities which seek to generate plans as a result of theatrical events. Theatre can involve professional or highly experienced actors as well as amateurs and people with no previous acting experience, particularly if skilfully facilitated. Processes which enable participants in change processes to become actors in their own plays can be particularly motivating and transformative.

Examples of use

Wan Smolbag in Vanuatu is a non-profit organization which now includes theatre alongside other complementary development activities to reach people across the country, the Pacific region, and in Asia. It employs experienced actors who produce short plays and films on social issues, such as environmental management, domestic violence, gender and transgender, and youth and reproductive health. The actors take their plays to rural areas and hold participatory meetings with community members to discuss issues and their relevance to each community, supporting change in engaging ways. Wan Smolbag has also developed smaller theatre groups on other islands and supported skills development in filming, lighting, recording, sound effects, music, and project management. In addition to stage theatre events, Wan Smolbag develops, produces, and uses high-quality films and radio shows to raise awareness and encourage public discussion on social and governance issues.

In Indonesia and Solomon Islands, SurfAid has supported villagers to develop, act, and film very small plays to address specific issues identified through village analysis. These films, made with a villager's phone and edited and shared within the village, generate high levels of interest, engagement, and change. For example, in one village in Indonesia, a small play was made, with actors from the village, about encouraging pregnant women to attend maternal child healthcare services. In Solomon Islands, villagers became aware of poor attendance at cancer-screening services, so they wrote a play, acted the parts, and made a film about the issue. They also wrote a song, broadcast on national radio, in local language, promoting attendance at health services. Rates of attendance increased significantly.

Selected references

Wan Smolbag Theatre, Vanuatu <https://www.wansmolbag.org/> [accessed 8 October 2021].

Guides about Playback Theatre from Tusitala Publishing <http://tusitalapublishing.com/> [accessed 8 October 2021].

Theatre for a Change <https://www.tfacafrica.com/> [accessed 8 October 2021].

Ferreira, P. (2018) 'Power of theatre in social change' [online] <https://www.iol.co.za/entertainment/movies/power-of-theatre-in-social-change-14536350

SurfAid <https://www.youtube.com/watch?v=ZyDT9mCEcxw&t=1s> [accessed 23 January 2022]

Music and dance

> If we think we can all agree that we need a better world, a more just world, why is it that we are not using the one language that has consistently showed us that we can break down barriers, that can we can reach people? What I need to say to the planners of the world, the governments, the strategists is, 'You have treated the arts as the cherry on the cake. It needs to be the yeast. (Sarabhai, 2009)

It is easy to incorporate music into any kind of change facilitation process. Music and dance are significant ways that people across all cultures form cooperative alliances (Hagen and Bryant, 2003), and thus can be relevant to and used for contributing to change. In the 1960s and 1970s, US musicians began to use lyrics and tunes more explicitly to engage audiences in change agendas (Reese, 2015), and the same phenomenon occurred in South Africa in relation to the anti-apartheid movement. Music can raise awareness and generate engagement in change by communicating, often in indirect and metaphorical ways, about issues to do with representation, justice and power, in many contexts. While music by itself may not be sufficient to bring about systemic change, it can contribute in multiple and unexpected ways.

The emotional and inclusion aspects of music make it a useful element for generating participation and teamwork. For example, musician contributors to an Australian article which pondered the question 'how can we use music to achieve social change? (Eslake, 2017) responded with various perspectives including:

- 'Whilst art may not necessarily have the answers, it should get people thinking' (Aidan Maizals in Eslake, 2017);
- 'Music along with all of the arts has the power to make us think and feel and consider what we stand for, what connects us, question the things we don't understand, and embrace and accept our differences. That is how music can influence social change and as musicians and composers we must not be afraid to ask the big questions or expose the hard issues' (Shannon Rogers in Eslake, 2017);
- 'Music only changes what people already want to change' (Marlene Radice and Hannah De Feyter in Eslake, 2017).

Incorporating music and dance into change facilitation processes can promote emotional engagement with other people and the world around us, both necessary for change to happen. Facilitators can encourage participants to use music and dance to communicate their ideas on change agendas and articulate their visions for the future, for example, or bring in musicians and dancers to engage with participants in similar ways to theatrical and story-telling methods. Wan Smolbag, mentioned above, uses music and dance as important streams in their social and economic development work in many media. It helped establish a Hip Hop crew, which tours rural villages contributing to community understanding about various opportunities for social change.

Why is music and dance useful for facilitating change across cultures?

All cultures incorporate elements of music and dance into the lives, rituals, and ceremonies of community members. People are largely familiar with and thus potentially able to express themselves and participate in change-related processes using these means (Clark and Koster 2014). Music and dance provide means to reach audiences in ways that the written or spoken word may not. They complement other ways of reaching and involving people in change processes at all levels, from village level to corporate- and government-level change.

Key elements

If agreeable to people within relevant contexts, change facilitators can simply ask participants to use music and dance to communicate change-related messages at any stage of a process, from articulating their priorities to expressing visions for the future. Alternatively, specialists can be included as co-facilitators for parts of the process, to build links with participants in specific or broad change elements. The limits of such processes are set only by the imagination of those involved. As with all facilitation methods, consideration should always be given to inclusive elements, such as ensuring people with disabilities can fully participate.

Example of use

In Kiribati, a school which had sought small grants over many years from various donors was advised that a formal strategic plan would be needed if it wanted longer-term funding. A facilitator was appointed to support the school's stakeholders – teachers, parents, children, and supporters – to develop the plan. Recognizing the importance of song and dance in Kiribati, the facilitator encouraged the stakeholders to present their future vision for the school in any form. One group developed a fun song with words that cleverly and beautifully articulated the school's priorities, such as fully trained teachers, access to learning materials, recognition by the Ministry of Education, more engagement by the broader community, a new school bus, and more accessible classrooms. Teachers, parents, and students sang for the rest of the participants. They owned the vision and shared it with others, and the key elements were documented and communicated to the external donor. With more secure funding, the school is now achieving its objectives.

Further reading

Reese, A. (2015) 'How can music inspire social change?' [blog] Facing Today, <https://facingtoday.facinghistory.org/how-can-music-inspire-social-change> [accessed 8 October 2021].

Aloe Blacc, *How 'message music' inspires social change*, TedX talk [video], <https://www.youtube.com/watch?v=M2mpE6Nwh2g> [accessed 8 October 2021].

Clark, M.K. and Koster, M.M. (2014) *Hip hop and social change in Africa: Ni Wakati*, Lexington Books.

Appreciative inquiry

Appreciative Inquiry is a strengths-based planning and organizational change method: the author's preferred facilitation method in many circumstances. It is particularly powerful for facilitating and planning change because it assumes the presence of existing strengths in every context and surfaces these strengths to generate agreed visions for the future, as well as motivation towards and engagement in the change process. When working across cultures, Appreciative Inquiry promotes shared recognition of what is valued in each context, thus has high potential for shared understanding of the cultural values which participants identify for themselves. When facilitators both espouse and demonstrate their own strengths-based approach and use Appreciative Inquiry, their effort is more coherent and the benefits significantly enhanced.

Appreciative Inquiry, developed by David Cooperider (1986) (Cooperider et al., 2003; Cooperrider and Whitney, 2007), is relevant to almost all types of change in all sectors where people's experience and motivation are relevant to the changes envisaged. Within western cultures, it is now used relatively widely in social work, youth services, psychology, education, community development, public health, and organizational development. It has also been used in international development in multiple sectors, countries, organizations, and programs (Winterford et al., forthcoming).

Appreciative Inquiry involves a process of appreciating and valuing what is best in a particular setting, envisioning what could and should be a different future and collaboration to determine the steps required. This contrasts with the dominant problem-based thinking and practice that permeates most planning and change processes.

Why is it useful for facilitating change across cultures?

When a facilitator commences a change process by asking for consideration about the strengths that exist in each context, they are in effect revealing and potentially generating a shared understanding about what is valued. This is a critical aspect of facilitation, but is rarely done in practice, since many initial engagements start with 'a problem to be fixed, a gap to be filled or a need to be met', rather than recognition of positive factors that are already present. When a facilitator from one cultural context uses Appreciative Inquiry in another, they are demonstrating an interest in and potentially an appreciation of what is valued in that context. Applying understanding of the cultural value differences described in Part 1, facilitators are thus able to both interpret for themselves and help the stakeholders to confirm what is valued, e.g. authoritative leaders or collaborative leaders, individual effort or group work. This process of surfacing and analysing existing strengths contributes to respect for others' cultural values, even if they are not necessarily shared. It also contributes to trust development between people and groups. Since respect and trust are key to effective cross-cultural collaboration, it is easy to see how Appreciative Inquiry is such a powerful method for facilitating any change.

A key benefit of the Appreciative Inquiry method is its ability to generate motivation and energy, among the people involved, towards doing something about change. This contrasts with problem-based approaches which may generate detailed knowledge of a problem and its causes, but often leads to negative feelings of hopelessness, disempowerment, immobility, or depression, not helpful in generating the energy needed for change.

Finally, the core elements of Appreciative Inquiry translate well into other contexts and other languages. There are no challenging new words or concepts to define and no particular props needed. The method can be used for all group sizes and all settings.

Key elements

While successful use of Appreciative Inquiry benefits from a mix of philosophical understanding and personal attributes of the facilitator, the method itself is remarkably simple. It involves framing interaction around four questions:

1. What has worked well and why?
2. What resources are available?
3. What is our (shared) vision for the future?
4. What steps will enable the vision to be achieved?

In the author's and others' experiences, the use of this method often very quickly leads to actual action towards change, even before the findings have been written up.

Example of use

When designing a new governance program in Vanuatu, Appreciative Inquiry was used as the framework for a workshop with fifteen stakeholders from two countries. The four questions were interpreted as general headings for various sessions. The length of the workshop (three days), the contents of each session, and session times were informed by understanding of the stakeholders and their context, the focus topic, and the scope of the intended program. The fact that participants all held leadership roles in their respective contexts as chiefs, diplomats, and academics also informed the design of the process.

Time was initially allocated for building on existing stakeholder relationships and negotiating ground rules or ways of working together. After discussion about the method to be used and its purpose, the first session was a simple 'brainstorming' undertaken in small groups to answer the question 'what has worked well in this space before, and why?' The session generated important and useful information about what was valued, what had been achieved previously, and success factors. After small groups presented their responses, the facilitator asked 'how do you feel about this list?' Responses confirmed that the participants were feeling respected, confident, motivated, and keen to move towards a new goal. The second session generated a list of combined 'resources' known to the participants, which was useful for confirming the breadth of support available and that the stakeholders were not on their own. The third session asked groups to envision their preferred future and find a symbol to explain this vision (see Symbols below). Negotiations resulted in a shared vision, with elements combined from all groups.

After the respectful starting conversations were held, stakeholders realized their detailed knowledge of the context was valued and their level of engagement was high. Participants were actively involved in identifying and negotiating a realistic vision for the context, and in the timeframe, based on their confidence and motivation. Once agreed, the task of determining activities was relatively straightforward and manageable, informed by experts in the room and the answers to previous questions. At the end of the workshop, several chiefs reflected on the method used and said they thought it would be useful for working with their own village communities as a respectful, portable, and effective means to generate shared goals and collective motivation.

How to ensure the method is applied in a culturally attuned way

The Appreciative Inquiry method uses accessible and relatively easily translated language. Explaining the method to participants and the concepts behind the method is important. In order for the process to generate answers to each of the key questions in Appreciative Inquiry, sessions need to be designed to suit each context. The time taken for each session should allow for appropriate engagement, reflection, and feedback. Since Appreciative Inquiry enables participants in a change process to express positive views about the existing context, the chances that hierarchy-related challenges will emerge are low. For example, those with power and those with less power are not likely to feel uncomfortable or threatened by critiques of negative aspects of the context. The method does not rely on individualized participation: collective small group work is key.

The method enables facilitators to use a mix of elements for each of the key questions. Discussions with people from the cultural context who understand culturally suitable activities are recommended when planning for events and processes using this method. For example, in the first question, small groups can be simply asked to list the answers and share them with the whole group, or they can be variously supported/asked to prioritize them, discuss them, present them in various ways, write them up, and place them for others to read and consider. In relation to the third question, participants could be asked to work in small groups to find a symbol, draw a picture, develop a song, tell a story, find a metaphor, create a skit/piece of theatre, brainstorm some words that would be included in a vision for the future or craft a vision statement or sentence. When presenting their responses to the whole group, a wide variety of formats could be used.

Further reading

Appreciative Inquiry Commons <https://appreciativeinquiry.champlain.edu/> [accessed 8 October 2021].

Cooperrider, D. Whitney, D. and Stavros. J (2003) *Appreciative Inquiry Handbook*, Lakeshore Communications, Bedford Heights, OH.

Centre for Appreciative Inquiry <https://www.centerforappreciativeinquiry.net/> [accessed 8 October 2021].

Cooperrider, D, and Whitney, D. (2007) 'Appreciative Inquiry: A positive revolution in change', Chapter 5 in Holman P. et al. *The Change Handbook*, Berrett-Koehler, San Fransisco, CA.

Art and visual methods

The use of art and other visual methods (including symbols – see below) for communicating change-related ideas is easily incorporated into any facilitation process and is increasingly common. Artists over millennia have used these means to address issues of the day and to stimulate change. Numerous contemporary artists demonstrate deep commitment to creating work that addresses political and social issues and seeks to change the way the world is perceived and understood.

Art can be used in many ways – to comment on, stimulate reflections on, respond to or advocate for change – in any context, including change facilitation processes. 'Socially engaged art can ignite outrage and demands for change, and/or provide a platform for reflection, collaboration, and building community. Art expressions can focus on the residents of a single city block, or reach out to a global audience' <https://bigideascontest.org/art-social-change/> [accessed 2 October 2021].

Community development practitioners explore the use of visual methods within the suite of participatory approaches, with the purpose of enabling participants to express ideas and create spaces for reflective dialogue as well as retain agreed plans for change. Methods can include spontaneous drawing, mapping, and photovoice (Wang and Burris, 1997) that are adjusted to suit various audiences, from children and youth to participants in formal and educational settings.

Why is art useful for facilitating change across cultures?

The production and sharing of art is common to all cultures and is another well-known means to distinguish cultures from each other. While cultural values have a deep influence on the way in which art is created and used in each setting, people from other cultures can enjoy and potentially understand messages inherent in art generated in different cultures. The connection between art and change is universally understood. For example, Shulman (2013: 1) noted 'art exposes and helps resolve issues of social justice. As a cultural tool, art helps humanize and actualize the emotions, grievances, and fears of those who may not have another place to voice concerns. As an illustrative and journalistic tool, art shocks and inspires us to action. What art depicts can elicit a visceral, almost cellular, reaction'.

In official contexts, the use of art and other visual methods may be best incorporated as part of a broader engagement process: it can often break down barriers to participation and expression associated with more formal methods. When used within change facilitation processes, art can support emotional engagement, even on topics that may otherwise appear bland and removed from human priorities. Art can also be used to promote inclusion, particularly for those who prefer visual means of communication and expression to written or verbal means. For example, a wide variety of simple, portable, inclusive, and accessible materials, such as clay, sand, leaves, and shells can be used to create change-related messages. Art-based activities, such as cartoons and story-boarding, can generate high degrees of creativity and energy as well as focus attention on messaging change-related issues (Margulies and Sibbet, 2007; Palus and Horth, 2007).

Where technology permits, facilitators can use art-based videos, creative or simple photos, graphical maps, and other means to stimulate discussions about and articulate visions for change.

Key elements

The production of art is limited only by the imagination of those involved – the facilitators, specialist art facilitators, and participants. While it may be easy to use readily accessible paper and some kind of drawing implements, there are multiple ways of creating visual representations of change-related messages. These range from natural resources (e.g. bark, seeds, and leaves) to more sophisticated sculptural items, use of cameras to produce photos (known as photovoice methodology), and use of software which enables people to express ideas in creative ways. Encouraging participants in a change process to both find the materials and produce art can add an extra layer of interest, collective teamwork, and engagement. If participants have something physical to take away from a facilitation process, changes can be embedded or extended. Demographic and cultural groups may engage differently with forms of art, which facilitators can take into account, when selecting methods.

Examples of use

In Fiji, a 3-day leadership development workshop provided an opportunity for nearly 90 Pacific leaders from multiple sectors to reflect on ways to increase their leadership of international development programs. An art activity was incorporated as a means for groups to communicate their vision about the future of Pacific-led development cooperation. Groups were provided with a broad remit, large pieces of paper, and pens/markers/pencils and time to discuss ideas and develop ways to communicate them visually. The ideas and means of expression varied widely. All participants were actively engaged in at least one aspect of the activity and took away a vision for their own leadership. Years later, when the facilitator met participants in other contexts, they remembered the activity, the image they created, and subsequent changes they made as leaders.

In Laos, children were given cameras to take photos in their rural schools as a means to communicate changes they valued as part of an internationally funded education program. The photos were shared among participating children: they selected those that best told their story, and drafted captions. Complementing other sources of information, including hand-drawn maps of the schools made by school community members, the photos were shown to senior officials at the national level to illustrate changes valued at school level. This method, called photovoice, contributed to national decisions to expand student-focused policies.

Further reading

Margulies, N. and Sibbet, D., (2007) 'Visual recording and graphic facilitation: helping people see what they mean', Chapter 61 in P. Holman, T. Devane, and S. Cady (eds), *The Change Handbook*, pp. 573–87, Berrett-Koehler, San Francisco, CA.

Institute of Development Studies, 'Participatory visual methods: a case study' <https://www.participatorymethods.org/method/participatory-visual-methods-case-study> [accessed 8 October 2021].

Palus, C. J. and Horth, D.M. (2008) 'Visual explorer' Chapter 65 in P. Holman, T. Devane, and S. Cady (eds), *The Change Handbook*, pp. 603–7, Berrett-Koehler, San Francisco, CA.

Wang, C. and Burris, M.A. (1997) 'Photovoice: concept, methodology, and use for participatory needs assessment', *Health Education Behaviour*, 24(3): 369–87.

Action learning and research

Action learning is commonly used in organizational change, community development, and research settings. Its benefits are best generated in longer-term change processes, although elements can be incorporated into workshops. It has particular benefits in promoting understanding of and respect for cultural value differences and indigenous knowledge. Defined as a 'structured change method that engages leaders and teams in a repeated cycle of reflection and action' (Hyatt et al., 2007: 481), action learning can be a powerful contributor to change. Action research is similar but places more emphasis on studying the process of taking actions at the same time as the actions occur. These methods can require high levels of resources over an extended time, but can have significant benefits in terms of sustainability and reach of change agendas.

Action research has been used in change processes for decades. It was first defined by Lewin (1946) as comparative research on conditions and effects of forms of social action and research which led to social action. He described the concept as a spiral of steps, each composed of a circle of planning, action and factfinding about the result of the action. Since then, the approach has been developed in various social science disciplines, and tools and methods have been proposed which apply these principles and steps. Hult and Lennung (1980: 242) wrote that:

> Action research simultaneously assists in practical problem-solving and expands scientific knowledge, as well as enhances the competencies of the respective actors, being performed collaboratively in an immediate situation using data feedback in a cyclical process aiming at an increased understanding of a given social situation, primarily applicable for the understanding of change processes in social systems and undertaken within a mutually acceptable ethical framework.

The method remains widely used in multiple sectors. Action research was described more recently as 'a family of practices of living inquiry that aims ... to link practice and ideas in the service of human flourishing' and 'not so much a methodology as an orientation to inquiry that seeks to create participative communities of inquiry in which qualities of engagement curiosity and question posing are brought to bear on significant practical issues'. (Reason and Bradbury, 2008: abstract)

Participatory action research is a particular body of practice now seen by many as a significant methodology for intervention, development, and change within groups and communities. Building on the work of Paulo Freire on critical pedagogy (Freire, 1970), participatory action research now has a wide following, particularly in Latin American contexts. The body of practice blends action, practice, and experimentation with evidential reasoning, factfinding, and reflection and learning. The many different tools and approaches share the idea that research and action must be done 'with' people and not 'on' or 'for' them. The work of Chambers (1983, 1994, 2002, 2005, 2008) popularized this principle, and supported the application of participatory action research, within the participation frame, as noted in Chapter 4. A guide developed on the application of these approaches (Pretty et al., 1995) is widely used across multiple sectors. The following principles to guide participatory action research (PAR) were proposed by Khan and Chovanec (2010: 36):

- The change process includes simultaneous change in the individual and in the culture of the groups, institutions, and societies to which they belong.
- PAR is a collaborative process that includes all those who are affected by the issue being researched.
- PAR practitioners serve as guides and facilitators.
- PAR practitioners ensure that participants, not just researchers, engage in theorizing and in gathering compelling evidence for validation of their practices.

- The PAR approach involves a continuous action/reflection spiral of planning, action, observing, reflecting, and then re-planning and so forth.
- PAR is a political process. Continual critical analysis of the distribution of power and the expression of resistance, playing out both within and between groups, is required throughout the PAR process.

The role of the facilitator in participatory action research is particularly important in mono-cultural, cross-cultural and multicultural settings. Recognizing facilitators' and participants' cultural and other values in an action research process contributes to understanding of power, politics, and race as well as co-creation of knowledge and plans. For example, Khan and Chovanec (2010: 35) wrote 'the relationship between the researcher and other participants should be one of co-researchers, thereby allowing input not only into results but also into the definition of the problem or issue to be researched. Proponents of PAR embrace the notion that knowledge is a social construction, that all research is embedded within a system of values, and that research promotes human interaction'. This was also emphasized by McTaggart (1999: 497) who wrote:

> In the qualitative research literature in particular, debates about the representation of the 'other' have called into question the practice of inscribing meanings on the lives of others. The conventional research purpose of generating understanding has been seriously challenged as a form of exploitation, typically imposing categories, meanings, homogeneity, and stereotyping on disadvantaged groups, all of which the people portrayed deny, resent, and regard as unhelpful. In cross-cultural situations, especially those where Western researchers work among indigenous people, these challenges are at their sharpest. In Australian Indigenous communities, for example, researchers face a difficult time gaining access unless they commit to the principles of participatory action research (Marika et al., 1992). But commitment is one thing. Just what professors should do in such settings remains both hotly contested and poorly understood by people who have not worked there (and by some who have).

McTaggart (1999: 498) also wrote:

> We conduct participatory action research to produce substantive change. We also do it to inform the debate around social issues, but we see ourselves as authorized to report only through our direct experience of trying to bring about change. It is worth emphasizing this ethical and political point ... In participatory action research, the key point of reference for writing is the perceived needs of the action program (and eventually others like it), not merely the sensitive production of accounts of the 'other.' In participatory action research, reflexivity refers to deliberate effects on social life of action and research together.

In community development, sustainable livelihoods, and international development the principles of participatory action research are applied widely, but for as long as they have been used there have been critiques. Critics often point to unrealistic expectations that participatory projects can transform existing patterns of power relations (Khan and Chovanec, 2010).

Why is action learning/research useful for facilitating change across cultures?

If undertaken in culturally attuned ways, which take into account aspects of power, politics, and race, action research and participatory action research provide important and potentially useful means for facilitating change. Understanding and exploring indigenous knowledge and expertise is a key element of culturally attuned action research. If cultural value differences are understood and appropriate methods used, then action research can support sustainable and relevant change.

The approach may be particularly useful across cultures given that many of the early ideas were developed in non-western cultures. Action research approaches have also been 'tested' in multiple contexts (for example see Conn et al., 2016 and O'Keefe et al., 2014) . Explicit acknowledgement of different cultural perspectives on the concept of research and knowledge is as useful for action research as it is for other approaches.

Key elements

Action learning and action research methods share a focus on continuous and simultaneous action and reflection, usually expressed in a cycle of different stages of inquiry. The emphasis is on deepening understanding over time, with increasingly more strategic actions taken once learning has been generated. Most methods include the following elements:

- clarifying the situation;
- framing the situation;
- exploration of various perspectives on the situation;
- reframing the situation;
- preparing to take more strategic action.

Example of use

A fascinating long-term action research program on mutton-birding in New Zealand illustrated the extraordinary richness of different cultural perspectives and their benefits for achieving a sustained positive benefit at ecological and social levels. It found:

> Core conditions for community engagement included trust between parties, effective communication of the science, equitable decision-making responsibility, and building scientific capability and monetary

support to enable meaningful participation. The most fundamental requirement is mutual respect for each party's knowledge. Attention to this inclusive, equitable, slow and prolonged process makes it more likely that the community will uptake results to improve sustainability of harvesting. (Moller et al., 2009:211)

Selected references

Action learning, Action Research Association, <https://www.alarassociation.org/> [accessed 8 October 2021].

Conn, C., Said, A., Sa'uLilo, L., Fairbairn-Dunlop, P., Antonczak, L. Andajani, S. and Blake, G.O., (2016) Pacific Talanoa and Participatory Action Research: *Providing a Space for Auckland Youth Leaders to Contest Inequalities*, Auckland University of Technology [PDF] <https://ccep.crawford.anu.edu.au/rmap/devnet/devnet/db-77/db-77-vcc-2.pdf> [accessed 8 October 2021].

O'Keefe, M., Sidel, J., Marquette, H., Roche, C., Hudson, D. and Dasandi, N. (2014) *Using Action Research and Learning for Politically Informed Programming*, DLP Research Paper 29.

Symbols

Incorporating symbology into change-oriented workshops is relatively easy for facilitators and potentially significant for participants in all contexts. The use of symbols to communicate an idea or message has long been and continues to be part of our identity and everyday lives (Tett, 2021). Symbols are often used to distinguish between and identify cultures and to bring people within a particular cultural group together. In modern times, symbols are used for many purposes – to know which bathroom to enter, how to turn on a computer, whether we have joined the right group, or when to cross the road or stop at an intersection, for example.

Symbols are often closely linked to power, and thus of particular benefit for change-related agendas. Symbols can raise the ire of others for what they represent or how they cause people to act in a particular way (Dean, 2013). Leaders, businesses, religions, and many other institutions use symbols to create memorable representations of what they stand for, and thus populations around the world become familiar with symbols as emblems of the ideas associated with them – change, strength, reliability, quality, belonging, or effectiveness, for example (Tett, 2021). Colours are representative of particular ideas or movements in some contexts, such as the yellow shirts worn by protesters in Thailand and Malaysia. Hand gestures are also powerful symbols of power and particular messages, such as the three-fingered protest sign in Myanmar following the 2021 military coup. Symbols are commonly used in many countries to signify a division between followers of particular leaders.

Engaging with the concept of change, symbols can make a useful contribution to defining change in multicultural contexts. They can provide a binding representation of concepts and means of communication for people in a group to explain to others. For facilitators of change, they can assist at individual and group levels to give a focus for a message or a structure on which to hang more nuanced ideas about how change happens. Siler's (2007) 'metamorphing' is an example of a symbolic modelling activity which bridges worlds of ideas and cultures.

Why are symbols useful for facilitating change across cultures?

Symbols can be applied positively or negatively in a context of change and used for good and bad purposes. As noted earlier, one person's or group's positive can be another's negative. Symbols can represent optimistic expectations of something good, which brings people together, or they can generate fear, threat, oppression, division, or other negative aspects of power. Facilitators of change can encounter both strong and positive aspects of using symbols as well as potential pitfalls. Bolman and Deal (2013) noted that 'facing uncertainty and ambiguity, people create symbols to resolve confusion, find direction, and anchor hope and faith' and also 'events and processes are often more important for what is expressed than for what is produced. Their emblematic form weaves a tapestry of secular myths, heroes and heroines, rituals, ceremonies, and stories to help people find purpose and passion'. Given the complexities involved, careful use of symbols in change processes is recommended.

If existing symbols are used as elements of division and separation between groups, it is likely they may not be useful when seeking to generate collective action towards a shared change. However, in some cases, they could be used to symbolize 'old ways' in ways that participants instantly understand, and other symbols can be created in order to represent and illustrate a new future, a new way of living, or a new idea that is more positive. Symbols or brands can be used to invite people to belong to a group which involves new attitudes, new behaviour, and new opportunities. As a symbol is a representation of an idea, it can really only be as useful as the deeper ideas and actions it signifies. Symbols can also be used in learning contexts to support people to gain and remember new ideas, methods, or techniques, for example.

Key elements

The elements associated with using symbols as part of change processes are:

- Symbols may be useful if they are either very familiar and recognizable for participants in a change context or easily explained.
- Symbols can be used to communicate messages to stimulate deeper discussion about existing or future scenarios.
- Symbols can be inspirational and also divisive, so even using them to stimulate conversations about what motivates people and how to work collaboratively can be useful.

- Symbols can be used to harness energy, to promote positive culture within groups, to attract loyalty, and increase morale.

Examples of use

In Vanuatu, as part of the design workshop described above (see Appreciative Inquiry), participants were asked to find a symbol from the surrounding environment to explain how they envisaged the interface between traditional (known as *kastom*) and introduced governance. Groups of people discussed their vision for the future then moved outside the meeting venue to find a symbol of that vision. The groups returned with a selection of natural elements: a palm leaf from the Chief's Palm (called namele leaves), a coconut, and a live gecko! Each group explained in extraordinary clarity why their symbol was chosen to describe the future. The namele leaf is a particularly powerful symbol in Vanuatu, representing peace, wealth, and power. If two leaves are placed across each other at the door of a business, staff will not enter until a problem is solved. If a person feels they have ownership of a particular fruiting tree, they hang a namele leaf on the trunk and could fine anyone who dares take the fruit. In this workshop, the group explained that the namele leaf is symmetrical with a strong central stem and the same number of leaves on either side, and thus it symbolized a future where both *kastom* and introduced governance were well balanced and could be used to keep the population stable and at peace.

In Fiji, at a UN agency staff retreat, nearly 100 participants from across many Pacific countries came together. They discussed contemporary development issues and particularly enjoyed a session where they found and described symbols of their engagement with selected priority issues. The session enabled small groups of people to get to know each other better, move out of the conference room and be active, relate to the natural world around them as well as articulate complex change-related ideas in relatable, memorable, and meaningful ways.

Further reading

Bolman, L.G. and Deal, T.E. (2013) *Reframing Organizations: Artistry, Choice and Leadership* (Fifth edition), Jossey-Bass.

Dean, P. (2013) *The Power of Symbols*, 4 Square Books, London.

Siler, T. (2003) 'Think like a genius: realizing human potential through the purposeful play of metaphorming', Chapter 30 in P. Holman, T. Devane, and S. Cady (eds), *The Change Handbook*, Berrett-Koehler, San Francisco, CA.

Village meeting style

Facilitators may explore ways to incorporate elements of traditional meeting styles in workshops and processes. Many cultures have developed ways of bringing people together to discuss issues that affect their lives, including plans for change. The nature of these events and processes varies widely, reflecting historical influences and deeply held values. Again, a major influence on the nature of village-style meetings is related to power, i.e. how egalitarian or hierarchical a culture might be and the nature of the relationship between leaders and others: the social contract. The way power is shared combined with cultural values about the expression of leadership shapes the degree to which those in power listen to those without power.

Village-style meetings may involve groups of people linked by geography (for example, village, island, valley, district), family, religious, or other characteristics or beliefs. In contemporary individualist cultures, community-level processes and events have often been replaced by other mechanisms to engage people as individuals. For example, the leaders of an organization could meet as a leadership team, staff in a workplace meet as a work team, members of a sports team meet to make plans, citizens in a government area meet as a community group, or officials on a board or committee meet with a shared focus on an organization. Members may have no other characteristics in common. Town hall meetings, a term originating in the US, are used in more individualist cultural contexts as a means for politicians to meet with their constituents either to hear from them or to communicate particular change-related ideas.

Village meeting mechanisms range widely in style from top-down to participatory. In some collectivist cultures, traditional meeting systems continue to be used as a means for including community members in decision-making. As part of a broader and growing recognition of indigenous knowledge, facilitators use these methods, sometimes adapted, to bring about change, as well as to undertake research on various topics of interest to particular cultural groups (Denzin et al., 2008; Chilisa, 2012).

Using, adapting, or adopting traditional village meeting systems to identify and plan for change is becoming increasingly feasible for those involved in facilitating change across cultures. For example, *talanoa*, meaning to talk, dialogue, discuss, or tell stories has been used for thousands of years in Tokelau, Fiji, Tonga, and Samoa, (Tunufa'i, 2016; Vaioleti, 2006). It has been used recently as a research method and a means to engage communities in determining and planning for change processes. *Talanoa* is a structured conversation using culture-specific processes and ceremonies, and usually involves a particular order of speakers and discussion. This approach has the benefit of potentially generating a consensus rather than pitting winners against losers. It contrasts with more individualist cultural styles which seek to generate an outcome that the majority support. If used respectfully and appropriately, the method may contribute to change processes in the countries where it originated (Tunufa'i, 2016) and its principles may be relevant in other collectivist contexts.

In India, the Gram Panchayat has been developed in the post-colonial context, as a means of engaging village/community members in social change, based on traditional ways of meeting, but with new aspects related to inclusion (e.g. see Chatterjee, 2014; Sinha and Jaiswal, 2020). The absence of inclusion is often noted as a critique of traditional village systems, but, again, if the principles are adapted to suit a contemporary society then they could still offer a means to generate shared agreement.

In Morocco, *jema'a* is another example of a traditional village system, responsible for decision-making. While again, it was traditionally comprised as a group of (older) men based on lineage structure of a village, recognition that a village could manage its own affairs, using systems generated within the cultural context, could be applicable elsewhere (Bergh, 2009).

In Indonesia, *musyawarah untuk mufakat*, a customary means to build consensus, is recently being noticed for its value in contemporary contexts. The method involves taking various perspectives into consideration related to decisions that are about to be made and is often conducted to reach a consensus (Kumawara, 2013; Sakkir, 2021).

Why is it useful for facilitating change across cultures?

If participants are familiar and comfortable with a particular means of engaging people, then the method can have the benefit of putting them at ease. Methods which generate strong levels of agreement, consensus, and commitment can be beneficial where this is preferred over methods which set up winners and losers or where individuals are expected to take sides or vote, for example.

Since some traditional village-style systems can be exclusive (i.e. they give voice to men, or inherited chiefs or leaders, or particular ethnic groups), discussions about ways to make them more inclusive may be a focus in facilitation. Methods which enable people to come together to consider whether traditional systems are still fit for purpose in a contemporary world and to envision a more inclusive approach are worth considering here.

Key elements

The elements of village meetings vary depending on values and contexts but tend to focus on certain principles related to leadership, listening, and decision-making. They may also include an order of ceremony, an order of speakers, and a means for generating a resolution or agreement, either by the group or by the leaders. Traditions may involve the sharing of food or drink, the officiating of steps in the process, and the definition of group members' roles and status. These elements could be developed within any group if participants are interested.

Example of use

A new Pacific monitoring and evaluation framework proposes ways of enabling reflection, learning and, data gathering using village-style engagement methods. Called *Rebbilib*, the framework describes a mix of indigenous frames of reference (Secretariat for the Pacific Community (SPC), 2020: 6). It includes a means of stakeholder engagement called *tekuhi*, a Melanesian fish trap, described as follows:

> As an object for gathering, the Melanesian fish trap was adapted and used as the stakeholder engagement and management strategy. The first and widest section, which opens up, is symbolic of the connectedness of Pacific peoples. The foundational partners reached across existing networks to bring in diverse stakeholders to seek evidence and knowledge from multiple voices through survey talanoa. The narrow or mid-section of the net represents the safe space where partners from across the region participated in deeper talanoa ... The third section widens outwards and is symbolic of sharing all the data obtained from respondents of the talanoa survey, interviewees of the talanoa interviews and respondents of the priorities and plans survey. The widening is not just symbolic of data-sharing but also the application of the principle of reciprocity from the perspective of the data collector, to gift something back to the respondents.

Further reading

Kawamura, K. (2013) *Consensus and Democracy in Indonesia: Musyawarah-Mufakat Revisited'* IDE Discussion Paper No. 308. Institute of Developing Economies (IDE-JETRO).

Sakkir, N.B. (2021) 'Musyawarah-Mufakat: Indonesian diplomacy through the Jusuf Kalla experience' [online], Jenggala Institute for Strategic Studies, <https://www.jenggalacenter.org> [accessed 8 October 2021].

Secretariat of the Pacific Community (SPC) (2020) *Pacific Monitoring, Evaluation and Learning Capacity Strengthening Rebbilib*, SPC [online] <https://www.spc.int/updates/blog/2020/08/pacific-mel-rebbilib-report-on-mel-capacity-available-for-download> [accessed 8 October 2021].

Networks and movements

The building of networks and movements are potentially useful methods for facilitators as critical elements in some change processes. Cultures have different approaches to the practice of building links with others, and facilitators need to research context-specific methods. While it is challenging to squeeze this category as a method of facilitating change, there are excellent examples of networking and movements across cultures that are worthy of consideration.

The development, strengthening, and support of networks within organizations and across sectors or borders are commonly used means to bring about and support change. Donors, for example, are turning to networks to deliver development programs, NGOs are working through networks for collective advocacy, and researchers collaborate across networks for greater policy influence (Hearn and Mendizabal, 2011). Network facilitators (or brokers) are engaged in various ways to encourage people from various contexts to join in a particular cause, work together for a specific purpose, or simply get together for the generic benefits of linking up with others. Change agents who have the skills to activate and extend networks can achieve more than those who cannot. Brokers who serve as bridges across a number of groups within networks can be highly influential. Being able to gather and disseminate information across diverse groups is a major contributor to change.

Applying a cross-cultural lens will help inform the purpose, nature, and support required for networks that operate in different countries. In highly collectivist cultures, people are more likely to be skilled in maintaining networks within their particular group, but less inclined to include people from other networks: for example other islands, other language groups, or other ethnic or religious groups. Particular efforts for finding commonalities and building relationships may be necessary for creating new networks in these contexts. In contrast, networks in more individualist cultural contexts are more likely to be successful when individuals with shared ideas come together, and other characteristics are less relevant.

Social movements are more widely studied and research confirms they have a role to play in bringing about change. While it would not be appropriate for a facilitator from a different cultural context to single-handedly initiate the formation of a movement outside their own context, they may well be involved in supporting the initiation, building, and work of a movement at the invitation of movement members. Movements including Arab Spring, Black Lives Matter, Women's Movement, and the Climate Change Movement all offer many lessons about how change happens across cultures, which will be understood differently through cultural and disciplinary lenses and generate reflections on appropriate methods. What is called success from one perspective could be seen as disastrous and failure through another lens. The key point in this context is that cultural value differences have an influence on the nature of networks and movements, how they are understood and portrayed, and how they might be facilitated.

Why are networks useful for facilitating change across cultures?

A facilitator of a movement or network is not necessarily a person who initiates or directs, but they may play a role of supporter, connector, provider of strategic linkages, or catalyst for change.

Key elements

Networks can be formal or informal, of any size, and have any kind of purpose. Some have no other purpose than to network based on certain membership criteria, while others may be formed as a united front against others or an issue, and yet others may have a specific or unspecified change agenda. Similarly, movements can have vastly divergent sizes, shapes, and characteristics. Facilitators may be asked to contribute to an existing network or movement, or may encourage people to form networks or movements in order to bring about a change.

Online networks are a major phenomenon contributing to social change in modern society, and are already used widely to bring about change. For example, in Australia, change.com and GetUp are influential in mobilizing large numbers of people to argue for changes in policies and practices in public and private sectors.

Example of use

A fascinating analysis of the power of cultural value differences for a global–local effort to forge a movement, by bringing together young people from around the world in relation to human rights, was undertaken by Fine et al. (2008). The story involved a diverse group of young people from marginalized ethnic communities brought together with the expectation they would present at a meeting of the United Nations Commission on Human Rights. In preparation, selected youth activists participated in a workshop called 'Amplifying Youth Voices Participatory Action Research Project', focused on rights, poverty, and discrimination. The facilitators of the workshop (co-authors of the analysis) reported that rich and unexpected issues emerged over the process, reflecting the mismatch between global/universal ideas and the reality of local perspectives and experiences, often deeply culturally bound. While the group did not end up speaking at the UN meeting, they did plan to meet with 'representatives of the international financial institutions and the donor community in Washington DC to advocate for "the unique circumstances of members of minority communities [to be] considered and strategies designed to affect them positively"'. (Fine et al., 2008: 176)

Further reading

Hearn, S. and Mendizabal, E. (2011) *Not Everything that Connects is a Network*, [online] Background Note, ODI <https://odi.org/en/publications/not-everything-that-connects-is-a-network/> [accessed 8 November 2021].

Fine, M., Tuck E. and Zeller-Berkman, S. (2008) 'Do you believe in Geneva? Methods and ethics at the global-local nexus', Chapter 8 in Denzin, N. et al. *Critical and Indigenous Methodologies*, Sage, Thousand Oaks.

This chapter considered methods that are well suited to facilitation in different cultures and readily incorporated into change facilitation workshops and processes. They all enable people to express ideas about change in culturally comfortable ways. Some require more courage and confidence than others, but all can contribute to change in different contexts. Other methods can also be included in a facilitator's tool bag, so consistent with the necessary commitment to ongoing learning required of all facilitators, there is value in remaining open to new ideas.

CHAPTER 10
Contemporary facilitation methods through a cultural values lens

The scope and nature of methods used to contribute to a better world are impossible to quantify or describe succinctly in an introductory book such as this. The range of settings, approaches, topics, and processes is enormous. From a volunteer in a village environmental education program to a multi-million-dollar global development program to improve access to safe water, huge numbers of people and organizations are involved in facilitating change, and they use an extraordinary range of methods. There is inevitably a massive body of research as well as considerable consulting and training work undertaken to support those involved.

This chapter does not aim to summarize or synthesize existing methods, but to apply a cultural values lens to dominant methods and assist facilitators to adjust practice to suit. Most change facilitators and current community and international development programs tend to use a relatively small range of methods, such as workshops, training, advising, coaching, and mentoring, though a much wider range is available. Factors shaping the selection of methods by governments and donor agencies are dynamic and easily contested, but they are not the main focus of discussion here.

All facilitation methods can be perceived and understood in different ways, for example through a power lens, a psychological lens, or an efficiency lens: the cultural lens gives just one view. Here, the focus is on the way these methods can be understood and applied across different cultures using the value differences explained in Part 1.

Workshops

Workshops, within and beyond organizations, are perhaps the most common feature of interaction in our modern diaries. Workshops can be organized for many purposes, not just to bring about change. They are used for convening people within or across organizations or sectors, planning, reflection, training, monitoring, designing new activities, sharing information, generating new ideas, motivating people, and evaluating previous efforts. Like all methods for facilitation, there are strengths and limitations associated with workshops, and the quality can range from awful to excellent, and the effects can range from negative to system-changing.

This section considers workshops through a cultural lens and offers ways to maximize their benefits in multiple contexts. Applying a cultural lens to the concept of workshops encourages reflection on how cultural value differences may influence their relevance and usefulness. This covers how they may be perceived, how people may engage with them, and how effective they may be in facilitating change in various cultural settings. Such analysis leads to reflecting on other practical topics such as how workshops are structured, the timing and mix of activities, the venue, and even the catering. Many a workshop has flopped because the wrong food was ordered or the venue was inadequate.

The underpinning idea of a workshop is that bringing people together to discuss and undertake a task adds value: many views are collated, many people hear particular messages, people hear each other, and the result is more effective than keeping people separate. In individualist and low hierarchy cultures, workshops are understood as the basic means for engagement between those with different or similar responsibilities, levels of authority, or interests. The assumption is that power is shared across the participants and the views of individual participants will be invited, surfaced, and considered by the others in the room. Workshop participants are generally expected to actively engage with the task, the process, and the outcomes.

What are the implications for a workshop, where participants may hold different values: for example, about power, voice, task, relationships, and risk? For example, there may be variations in: the degree of familiarity of participants with the protocols associated with speaking up in plenary and small groups in workshops; the degree of comfort for those who feel marginalized in speaking in front of those with power; and with the extent to which people will express views that may result in punishment or ridicule after the event.

Benefits of convening groups can be significant: planning workshops and similar events in a culturally attuned way will only enhance their relevance and likelihood of success. For example, the selection of participants should take account of the way in which those with and without power may interact with each other and include means to address the various options. Similarly, the way in which interactions are supported should reflect understanding of the dominant cultural values that shape communications and the sharing of information, even if these are then challenged in the workshop process. Challenging values and stimulating conversations about whether prevailing values remain fit for purpose are reasonable and appropriate approaches as long as they are done respectfully, transparently, with the knowledge and agreement of those involved, and where risks are understood and mitigated, particularly for those with low levels of power over their own lives. Given the critical importance of shared commitment to change and the shared experience of global change issues, those who are facilitating such challenges should also demonstrate commitment to reflecting on their own values.

Though workshops are more prevalent than ever, there may be varied degrees of familiarity with their protocols and practices. People's comfort with sharing ideas in front of others and their skills to organize and share information within groups varies between settings. Facilitators' abilities to read and understand group dynamics, which may be complicated by cultural value differences, is critical here. A culturally attuned facilitator may be more aware about the influence of cultural values on the people speaking and the people keeping quiet – often associated with hierarchical values.

Co-facilitation with those more familiar with the cultural context and learning styles, the use of cultural guides, as well as incorporation of elements described in Chapter 9 will contribute to maximizing the cultural relevance of change-related workshops. While there may be value in introducing workshops as a means for participants to learn about the value of the process or methodology, respectful negotiation with local leaders about potentially different expectations and consequences is recommended.

Training

Informal and formal training is used globally, extensively, and increasingly virtually as a means to contribute to change. It can take extremely varied forms. Adult learning principles have been a strong theme in community and international development practice for decades (e.g. Knowles, 1970; Korten, 1980). A wide range of activities, including those listed in Chapter 9, can be incorporated into training programs. The focus of this section is not on how to undertake training when facilitating change (there are plenty of resources available elsewhere), but on the implications of cultural value differences for facilitators of training. These relate to selection of training as an option to contribute towards change, as well as design and delivery of training.

Training in formal settings and adult learning in multicultural and different cultural settings are the subject of considerable research and advice (e.g. Leask and Carroll, 2013). Specialists in particular disciplines tasked with running training courses within topic-specific or partnership contexts tend not to consider this research: their primary focus is usually the technical content. The author has witnessed multiple training-centred programs which focus almost entirely on the technical content and seriously ignore or downplay the pedagogical aspects of adult learning in different cultural contexts, let alone the relevance of the content to the particular setting. The mistaken belief that an appropriate response to an identified priority or a desired change is to run a short training course prevails in many development settings.

A strong emphasis on 'picking the right participants' or 'ensuring participants apply their learning in practice' is often a sign that the training is poorly contextualized in the first place. If participants have been consulted about their learning priorities and training is then contextualized, learners will be keen to participate and then apply their learning: they will not need to be badgered, cajoled, or contracted into doing so.

Trainers who take account of the values that inform learning in each context are better able to engage participants in change-oriented learning processes. That is, they will seek to match their teaching style with the learning style of participants. Those with the skills to shape, deliver, and adapt their courses to suit will more successfully achieve the outcomes sought. This section addresses two topics: what to consider when conceptualizing and reviewing training, and steps to take when planning and delivering training. These are discussed under the following headings: teaching styles; learning styles; course/curriculum design, including assessment; online learning; and formal training in international settings.

Teaching styles

Teaching styles vary between cultures, largely reflecting sociocultural and political values about how information is transmitted, how knowledge is regarded, the respective roles of teachers and learners, and expectations about power in decision-making over curriculum and education.

Those asked to 'run a training course' based on their particular technical expertise would be wise to consider learning styles through a cultural lens. In the western world, Bloom's cognitive taxonomy, developed in the 1950s, was an influential effort to categorize different levels of complexity associated with teaching, to inform teachers about curriculum development and classroom practice (Anderman and Anderman, 2009). Bloom offered a simple hierarchy of levels of thinking: with the acquisition of knowledge at the base of a pyramid shape, going up to understanding, application, analysis, synthesis, and evaluation at the top. The taxonomy has been critiqued since (e.g. Reiner and Willingham, 2010), including for its portrayal of 'lower order' and 'higher order' thinking, and adjusted in various ways, but is still applied widely to differentiate between varied emphases in teaching. Those involved in adult learning have referred to this taxonomy to distinguish between the emphasis of teaching in different cultures. For example, Wang and Farmer (2008) used Bloom's taxonomy to compare adult teaching methods in China and the US, finding that in China, teachers prioritized more teacher-centred didactic teaching (focusing on Bloom's lower order levels: knowledge, understanding, and application), while US teachers preferred student-centred teaching (focusing on higher order levels: analysis, synthesis, and evaluation). For adult learners, this latter style, known as andragogy (Knowles, 1978), is now widely used. It is premised on the idea that adults are responsible for their own learning, so there is a partnership between teachers and learners, rather than an expert–follower relationship.

The influences of cultural value differences on teaching styles often reflect polarized perceptions of teachers and learners. In individualist cultures, initiative by both teachers and learners is rewarded and valued, while in more collectivist cultures, compliance with group norms is expected and prioritized. In more egalitarian cultures, trainers of adults will more likely seek collaborative relationships with course participants, reducing the gap in power. In contrast, in more hierarchical cultures, teachers are more likely to be regarded with considerable respect as experts and gurus (the Bahasa

Indonesia word for teacher), and the gap in power is widely understood (Ziegahn, 2001). This diversity in the degree of respect shown to teachers was confirmed in an interesting survey of the status of teachers around the world (Dolton et al., 2018). Another study by Guthrie (2021) also highlights the central role of cultural value differences for classroom teaching and learning styles around the world, based on experience in international development programs.

A suite of concepts and frameworks about adult learning has been generated in western cultural contexts (Tendy and Geiser, 1997), presenting trainers with many options and decisions to make. Commonly used frameworks include: competency-based training (Blank, 1982); double-loop learning (Argyis, 1977); growth mindset (Dweck, 2008); adult learning styles (Felder, 1998); and reflective learning (Ramsey, 2006). Finding accessible training frameworks generated in non-western cultural contexts is more challenging for English-speaking facilitators. A qualification framework for the Association of South East Asian Nations (ASEAN) for example, includes few signs of cultural relevance: all references are from Australia or Europe (ASEAN, 2016).

When trainers and facilitators from one cultural context design training courses in other contexts, awareness of the values that influence perceptions of trainers, as well as the ways in which culture shapes behaviour and attitudes among learners, is essential (see below). When planning for training workshops, there is value in considering the implications of value differences for the nature and expected benefits and results of training. For example, the selection of trainers, the venue, the types of information provided, the teaching styles, and the assessment mechanisms can be considered through a cultural lens.

Learning styles

The fact that learning styles vary within and between cultures is widely understood, but efforts to define and describe the differences have often encountered controversy. Guild (1994: 16) noted that 'cultures do have distinctive learning style patterns, but the great variation among individuals within groups means that educators must use diverse teaching strategies with all students'. Guild described three elements of the controversy: the reluctance to generalize about a group of people, leading to naïve inferences about individuals within groups; sensitivity relating to explaining achievement differences between minority and non-minority students; and philosophical issues about equity and pluralism. Felder (1998), reflecting his teaching of engineering in the US, is one of the early proponents of the idea that people have different preferred learning styles and that when there is a mismatch between these and teaching styles, learning outcomes are negatively affected. Debate on this proposition is now widespread within western settings (Reiner and Willingham, 2010), but there is more evidence of different learning styles between different cultures (Wang and Farmer, 2008).

Differences in learning styles generally reflect a combination of sociocultural and psychological issues. At the cultural level, values about the degree of respect for and the sharing of knowledge and connections between knowledge and power within societies are relevant to perceptions about learning. This is illustrated in 'one of Confucius's cardinal principles which was to let teachers be teachers and let students be students' and that 'the hierarchical structure reinforces China's pedagogical approach to adult education' (Wang, 2007 quoted in Wang and Farmer, 2008: 6). Access to information varies between cultures: information can be seen as something readily accessible for all in more egalitarian cultures but something to be held in the hands of the few in more hierarchical cultures. The globalization of the internet has changed practical accessibility to a large extent, but has not necessarily resulted in changing values about power. In individualist cultures, learners are more likely to learn through individual endeavour, compared with collectivist cultures, where group learning is generally preferred.

For training facilitators, it makes sense that consideration be given to the learning styles of participants, although there is no simple way to do this. Guild (1994) rightly cautions against assuming that raising cultural awareness of trainers is appropriate, if it leads to inappropriate stereotyping and differentiated or segregated approaches. He also notes the issue that raising awareness of trainers is not necessarily going to address the 'systemic inequities' that exist in many contexts. However, ignoring the relevance of cultural values on participants' learning also raises the risks of irrelevancy and creating unnecessary efforts for participants to achieve desired outcomes.

Drawing on the expertise of trainers with cultural knowledge of particular participants is an obvious means to inform the design and facilitation of training so it is more culturally relevant. Use of a considered mix of methods (see Chapter 9) is also likely to appeal to those with different learning styles. At the level of sustainable development, questioning the use of external trainers may be useful in many cases, in favour of promoting the strengthening of national training systems and processes which draw on cultural preferences and styles in teaching and learning. For example, rather than bringing in an external nurse educator or flying groups of nurses to a donor country, funding processes to strengthen local nurse education skills and systems, will be more sustainable.

Considering symbols of learning in each cultural context may be a useful means for facilitators to identify options. An example of an interesting intercultural learning space in Papua New Guinea was described by Pamphilon (2015). She referred to the symbol of the *bilum* (a Papua New Guinea traditional woven bag or basket) for explaining the 'weaving of knowledges' as a process to describe engagement between smallholder farmers and external experts. The *bilum* patterns were described as combining the range of people who hold different knowledge (the range of coloured yarns) and providing an environment for participants to identify and share the knowledge they bring (recognizing there is a place for each colour) in order to produce a local outcome (the *bilum*) that is a new creation made up of the collaborative inputs of all (Pamphilon, 2015). Similar symbols will likely exist in other cultures and be useful means to support learning towards change.

Course/curriculum design, including assessment

The identification of appropriate content and design of activities in training programs is a time-consuming and challenging task within one's own culture. It requires significantly more effort when working across cultures, another reason why co-facilitation of training courses is useful.

Research undertaken in western contexts about how to maximize learning outcomes for international students is a potential source of advice for change facilitators. Leask and Carroll (2013) produced a useful set of *Good Practice Principles and Quick Guides* for training international students, which may apply when working internationally. Noting the importance of building on and using participants' cultural and social capital and individual differences, as well as the importance of institutional support for teachers to work in inclusive and culturally respectful ways, they provide extensive suggestions on how to apply principles in practice. They address the setting of assessment tasks in ways which acknowledge different values and experiences of international students, although there are ongoing controversies about the ways in which universities in western countries respond to different forms of learning and assessment for students from different cultures.

Designing courses which consider learning and teaching styles in each context is important, but other factors are relevant. For example, the degree of effectiveness of training a group of public servants in how to use a new technique could depend on whether they were involved in its development, whether their leaders support its use, whether the resources are available to support practice, or whether the new way of working resonates with or clashes with current values and practices.

Training in new ways of working benefits from co-design, where those involved in the change process are engaged in determining the means of communication and engagement with trainees. Trainers who develop materials in their own (external) context, and leave a few blank slides or pages for the local voice to be added miss the critical value of co-design and co-creation of ideas.

Online learning

With increasing prevalence of online learning for learners in any location, there is now a body of research about cultural value differences in this context. Rogers et al. (2007) were among the first to consider the experience of instructors faced with developing online curriculum in cross-cultural contexts. They concluded that teachers themselves experienced barriers to the extent they could be culturally attuned, in the broader system, including over-focus on content development. They found additional efforts were needed to educate and get buy-in from other stakeholders (i.e. beyond the instructors) to engage in more learner analysis and evaluation.

Further recognition has been given to cross-cultural aspects of online learning. For example, Tapenes et al. (2009) found that a student's culture heavily influenced their perceptions of an online course, with collectivist learners feeling the instructor did not consider culture when facilitating. Milheim confirmed that 'culture plays a critical role in the [online] classrooms' (2014: 5) and 'an instructor's understanding of a student's cultural background is important to online learning' (2014: 3). She identified ways in which instructors can better engage students from different cultures and the need to continually reflect on and build a community with students, providing explicit opportunities for sharing cultures and understanding. Milheim's research identified the benefits of cultural value differences for rich learning and promoting curiosity, particularly when students' cultures are recognized and valued. In 2020 and 2021, the major shift towards online learning has been a necessary aspect of lockdowns, border closures, and other restrictions associated with the COVID-19 pandemic: more research can be anticipated.

Understanding where learning takes place in different cultures – the location of learning – can help maximize the benefits of online training. Do learners gain more in informal settings, in classrooms, separate learning centres, or in their workplaces? Do they benefit from quiet places on their own, or in groups? One piece of research about online learning, concluded 'the task of the online distance learning instructor is to create learning spaces that provide learners with optimal benefits and facilitate their learning experiences' (Star-Glass, 2013: 65). Since the options for locations are endless, discussions with participants about what works for them are always worth having.

Formal learning in international settings

Scholarships for international education are a core element in most international cooperation, development, and diplomacy programs, generally framed as contributions to change in developing countries. Scholarships are also widely used for change-oriented purposes related to indigenous students or those from other cultural backgrounds. A core belief in this effort is that scholars will learn new information from 'other' contexts which will transform or at least shift practice in their respective disciplines when they return to their home or organizational context. A great deal has been written about the benefits and limitations of scholarships more broadly, with some considering the issues of education through the cultural values lens (e.g. Jelavic and Salter, 2014; Gay, 2015) and in terms of cultural relevance (for example, Gaulee et al,. 2020).

When scholarships are used either separately or as part of a suite of methods to facilitate change, many cultural-value-related issues should be considered. For example, how relevant is the content of formal education in one cultural context to another context? Can a Fijian student undertake a Masters in Human Rights Law in Scotland (focused on Scottish case studies), for example, and expect that the course content will be relevant to their future work in the Pacific? How much should the student be expected to adapt the content of their learning from one cultural context to their own and how realistic is it for them to do so, if the content is completely unfamiliar? How much should teachers and universities be responsible for supporting students to adapt, interpret and consider information taught into a different context? When language challenges are added, the burden of 'translation' on international students is particularly heavy.

The many benefits that may accrue to individuals from the cross-cultural experience may be countered when they seek to apply knowledge developed in one culture to their own, or when they seek to communicate ideas in ways that differ from the norms at home. For example, when students from hierarchical cultures undertake studies in low hierarchy cultures, they learn to speak up to power and challenge dominant ideas. When they return home, they may experience potentially serious negative reactions from those in power. While this may not prevent returning scholarship students from succeeding in many cases, it raises questions about expectations that investing in small numbers of students is beneficial in contributing to systemic change. This does not assume that hierarchical cultures need to change, or that people in hierarchical cultures have to learn to speak truth to power and challenge dominant ideas, but simply that cross-cultural aspects of translating ways of working and thinking from one context to another need to be considered.

Advising

International development programs frequently use the placement of international advisors as a primary means to bring about change. Sector specialists undertake advisory roles related to multiple topics ranging from public sector financial management and health systems strengthening to gender-based violence, police service development, and disability inclusion. The role of advisors usually includes a mix of direct technical work, for example setting up a new system or introducing new ways of working, plus some form of 'capacity development'. Sometimes, they hold in-line positions, where local specialists are not available. Advisors can hold positions from weeks to several years and work with one or more colleagues in many different settings, often public sector organizations.

Through a cultural values lens, both the strategic intent of placing international advisors overall and advisors' ways of working can be considered. As a strategy, the placement of advisors from one cultural context working in another implies the expertise in the source country is of a higher level than that available within the country of placement, and that advisors can be made responsible for the achievement of particular changes. In a globalized world of education, where specialists from different countries may have attended similar universities and conferences, this may not always be the case. The placement of advisors can also be understood as a partnership, whereby the combined expertise of people from different contexts contributes to the achievement of shared change-related objectives. At a strategic level, the intention of advisor placement has an influence on how the advisors are expected to work, then managed and assessed. Cross-cultural perspectives on the relevance and nature of change-related concepts and approaches need to be understood at this strategic level in order to shape advisors' ways of working.

Advisors are expected to work closely with their colleagues, finding ways to minimize direct work in order not to substitute themselves for national workers, while supporting various practical changes. Finding this balance and working with it over a sustained period is a common challenge for many advisors, particularly if there are unresolved differences at the strategic level about the intent and nature of overall collaboration and expected changes. Working cross-culturally on a day-to-day basis can also be challenging for individuals, especially if they have been selected and placed according to their technical expertise and not supported in their cross-cultural practice. Supporting technical specialists to work as advisors in cross-cultural settings requires specific and systemic effort beyond wishful thinking and goodwill. Training, culturally attuned monitoring, and ongoing leadership support are all valuable in this regard; however, these are often minimized when funding is limited, with more effort given to assessing advisors' performance according to set criteria. This potentially reduces the achievement of culturally relevant and sustainable outcomes, even if short-term tasks are completed to meet externally determined definitions of success.

For individual advisors, cultural value differences present challenges and opportunities, depending on their own openness to learning, flexibility, curiosity, ability to play a back-seat role, and other personal qualities. While perspectives of those being 'advised' are not always prioritized when it comes to cultural relevance, when they are heard, they tend to give greater value to those advisors who have been culturally respectful, attuned, and responsive.

Coaching and mentoring

Coaching and mentoring are popular means to facilitate change at individual or small-team levels and sometimes for large cohorts. They are standard options in many community development and international development programs. Coaching and mentoring are designed to contribute towards individual growth in confidence, knowledge, skills, networks, understanding, self-esteem, and motivation and can enhance individual performance. Without complementary support, it cannot be assumed that these methods will lead to organizational or systemic change in a linear or sustainable manner, but they are well regarded in individualist societies. Undertaking both coaching and mentoring across cultures can be challenging, reflecting not only different cultural values, but also the fact that coaches and mentors are usually expected to support people to succeed within their particular context, which is hard for people from other contexts to appreciate. A British or Canadian public servant may have good knowledge in how to succeed in the British or Canadian public service, but this expertise may not translate well in an Indonesian or Chinese ministry context, for example.

Through a cultural values lens, a coaching or mentoring system should take account of the particular values that drive individual performance and motivation in different contexts, as well as the broader context in which coachees and mentees live and work. For example, suggesting a coachee in a high power distance culture should challenge their leader may involve risks that may not exist in a low power distance cultural context. In a multicultural setting, different values influence the degree of engagement between coaches and mentors, the nature of interactions, and the chances of success.

Successful mentors and coaches have a good understanding of the cultural context in which mentees and coachees operate, ensuring their contributions are relevant and meaningful. Since a mentor–mentee relationship is generally understood as a teacher–student relationship, those from hierarchical cultures may be quite comfortable, but culturally respectful communications are obviously crucial.

Strengthening knowledge systems

One method that potentially recognizes cultural values in change processes could be labelled as strengthening indigenous knowledge systems. This is a contentious idea for various reasons, through the lens of disciplines such as anthropology, politics, and history. However, if facilitators are working in trust-based and culturally attuned relationships, it is worth considering as an option to contribute to change. At its core, this method involves the identification, collation, and recording of indigenous or traditional knowledge about any particular aspect of the world (for example, Indigenous Australians' use of fire to manage the environment, or Pacific Islanders' understanding of weather patterns for predicting cyclones), so that it can be shared, reflected upon, communicated, and potentially applied more broadly to bring about desired change, where appropriate.

The idea of recognizing indigenous knowledge in change processes is not particularly new but is now attracting greater attention. According to Thompson (1996: 105) 'the detailed study of indigenous knowledge dates back to the late 1970s when two seminal collected works drew together research that examined the capacities, skills and rationale of peasant farmers and pastoralists'. As the interest in indigenous knowledge grew, shifting from social anthropology to other sectors, Thompson (1996: 106) noted two emerging approaches: one which considers knowledge using 'the conceptual apparatus of western science' and another which 'sees the cross-cultural study of agroecological and sociocultural beliefs as challenging the basic conceptual apparatus of western science'. Dawning recognition that frames of reference are directly conditioned by the history and geography (and cultural values) of a discipline has led to an opening up to new frames of reference. This includes opportunities taken by indigenous people around the world in more recent times to articulate knowledge more explicitly. The work of Denzin et al., (2008) who edited a collection of articles on indigenous inquiry methodologies epitomizes this shift.

Methods which explicitly showcase indigenous knowledge, norms, and ways of being and seeing the world can be incorporated into change facilitation processes, particularly if there is trust, respect, and good collaboration. Such methods cannot be co-opted by change facilitators from one culture and applied to another, but there are potentially respectful ways of supporting their use. The assumption that it is possible to integrate local knowledge into existing western constructs about knowledge and systems is easily challenged. Thompson (1996: 108) wrote that indigenous knowledge 'is not an accumulation of "facts" but involves ways of comprehending the world: knowledge is always in the making'.

Contemporary development programs commonly include the establishment of systems for collating and sharing information, reflecting the belief that when knowledge is shared, organizations, systems, and sectors are strengthened, and positive change is more achievable. In addition to the questions raised by Thompson (1996) and many others since about the idea of handling indigenous knowledge in the same way as western forms of knowledge, different cultural values apply to sharing information. The assumption that information is freely exchanged between people and groups does not apply in all contexts. In low power distance and individualist cultures, where encyclopedias and the internet first emerged, information is relatively freely shared and everyone is expected to be as informed as possible to enhance their life prospects, achieve tasks, and much more. Sharing information is a critical aspect of contemporary low power distance cultures and it is largely assumed this is a shared value globally. In high power distance and collectivist cultures, even with the widespread uptake of the internet, it may be more likely assumed that some information is kept in the hands of a few, the leaders, or shared within a particular small group, rather than widely shared. Strong connections between power and information mean that those with power often keep information to themselves, and those without power expect their leaders to make appropriate decisions on the basis they are best placed to do so. Consistent with ideas about rote learning in high power distance cultures, (in contrast with critical analysis found more often in individualist cultures) there is also potentially more interest in the 'right and wrong' aspects of information than the nuances between different frames of reference.

For change facilitators, discussions with cultural guides about whether indigenous knowledge systems and understandings of change can be included in change processes are the key. If there is interest in this method, then co-facilitation with indigenous facilitators is a minimum requirement.

Partnership brokering

Partnerships, when undertaken in ways that reflect the true definition of the term are potentially significant contributors to positive change and are increasingly used in contemporary change contexts. Cross-cultural partnerships in particular, when operating successfully, are probably the most critical means available to address some of the global challenges faced by humanity: their absence is evident in most global conflicts. Facilitation and management of partnerships are now key tasks for those involved in change-oriented programs. Facilitators can learn to broker new partnerships, support the process of partnerships, as well as monitor partnership-related changes.

Several global networks have been established in recent decades to support the quality of partnerships, for example The Partnering Initiative <https://thepartneringinitiative.org/> [accessed 7 October 2021] and the Partnership Brokers Association <https://partnershipbrokers.org/> [accessed 7 October 2021]. These offer training, consulting advice, and other resources, including resources for those who work remotely. Through a cultural values lens, taking account of different perceptions of power is one of the most critical aspects of partnerships and relationships. Rarely are two entities equal in their power when they come together to achieve a particular change. While one may have more funds or resources, for example, another may have more knowledge of the context, relevant local networks, what has worked and not worked previously, and what is more likely to succeed. Awareness of the cultural values of each partner and their influence on how power is understood and shared, how information is regarded and shared, and how one partner views another is crucial. Similarly, steps taken to plan for change, describe change, monitor change, and determine success can be understood differently through cultural value lenses, alongside all the other factors that influence partnerships' success.

Culturally attuned partnerships will include all the standard elements plus a focus on deepening shared understanding of the values and norms which influence each partner's views of the world, of each other, the process of collaborating, and the purpose of the partnership. They would also include efforts to affirm respect for each other's cultural values within the principles of collaboration and shared commitment. Culturally attuned partnerships could provide appropriate locations for the kinds of conversations that address values, asking the questions about whether prevailing values are still fit for purpose, for example.

This chapter considered common change-oriented methods through a cultural lens, acknowledging that other lenses are also important.

It identified some of the nuances and pitfalls associated with popular forms of engagement with people when cultural value differences are considered. While each method has strengths and limitations, there are ways to maximize cultural relevance and therefore value and effectiveness, when appropriate consideration is given. However, it is also likely that different perspectives will emerge on the value of engagement methods, for a multitude of reasons. The following chapter considers conflict and related issues through a cultural values lens.

CHAPTER 11
Cross-cultural conflict management methods

> When people become more confident in their ability to address conflicts, they begin to see it as a natural process. They learn to look for ways to create mutually beneficial outcomes from it. They also recognize that working through conflict can help bring people closer, particularly when the individuals involved have shown respect for each other and for their respective cultures. (Runde and Armon, 2016 p. 70)

Facilitators of change who understand connections between cultural values and conflict and have skills to understand, mediate, and navigate conflict in change processes can make a valuable contribution to positive change. A cultural values analysis of everyday news bulletins and history books confirms that differences in values are connected to a large proportion of global and local disagreements, disputes, clashes, conflicts, and wars within and across borders. The nature and extent of links between values and conflict varies from 'limited association' to 'directly causal'. The stronger a person or leader identifies with their cultural group and values, the more motivated they may be to defend the interests of that group and try to defeat the 'other' group. This often leads to pitting values of one group against another and thus conflict between those who seek a particular change and those who do not. Some leaders even consider that conflicts and wars are necessary when cultural values are different. As cultural values shape the way that groups and issues are defined and separated, the connection between cultural values and conflict is clear.

Acknowledging the enormity and complexity of the topic, this chapter focuses on four practical approaches that enable facilitators to address differences and conflicts within change facilitation processes across cultures:

- building shared culture;
- cross-cultural dispute resolution and negotiations methods;
- use of trained mediators with an understanding of different cultural values;
- contestation-based community development methods.

Change processes by definition are likely to generate or reflect conflict of some variety and degree of gravity. Members within and between groups may have opposing ideas and degrees of interest in the change agenda. Those with and without power may have different ideas about how power should be shared. For change facilitators, these differences have at least two major implications. First, facilitators themselves need to develop conflict management skills and the ability to understand how conflict is expressed and managed differently in various cultures (e.g. Hammer and Wiseman, 1978; Augsburger, 1992; Ting-Toomey, 1994; Hammer, 2005). Second, there is value in supporting or contributing to the capacity of facilitators within communities and organizations to manage conflicts in culturally attuned ways, including the use of mediators.

Common sources of disputes in all cultures involve issues associated with relative power and status, roles, emotions, misinformation (and misinterpretation), and values. Even in mono-cultural contexts, these may be present, but when people from different cultural backgrounds come together, such as in a multicultural or cross-cultural change facilitation workshop, the potential for conflict to come to the surface in a harmful way, increases. Negative impacts of such problems affect many people significantly at various times, particularly in times of crisis. Not all disputes between people from different cultures have cultural elements, but culturally attuned facilitators are likely to use approaches and methods which can work in any context.

Change facilitation processes, from simple to complex, inevitably challenge the status quo and risk undermining positive (and negative) culturally embedded relationships. When existing relationships are challenged, this may cause harm to marginalized or 'low power' groups in high power cultural settings. For example, by putting individuals from a marginalized group 'in the spotlight' and asking them to identify a change they want to see, they may be chastised or further alienated later by those in power if the change they seek is perceived to undermine them. Thus, culturally attuned monitoring of the quality of facilitation, the nature of engagement, issues arising, and other aspects of change processes is particularly critical.

Effective practices for negotiating, mediating, arbitrating, and navigating differences in conflict settings have been given considerable attention in research, with a large number of guidelines produced. While not all of this literature pays attention to the cross-cultural elements, a few researchers and institutions have specialized in this area (e.g. Avruch and Black, 1993; Ting-Toomey and Oetzel, 2001). The business world's interests in globalization have generated a body of work in cross-cultural negotiations at a generic level (e.g. Khan and Ebner, 2019) and at a specific country level (e.g. Sebenius, 2002). When added to literature on international peace negotiations, peacebuilding, and serious conflict management, there is no shortage of advice, a plethora of methods, and tomes of lessons learned.

Change processes attract supporters and detractors: facilitators, both individual and organizational, are therefore likely to encounter the need for negotiation and conflict management in their work. Even if they seek to focus on collaborative rather than contested approaches to supporting change, facilitators will encounter different perceptions of issues associated with different group identities. Understanding cross-cultural conflict management and strong negotiation skills are relevant for those involved in facilitating change, even if the major focus is on preparation for minimizing the risks of conflict over time. While lessons learned from the vast body of work on cross-cultural conflict may be helpful, some ideas are contested. Those involved in cross-cultural partnership brokering and support particularly recognize the value in understanding conflicting perspectives to bring about change (Dwonczyk, 2015).

Generic concepts have been referred to throughout this book about ways in which cross-cultural disputes and conflicts can be prevented, avoided, or minimized. These include:

- continuously deepening understanding about one's own and others' cultural perspectives;
- being attuned to the multiple layers of history, past experience, process, and outcomes associated with previous conflicts and systemic oppression;
- contributing to the understanding of others about the links between cultural values, norms, and behaviour at all levels, as well as complexity and how power can be understood differently through cultural lenses;
- seeking to show respect for others' views;
- ensuring organizational systems (policies, leadership practice) prevent discrimination;
- use of skilled and respected cultural guides and interpreters;
- leading, demonstrating, and promoting high-functioning inclusive teams which value diverse perspectives and promote a sense of well-being for all team members.

Particular frameworks and guides to support the management of conflict across cultures can be useful for change facilitators (e.g. Oetzel and Ting-Toomey, 2001; Runde and Armon, 2016). The work of Hammer (2005) is also useful for generating understanding about different approaches to conflict in various cultures. Hammer's research identified four different styles in approaching conflict in different cultural settings (discussion, accommodation, dynamic, and engagement). These reflect a mix of emphasis on two elements: the degree to which content is communicated (from direct to indirect) and the degree of emotional commitment (from reserved to expressive). Hammer's research allocated different cultures/nations to each category, but most benefit (from the author's use of this framework) comes from increased self-awareness. Enabling people to understand their own style and how it may be perceived by others can help them navigate future conflict more effectively. Other guides on cross-cultural negotiations, most relating to business negotiations and cross-cultural staff management in multicultural organizations, may also be potentially useful for change facilitators.

Change facilitators working cross-culturally can particularly benefit from understanding the concept of 'face', which has a key role in many cross-cultural conflicts. The idea of 'face-saving' or avoiding 'loss of face' is found in many cultures but is significantly more prominent in some, usually collectivist cultures. As noted by Ting-Toomey and Oetzel (2001: 176), individualists are more concerned with problem-solving and closure, while collectivists are more concerned with facework and process management issues. In cultures which prioritize avoiding the loss of face, increased attention is given to maintaining social standing and reputation. This means that people in these cultures tend to minimize others' loss of face. In summary, 'face is an explanatory mechanism for culture's influence on conflict behavior' (Oetzel and Ting-Toomey, 2003: 1).

Skills that facilitators can find useful in conflict situations include self-awareness, the ability to regulate emotions, the ability to support respectful engagement, and mindfulness. Their ability to help others generate these skills may also be useful. For example, Runde and Armon (2016) describe a set of leadership and related skills to support cross-cultural conflict management. They refer to the importance of efforts to support people and organizations involved in conflict to enhance self-awareness, regulate emotions, slow down and reflect on conflict, engage constructively, as well as create effective teams and organizational norms.

Building a shared culture

Change facilitators who can contribute to the development and adoption of a 'shared culture' in teams, organizations, and networks can work well across cultures. This is not only a means to set a positive foundation for cross-cultural collaboration, but a specific method to help prevent conflicts and strengthen people's abilities to navigate conflicts themselves when they arise. This method can contribute increasing understanding among people about different values that prevail and how they can be understood neutrally rather than as better or worse than their own values.

Acknowledging the importance of cultural backgrounds respectfully and constructively from the outset can help groups of people, who come together for any purpose, to avoid conflict or to manage conflicts better when they arise. Regular reflection and review processes can support multicultural groups to assess whether they are working well and what might need to improve over time. The practice of talking about cultural value differences and applying them to real-life work or teams helps make participants better equipped. Support from leaders for such efforts is critical for success.

A simple method for building shared culture in any context is called 'Map Bridge Integrate' (MBI) (Maznevski and Di Stefano, 2003). This method includes the following:

- Map: enables cultural groups to consider what values, norms, and behaviour are important to them in the particular context. For example, if a facilitation process includes a group of participants from India, Fiji, and Mauritius, each group would work together to document what values, norms, and behaviour are important to them.

- Bridge: this step enables people from each group to share their different perspectives with the other group, talk about the differences, and practise the idea of 'walking in the other's shoes'. This can be done using a variety of creative activities, such as pair discussions, use of symbols to exchange information, and story-telling.
- Integrate: this step involves the whole group negotiating collaboratively to determine agreed values, norms, and behaviour for the group members while they are working together. Specific consideration of conflicts – how they might be understood differently, how they might be handled, and which strategies would suit all participants – is included.

MBI recognizes the value that differences can have for bringing about change and actually seeks to nurture the differences. The tool can be applied in a wide variety of contexts and settings: change facilitators can deepen practice over time, extending the capacity of groups, teams, and organizations to deal constructively and creatively with different perspectives.

Cross-cultural dispute-management and resolution methods

> Participants in an effective multicultural collaboration must have inclusive leadership that understands and strives for diversity, while dealing with problems and conflict along the way. If the focus remains on the common goal and equal power for everyone involved, the collaboration will have a great chance of success. (Brownlee, n.d.)

Facilitators can work within systems (organizations, networks, relationships, partnerships etc.) or as outsiders, but are rarely in a position to substantially resolve conflicts themselves. This section addresses a range of dispute resolution methods, recognizing that the perceived and actual power associated with the selection and appointment of a facilitator will affect their ability to play an effective role. Even expert facilitators cannot overcome the wider systems in which conflicts may exist, though they may assist those in a context to understand those systems themselves, including through a cross-cultural perspective.

The role of facilitators in supporting people to address conflicts across cultures will vary widely. Their own cultural background and perceptions of it will influence the receptiveness of groups of people to their contribution, but if culturally attuned, they can make a more relevant contribution. Avruch and Black (1993) advise that any process of intercultural conflict resolution will benefit from a preliminary cultural analysis which at minimum makes explicit the underlying assumptions and understandings of conflict and conflict resolution held by all parties to the conflict, as well as the mediators or third parties. This process enables each party to gain an understanding of the cultural meanings of the other, along with a clearer understanding of their own.

Methods which enable those in conflict to understand the perspectives of others are best contextualized within broader respect-based systems.

It is difficult for an external facilitator to use the kinds of methods which are based on respect, within a context which is discriminatory, excluding, oppressive, or otherwise systemically undermining of respectful relationships between people. If the context includes regular opportunities in which people are able to safely express their views and concerns, and have their concerns heard and understood, then when a conflict arises, a facilitator is more likely to be able to address the specific issue at hand. Generally, a facilitator who is able to provide a safe place for people to express their concerns and to help others to understand the situation from another perspective will have more success if the participants are familiar with such an approach. Facilitators can seek to work patiently, flexibly, and in a way which illustrates their humility and willingness to learn, as well as use a mix of creative activities.

Mindfulness is highlighted in one of the few specific resources that exists on conflict management for those involved in cross-cultural facilitation. Ting-Toomey and Oetzel describe mindfulness within 'constructive conflict skills dimensions' (2001: 179). Mindfulness is not something that can be suddenly applied when there is a conflict, so needs to be part of a broader approach to interaction with others and life itself. The constructive conflict skills suggested by Oetzel and Ting-Toomey include: mindful observation, mindful listening, mindful reframing, identity validation, facework management, productive power balancing, collaborative dialogue, problem-solving skills, transcendent discourse, and interaction adaptability. To illustrate these options, the mindful observation method involves four steps, which seek to prevent the rapid escalation of a conflict or a negative conclusion. The four steps are 'observe, describe, interpret, and suspend evaluation' (ODIS). This method enables a facilitator to support people involved in a conflict to make sense of another's perspective of their own and others' behaviour in a way which works towards de-escalating a conflict (Ting-Toomey and Oetzel, 2001).

Facilitators looking for a 'best model' to address cross-cultural conflict in multiple contexts, beyond the suggestions proposed by Ting-Toomey and Oetzel, may struggle to find something. This suggests that context-specific analysis and collaborative approaches are the most useful.

Use of and support for culturally attuned mediators

Beyond the promotion of skills to understand the views of people from other cultures involved in conflicts, it may be necessary for facilitators to seek specialist expertise. While cross-cultural mediators may be hard to find, and some take a more legalistic slant than others, increased demand for such skills may contribute to growth in this area. Cultural guides or mentors may also be helpful.

Mediation involves a third party acting in the role as a 'go-between' or facilitator to provide both parties with opportunities to put forward their views, analyse the situation, and find a way forward that is satisfactory to all. When a conflict is related to a cultural misunderstanding, then engaging someone with cultural skills, able to help explain a process which is acceptable to all parties and support its implementation, can be critical.

Efforts to train or skill up mediators with cross-cultural expertise may make a sustainable contribution to multicultural and cross-cultural partnerships and collaboration, potentially covering all sectors, and all contexts, from communities to multilateral agencies.

Contestation methods

Facilitators working across cultures are more likely to be familiar with methods which seek to build collaboration between people than create contestation. However, community development practice distinguishes between collaborative and contested ways of achieving change (Weeks et al., 2003). Contest-based change facilitation methods are used across cultures and are particularly relevant to movements for change. The Black Lives Matter movement and the Climate Change movement use a range of facilitated processes which explicitly mobilize people to contest harmful and negative dominant systems. While these movements vary in nature in different settings, the fact that they seek to challenge systems and leaders means they are valuable sources of information about how change happens in different cultural contexts. Understanding the way that cultural values shape perceptions of conflict is highly relevant to change facilitation in each context.

The discipline of community development has a great deal to offer facilitators involved in change processes which are largely based on some kind of contested idea, policy, or program. Community development practice draws on theoretical frameworks to support communities involved in disputes, for example with governments or businesses which are perceived to cause harm. Examples of governments or businesses undertaking major infrastructure projects or environmentally harmful projects can be found worldwide, and these are often complicated by cross-cultural elements, such as when a dominant culture is in government or has power and a minority group is in conflict with them. In these contexts, the cross-cultural elements add complexity to existing issues related to the conflict, such as power and discrimination.

Approaches which may be useful in contested contexts are not dissimilar to others referenced in this book. For example, a facilitator may be involved in processes which seek to: build understanding through analysis of power, gender, class, and race; build social movements; strengthen inclusive leadership; support planning and decision-making processes; mobilize people and enable citizen participation; build organizations; support networking and communications systems; and undertake public advocacy campaigns. Conflict resolution processes may be relevant in all aspects of contested spaces, particularly in threatening and urgent contexts, and an understanding of the cultural drivers for a particular group's conflict and their cultural preference for managing conflicts is often critical to the achievement of resolution.

A facilitator's tasks in these contexts may vary widely at different stages of the process. Facilitators may be asked to support the formation of a movement or articulation of advocacy messages, activate aspects of advocacy, or help people to celebrate or manage the grief associated with final outcomes (Weeks et al. 2003). Awareness of conflict issues and skills in negotiation are therefore critical.

Change facilitation methods can include means which base group collaboration on the need to challenge 'others' as causes of problems or the need to respond to threats. Black Lives Matter is a contemporary example of this concept whereby a movement of people comes together in unity and with a collective voice to challenge the leaders and systems which are seen as oppressive. Similarly, the Climate Change movement is generating collective efforts to challenge dominant leaders and systems which perpetuate the causes of global warming, causing catastrophic harm to the planet, including the natural environment and the future of humankind. As noted in Weeks et al., (2003), contestation-based approaches are a common context in which facilitators can support and mobilize change. Activism at global, national, and local levels is an increasingly prominent means to either bring about change or block undesirable change. Cross-cultural movements are likely to encounter similar kinds of issues as any other kind of cross-cultural engagement, even when the common bonds are clear and strong, since there are always different perceptions about the means to achieve or block change, depending on cultural values and other factors.

Building transnational solidarity to address human rights, social justice, and climate change is an increasingly common phenomenon. Regional and national efforts to advocate for changes to unacceptable policies and laws similarly can involve cross-cultural collaboration, supported by facilitators either within or outside each context. The link between social movements and cultural values has been considered in western-sourced academia since the mid-1990s (e.g. McAdam, 1994), but sources from other cultural contexts are not readily accessible.

This short chapter offers a number of practical ideas for facilitators of change in conflict contexts, acknowledging that a cultural values lens is significant but there are many other sources and frames of reference on this topic. Methods mentioned in Chapters 9 and 10 can support movements which contest ideas, leaders, and systems and enable disparate groups to navigate conflicts. Methods which build solidarity; mobilize people to plan and decide on strategies; invoke strategies and campaigns to suit the groups' understanding of opportunities and norms; and assess progress and results may all be useful in these contexts. Additional methods which strengthen group members' commitment to the group, against the 'common enemy', may be sought, including training in social movements, campaigns, group mobilization, analysis, and strategizing, for example.

CHAPTER 12
Evaluating change across cultures

All aspects of change can look different when viewed through a cultural lens, including definitions of success. This applies to perceptions about the concept, value, and reality of change, the processes which take people on a journey towards some kind of change and the role of facilitators. It is inevitable that when it comes to assessing whether change processes are on track or have been successful, and whether a facilitator is doing a good job, a cultural lens is necessary. As cultural values shape societies' perceptions of change, there may be a lack of shared understanding between different cultures about the necessity of and approaches to assessing change processes, despite the impact of globalization on many similar concepts. Not everyone wants to know whether a particular program was successful: they may have other priorities and interests, not necessarily served by 'evidence of success'.

Facilitators of change are often engaged directly in monitoring and evaluation processes themselves, for example as evaluators or program managers. Opportunities and complexities involved in assessing change through a cultural lens require consideration in nearly all elements of the process, from conceptualizing a monitoring plan to communicating evaluation findings. Change processes inevitably include elements of monitoring, evaluation, and learning, variously resourced and supported. Projects, programs, partnerships, and other funded initiatives commonly identify high-level objectives or expected outcomes from the outset, and either a set of indicators or other means of assessing performance. A large body of literature and advice has developed since the 1980s about the many philosophical and practical aspects of understanding and evaluating change. Most accessible information has emerged from western cultural contexts, reflecting low power distance, individualist, task/performance-oriented, and low uncertainty avoidance values which dominate these cultures.

This chapter discusses ways in which change processes are considered and assessed through a cultural lens, addressing just four of the many elements: approaches for monitoring progress over time; approaches for judging/evaluating the results of change processes or success; communicating information about progress and results; and skills that facilitators will find useful to work cross-culturally in these particular aspects of change-oriented work.

As is the case with other topics discussed in this book, there is a large and growing body of work related to monitoring and evaluation across cultures, as well as a related body of literature on research through a cultural lens. The idea that different cultures see the world differently, and therefore consider changes to their own world or the broader world in diverse ways is now increasingly accepted (Mertens, 2016), albeit not necessarily widely applied in various disciplines. Since the 1990s, the practice of evaluation in particular has become more 'mainstream' and the recognition of cultural values within the field of evaluation more prominent. Substantial growth in the number of people who specialize in evaluation and make a career in evaluating programs and policies attests to this change, as well as increasing demand for evaluation from government and non-profit organizations. Evaluators are commonly engaged in facilitating reflection and review processes which can be understood to be part of change itself, so facilitators and evaluators can share approaches and skills.

Monitoring across cultures

The processes associated with determining whether plans are on track, commonly referred to as monitoring, largely reflect cultural values related to task and performance. In contrast, in cultures which place more emphasis on relationships than task, there is little need or demand for separate systems to determine if relationships are being maintained in harmonious ways: people know from their immediate feelings and experiences if this is the case.

People and institutions in largely task- and performance-oriented cultures have invented a vast array of systems, structures, concepts, tools, and practices associated with production and performance, particularly since the Industrial Revolution. These are so entrenched in cultures that they are often understood to be universal; however, it is increasingly clear this is not the case. Other forms of knowledge, ways of life, and frames of reference, particularly related to harmonious living with the natural environment, are being recognized outside indigenous contexts as important for the whole of humanity. The dominance of task-oriented values and constant growth is increasingly seen as having limitations and negative effects on the planet and the future of humankind.

Interest in monitoring progress in task-oriented cultures has led to the development of a range of systems, specialists, structures, and processes. Whole businesses help other businesses to manage data for monitoring purposes. People's sense of purpose, achievement, and career success can be based on their achievement of particular targets. The many manifestations of the cultural values that drive societies' task orientation, their interest in 'getting stuff done,' include planning, tracking, project management, and deadlines. Performance-orientation values generate practices associated with incentives, standards, continuous improvement, targets, and indicators. When combined and promoted as essential for success (economic, social, and otherwise), it is clear that different cultural values about harmonious relationships have been subjugated. Exceptions include Bhutan which measures national happiness (rather than economic growth) and New Zealand which currently uses a well-being approach to budgeting.

For those involved in monitoring across cultures, the assumption that everyone has the same interest in knowing about 'how things are going' needs to be questioned. At a minimum, acknowledging different expectations about the need to know, kinds of information that have meaning in that context, and ways of making sense of that information is going to be helpful. For example, a person from a highly relationship-oriented culture could be expected to be more interested in the nature of relationships than whether a set of tasks has been completed as planned. If asked to be engaged in a process to determine whether tasks have been completed satisfactorily, they could view this through a relationship lens, for example asking 'did the right people complete the task?' or 'did the people get on?' rather than 'were the standards met?' Similarly, if they are more interested in past timeframes than the future, assessing whether something was completed 'on time' has less meaning for them than it would for someone who is interested in deadlines.

For facilitators of monitoring processes, strategies described in Chapter 7 are relevant here. Setting the 'right climate' for effective cross-cultural collaboration in monitoring requires many of the same elements. In practical terms, this means that in each cultural context, conversations could be held to consider:

- Values that shape the participants in a change process, e.g. what is important in relation to progress towards change, what do people value, and how are these priorities expressed in the change process?
- The kinds of leadership that are valued, e.g. what kinds of information are sought by leaders and useful for them to pursue positive development processes?
- The kinds of information sought by everyone, including marginalized people in a context, e.g. what do young people, or people with disabilities, or ethnic or religious minority groups really want to find out?
- The data that will help build stronger collaboration and collective action, rather than simply report to an external party with no accountability to the participants in the change process.
- The kinds of information that will contribute to ongoing learning and reflection, e.g. what are we learning that can help us more broadly to achieve our own objectives?
- The kinds of information which address the really important priorities, rather than a lower-order topic that is not necessarily going to be sustained or systemically address the most significant issues.
- The kinds of information which recognize the strengths in the context.
- How information will be collected and analysed in ways that make sense for the cultural context in which the change process is occurring.

Methods described in Chapters 9 and 10 and those labelled 'participatory methodologies' proposed by Robert Chambers over decades are useful for reflection and monitoring processes. Many different ways can be found to support people in a context to reflect on and understand their lives and changes that have occurred: emphasis should be on the selection of methods which enable people to express their views and experiences in comfortable, safe, and meaningful ways. While program implementers and donors tend to be more interested in whether their particular activity has 'made a difference', culturally attuned monitors know that this may not be the interest of the people in the context. People's lives are inevitably more complex than can be captured in a single-focus survey about whether they are happy with an NGO's Program Officer, whether water is more accessible, they have more cows, or the number of people trained in disability inclusion has increased by 10 per cent.

Culturally attuned monitoring methods, when developed and applied in **participatory** ways, and after deep reflection about '**who finds out, who learns, and who is empowered**' (Chambers, 2008) in each context, include:

- action learning and action research processes;
- Appreciate Inquiry;
- co-facilitated reflection workshops or meetings;
- group or individual drawing, art, sculpture, theatre, film, music, or dance to explore and explain changes;
- mapping and counting;
- most significant change;
- narrative and story-telling;
- open space;
- outcome mapping;
- participatory democracy methods such as citizens' juries;
- theatre-based processes.

Information about these methods is readily accessible with a simple internet search. The key message about monitoring change across cultures is to consider why and for whom monitoring takes place, and then what is being monitored and how, through the lens of the culture in which the change is expected. Facilitators may well be involved in translating information to cultures which place more emphasis on monitoring data and accountability, affirming the value of translation skills.

Evaluation across cultures

There is now increased understanding across the evaluation profession that cross-cultural understanding is a priority for those working in communities and countries which are different from their own, to inform appropriate approaches, tools, and processes. However, before evaluators jump to selecting tools, it is worth considering how the concept of evaluation itself could be seen through a cross-cultural lens. The idea of evaluation reflects values about change, development, and risk; knowledge and wisdom; access to information and education; and the completion of tasks or the maintenance of harmonious relationships. These values are not necessarily shared universally. Political aspects of evaluation are influenced by cultural value differences, as highlighted in Chapter 3 and by Roche and Kelly (2012). Links between understanding differences in cultural values and the practice of evaluation are discussed here, before considering the selection of methods.

Cultural views of evaluation

The Australian Evaluation Society (AES) defines evaluation as 'the systematic collection and analysis of information to make judgements, usually about the effectiveness, efficiency and/or appropriateness of an activity' (Australian Evaluation Society, 2010: 3). From the perspective of a task and performance-oriented culture, there seems to be few contentious elements of such a definition. However, through a cross-cultural lens this definition reveals the potential for contested understanding. Given increasing interest in the intersection between different worldviews and evaluation methods, change facilitators will likely need to consider this in multicultural and cross-cultural contexts.

Core elements of evaluation include the collation and sharing of information, the forming of judgements about change, learning and success, and the use of evidence to enhance understanding and decision-making. In low power distance cultures, value is commonly placed on the sharing of information and on equitable access to education and resources, which means generally speaking that everyone is expected to be able to know, learn, have a critical perspective, make judgements and choices, as well as make sense of information themselves. In contrast, in high power distance cultures, value is generally accorded to the idea that those at the top of the power hierarchy will have information and access to education and wisdom, and therefore will be best placed to make sense of information and make judgements and decisions for others' benefit. Therefore, the idea that some kind of independent process or team can facilitate knowledge or make judgements, rather than those in power, may not resonate with or be welcomed in high power distance contexts. Globalization processes are obviously influencing these differences, particularly in urbanized settings, but not all evaluations take place in contexts where there is a shared understanding of why projects and programs are evaluated or how they could be evaluated by people other than local leaders.

In evaluation contexts, understanding about different ways in which people in individualist and collectivist cultures answer questions is important. In collectivist societies, it is common for members of a group to check with each other before answering a question definitively. From an individualist perspective, this may appear as collusion or influence, but from a collectivist perspective, such an approach minimizes the risk of exclusion from a group, the consequences of which can be highly negative. Dinh (2019a and 2019b), for example, describes the relevance of Confucian and Buddhist world views on the ways in which evaluation-related information is considered, shared, and acted upon.

Distinctions between task and relationship orientation also have major implications for evaluation practice. The project management cycle is a manifestation of task orientation and can sometimes be seen as a threat to the harmonious maintenance of long-standing relationships from the perspective of relationship-oriented cultures. From that view, evaluators who focus entirely on 'getting the job done' at the expense of understanding, building, and managing relationships can be seen as lacking capacity.

Evaluation and cultural values

Some evaluators and facilitators of change know to take cultural differences into account and this is increasingly acknowledged in the literature (Kirkhart, 1995 and 2005; Sen Gupta et al., 2004; Chouinard and Cousins, 2007; Quinn Patton, 2011; Mertens, 2012 and 2016). For many evaluators, emphasis has been on how people from one culture can most effectively extract or generate data *from* those with another cultural background. It has been assumed that evaluators can in fact *overcome* cultural differences in order to generate meaningful findings, and that sensitivity to different views of the world can contribute to effective evaluation processes and outcomes. There is now greater recognition and valuing of different frames of reference about evaluation and knowledge that applies in 'other' cultures, particularly indigenous cultures.

Consideration of the role of cultural value differences in evaluation appears to have occurred concurrently with the emergence of ideas about indigenous knowledge and perspectives in the broader field of qualitative research (Denzin et al., 2008). Without entering into the complex and contested world of ideas about post-modernism, there are clear links between the global process of decolonization and recognition that indigenous ways of knowing about the world are significant, both in terms of explaining different responses to the world, and in improving humankind's overall engagement with the world, particularly the physical environment. Indigenous knowledge and ways of seeing the world embody cultural values as well as cosmologies and relationships. Efforts to understand how cultural values shape knowledge, values, and identity are now considered important in the field of research and evaluation, though there is a long way to go before all disciplines integrate or acknowledge this in practice.

Evaluators who have raised issues about the centrality of cultural values include Kirkhart (1995 and 2005) and Mertens (2012 and 2016). In summary, Kirkhart recognizes that different cultures consider information differently and that evaluators therefore need to consider multicultural perspectives. Mertens advocates for understanding the implications that cultural value differences have for the quality of evaluation work. Her book *Indigenous Pathways into Social Research* (with Kram and Chilisa, 2016) addresses different ways of knowing from those understood in traditional (western) scholarly models and encourages more sensitive and collaborative research and evaluation practice.

Cultural value differences need to be understood by both those commissioning and implementing evaluation processes, including facilitators engaged in evaluations. At the strategic level, the question 'what values underpin the idea that evaluation should occur and could these values differ between cultures?' should be considered. Questions emerging from this understanding could include: 'should evaluations be undertaken by people from one cultural background about people from another cultural background?' At a more tangible level, questions may include: 'how do cultural values influence what we are looking to find out?'; 'how is evaluation best approached in different contexts?'; and 'what is the value of the evaluation findings to different cultures?'

At the practice level, dominant values relevant to evaluation, while changing over time and between sub-groups and organizations, tend to emphasize certain approaches. For example, ideas that equality of participation and access should be prioritized, that all voices are valid, and that people have volition to say what they think are deemed central in most evaluation texts. These premises reflect low power distance and individualist values. The fact that an evaluation process is by definition a set of tasks to be completed (as in a cycle from design to communication of findings) reflects task and performance-oriented cultural values. The fact that evaluations are often integral elements in change and innovation processes (proving or improving policies and programs, for example) reflects task and performance-oriented values and low uncertainty avoidance values.

In countries where most international development programs are implemented and where many migrants to European countries, US, and Australia come from, these values related to evaluation are not necessarily shared. According to Hofstede and the GLOBE Study, values are more likely to be at the opposite ends of these dimensions. For example, people living in communities in Melanesian countries neighbouring Australia tend to value high power distance concepts, collectivist decision-making, harmonious in-group relationships, and maintenance of the status quo. These differences mean that the idea that everyone might want to or has the right to have an individual view about a change process – what is 'good' or 'beneficial' or 'a positive change' – may not be shared or accepted. The idea that evaluators can listen to many individual perspectives and draw conclusions about them may be flawed. For example, in collectivist societies, the preference for people to consult others and consider the views of others, rather than their own interests, before communicating a response to a question, could significantly influence both the data collection processes and the meaningfulness of data collected. This concept is well considered in literature on indigenous research methodologies (Denzin et al., 2008) but less prevalent in international development evaluation.

Evaluations tend to have a particular view of the past, the present, and the future, which also raises potential issues across cultures. As discussed in Chapter 2, cultures give more or less value to planning for changes in the future (Hofstede 1980; House et al., 2004; Gesteland (2005). For example, reflective practices in cultures which are highly future-oriented tend to seek lessons and generate shared understanding of processes. In contrast, in low future-oriented cultures, people may seek information which affirms and celebrates those with power, facilitates greater collectivist practice, or values traditional practices.

Evaluators tend to be sensitive to issues relating to power, but those from low power distance cultures expect they can maintain neutrality and independence and be seen to hold low levels of power, when, through another lens, the opposite may be true. When coming from countries with sufficient funds to pay for projects and travel expenses, evaluators may be seen by people in low-resource settings to automatically hold considerable power and thus authority over others. Decisions about who should participate in evaluation processes (e.g. groups of women or men, community representatives, local stakeholders etc.) and what questions are asked are usually made by evaluators, even if they are informed by local perspectives. Increasing interest in joint research across cultures is emerging at the time of writing, responding to pandemic-related travel restrictions.

Culturally attuned evaluation

With increasing attention being paid to cultural value differences in research and evaluation, more methods for conducting cross-cultural evaluations which recognize different world views and maximize culturally attuned engagement are also emerging (Denzin et al., 2008; Wehipeihana et al., 2010; Mertens, 2016). These approaches variously take account of power differences, language and access, and other contextual issues. Facilitation elements described in Chapters 9 and 10 may be relevant, depending on the purpose and context of evaluations. Options include:

- joint evaluation with people who have deep cultural knowledge of the context;
- inclusion of cultural guides or mentors to support evaluation processes;
- strengths-based approaches, such as Positive Deviance and Success Case Method (explained below);
- action learning and research;
- emphasis on shared learning journeys rather than data extraction processes;
- emphasis on participant analysis, such as collective sense-making, rather than analysis by external 'judges';
- methods which work with and support deepening understanding of power relationships and dynamics in order to identify better futures for all;
- methods which accentuate people-centred agendas and resist top-down, donor-driven agendas;
- methods which generate discussion to support deepening understanding of the context;

- methods which explicitly consider all aspects of 'do no harm', particularly for marginalized groups of people within a community, organization or society.

Positive Deviance and Success Case Method are two methods which focus attention on exceptional positive results, as a means to better understand success factors and communicate them to promote replication or copying. For example, in the context of a micro-credit program, monitoring processes may have identified that several women's businesses become particularly successful: a Positive Deviance evaluation method would seek to find out what factors contributed to this success and how these factors might be replicated for others. Positive Deviance emerged in the field of international public health (child nutrition) and is now used widely in a range of health and social change contexts (see <https://positivedeviance.org> [accessed 7 October 2021] for resources and examples). Success Case Method (Brinkerhoff 2003) similarly seeks out the best stories associated with a change process, and considers them in-depth to understand success factors in each context. Both are potentially useful across cultures because of their focus on engaging positively.

Communicating findings from monitoring and evaluation across cultures

Ensuring that information which has been contributed by people to an evaluation process is given back to them is widely recognized as a critical step but not one that is always taken. Commissioners of evaluation are more often seeking to communicate findings and key messages in more accessible ways to busy leaders in their own culture, for example using graphics, pictures, and videos rather than heavy printed reports. Taking account of cultural value differences and considering culturally meaningful modes of communication are important aspects of this, in addition to the more practical aspects of languages, representation, and accessibility to online information.

Assumptions about how information should be shared need to be considered through a cultural lens. For example, an assumption that the participants in an evaluation process will be readily able to access information presented using sophisticated graphics and online systems may need to be checked for each context. The assumption that information needs to be made 'simple' should also be checked for each context – people who do not speak English as a first language do not necessarily need simplified messages, but messages in their own language, and these can be complex and nuanced if people want that kind of information.

The kinds of methods that apply to all types of information could be considered as means for communicating evaluation findings – brochures, posters, videos etc. – and assumptions about how information might be used and applied may also need to be tested in each context.

Skills for facilitators of monitoring and evaluation processes

When working across cultures, facilitating monitoring and evaluation processes requires additional considerations and steps. These include the particular role of the facilitator in gathering and analysing information in terms of independence and relative status, and the specific cross-cultural engagement skills relevant to assessing change in different settings.

A critical implication of different cultural perspectives in evaluation relates to the independence of evaluators. In task-oriented cultures, evaluators are expected largely to be independent and detached from a particular context in order to give an objective perspective. In relationship-oriented cultures, the generation of 'reliable' data may actually require evaluators who have strong existing relationships, deep trust, and significant understanding of power relationships in a particular context. In such contexts, if data is collected in a way in which the evaluator is highly separate from participants in the evaluation, the validity of such information could be seen by certain disciplines to be questionable. Positivist research methods generally argue that relationship-embedded data is less valid than objectively collected data, and the former could be portrayed as 'contaminated'. A variety of other social science research approaches counter such a connection (e.g. Denzin et al., 2008) and suggest that in relationship-oriented cultures, it is possible that relationship-embedded data is much more 'valid' and useful. Relationships, particularly those based on trust and respect, are thus critical for the generation of meaningful data in this way of thinking. When development agencies commission short 'fly-in fly-out' evaluations of development projects, rarely is it possible for such relationships to develop. This forms a critical limitation to the validity of findings. For practitioners working in cultures where harmonious relationships are prioritized, awareness of this tension is important.

Perceptions of an evaluator's critical analysis skills also vary across cultures. In a low power distance and individualist cultural setting, where critical analysis is highly valued, an evaluator's skills to observe and make judgement about worth and value are also valued. However, research on the qualities for cross-cultural adaptability (Kelley and Meyers, 1995) suggest that those who can separate the practice of observation from the practice of judgement are more likely to succeed. A culturally attuned evaluator may need to separate out two aspects of the process of critical observation, so as to minimize inaccurate judgement through their own cultural lens.

An evaluator's skill in understanding cultural values in contexts other than their own cannot be assumed, based on the training provided to evaluators or the requirements set by commissioning organizations. However, these skills are essential for evaluators to be able to navigate different perceptions of change, information, power, relationships, and many other key elements of life and work. Relationship management skills are important for evaluators, but in cultures where the maintenance of harmonious relationships involves ideas such as minimizing loss of face by leaders and ensuring communications are indirect, subtle, and ambiguous, asking people for 'the truth' about their situation is not as easy as it may seem from task-oriented cultural perspectives.

The extent to which an evaluator from one culture can successfully undertake evaluations in another is likely to involve a mix of personal commitment and experience gained over time. One perspective is that 'cultural competence cannot be determined by a simple checklist, but rather is an attribute that develops over time' (Endo et al., 2003 quoted in Mertens, 2012: 167). Others place more emphasis on the process than the attributes of the evaluator. For example, Sen Gupta, et al., (2004: 13) consider that 'cultural competence in evaluation ... is a systemic, responsive inquiry that is actively cognizant, understanding and appreciative of the cultural context'. Interestingly, another argued 'an evaluator is not culturally competent, but with appropriate understandings and experiences, an evaluator can conduct a culturally competent evaluation' (Lee 2009, quoted in Mertens, 2012: 165). Lee identified that 'an evaluator needs awareness of important cultural dimensions, cognisance of multiple social identities and group memberships and transparent discussion of relevant issues of power and privilege'.

An evaluator's ability to know their own cultural values and the influence of these on their beliefs and practices cannot be assumed: again, such ideas are not widely taught or factored into evaluation designs. The skills to manage cross-cultural challenges, understand different cultural perspectives, adapt to different cultural contexts, and deal with difficult physical or security contexts requires adaptability and resilience, which evaluators may or may not have. Issues associated with making sense of information in cross-cultural contexts are not straightforward. Issues related to informed consent, not just to participate in evaluation processes but to the meanings derived from evaluations or other research need to be considered (Australian Council for International Development, 2015). The skills to navigate cultural differences can be honed through years of practice, particularly if there is value placed on such skills by those commissioning evaluations, but in many cases, 'cross-cultural experience' is the last of a long list of criteria in terms of reference, and rarely prioritized.

In summary, in addition to the remarkably long list of qualities commonly asked of evaluators, specific skills and attributes are required for cross-cultural facilitators in evaluation contexts, for example:

- the ability to observe and understand others through a different cultural lens;
- the ability to engage with/lead/listen to people from different cultures;
- the confidence to initiate and respond appropriately, and navigate complexity;
- the ability to show respect to others' cultural values and lead inclusively;
- the communications ability to explain events in culturally respectful ways.

Finally, facilitators of change processes are often involved in complex translation processes, so it can be difficult for them to simultaneously monitor their own performance, the quality of the group's engagement, and the extent to which shared values are being applied and changes achieved. Thus, working with cultural guides to monitor and make sense of processing events can be a useful approach to maximizing relevance and therefore benefits.

CHAPTER 13
Conclusion

This book takes a positive approach to the facilitation of change through a cross-cultural lens. It seeks to bring together contemporary understanding about change, facilitation, and cultural values from various disciplines in order to support those who may be asked to facilitate change in a cultural context different from their own. In some ways, the book deliberately or necessarily skates across the top of highly complex issues for the purposes of accessibility, while synthesizing ideas and practices that have not necessarily been brought together before.

The contexts in which change is already happening or sought are increasingly complex. Many historical and contemporary leaders are adept at dividing communities on the basis of ethnicity, values, and cultural differences for the purpose of amassing or retaining power. They seek to convince their followers of the benefits that will flow from strategies that exclude or harm others who are not members of the defined group. Social contracts that exist between leaders and followers confirm this reality in many parts of the world. The practice portrays 'others' as lesser in value and ignores the value of and need for collaborative efforts for the benefit of all. Many authors describe this phenomenon, including Harari (2014) who argued that it emerged early in the history of humankind and has continued ever since. An inward-focusing leadership stance has become particularly evident at national and other levels during the writing of this book at the time of a global pandemic: many leaders seek to undermine collaborative cross-cultural efforts at the global level.

In contrast, this book is intended for those interested in bringing about change through encompassing diversity and collaboration: it proposes a shift in attitudes and new ways of working. Ideas included in this book are premised on the value and benefits for all of generating mutual understanding and respect, shared values and plans, collective action, and shared responsibility for success and risks, not just in the context of cultural differences, but as a result of them. The promise of increased global collaboration has emerged since World War II in various movements, systems, and structures, and has been particularly strengthened through globalization of the internet. More widespread recognition of the global nature of challenges facing humanity means that respectful collaboration across different cultures and concerted efforts to build shared movement towards positive change are even more crucial. The United Nations is founded on these principles and is the source of considerable experience and guidance in this regard.

It is broadly accepted that cultural value differences exist, but being definitive about the nature and scope of these differences is challenging. While past and current researchers on the GLOBE Study (House et al., 2004) have tried hard to quantify variations, others hold different philosophical views about the validity of their efforts. While it is possible to study the concept of culture in many disciplines, in practice, any frame of reference is probably best kept in one's back pocket, rather than applied in too definitive a way. Categorizing cultures too definitively is particularly best kept away from technocratic approaches to change, which seek to box people and cultures, and neatly categorize plans and systems. The most significant key message is that 'people see things differently,' so the most significant approach is to seek to facilitate respectful and power-sensitive conversations about how we all see the world differently and then apply this learning to our collaboration.

The strategies proposed in this book extend and complement great work undertaken by many thinkers and practitioners around the world. They add another dimension, a critical cultural values dimension, to understanding about how change happens and the role of facilitators from other cultures in change processes. The methods discussed through a cultural lens provide options for consideration and food for thought, rather than an exhaustive list or a set of perfect tools.

If readers have found this book and flicked through to the end to find short lists of key messages, here they are:

Principles

1. People who participate in change processes place a high value on cultural understanding by facilitators and partners.
2. Cultures have different perceptions of the purpose of facilitation and the nature of change, which need to be recognized.
3. Defining inclusion in context-specific ways is necessary.
4. Generating shared culture and building trust are key to effective collaboration.
5. Adaptive and flexible ways of working are essential for intercultural collaboration.
6. Cultural understanding is relevant throughout a program cycle, including in monitoring, evaluation and learning processes.

The role of change facilitators

1. Change facilitators can play an important role in contributing to a better world.
2. If they are culturally attuned, change facilitators' contributions will be more relevant and thus more likely to generate positive change for all.
3. An effective change facilitator will recognize that changes, including both processes and results, are understood differently through various

cultural values lenses – what is positive through one lens can be seen as unrealistic, or worse, through another.
4. Change facilitators can help identify, for all participants, the critical influence of cultural values on how change occurs and on how it is received.

Strategies for change facilitation

1. Analyse the context in which change is expected to happen, and also the collaboration context, using a Cultural Landscape Analysis.
2. Build strengths-based collaboration between people who seek to bring about change.
3. Collectively choose and use a mix of facilitation methods to suit each purpose and context.

Methods

1. There are many potentially useful methods to choose from, some of which are more attuned to the expression of cultural values, and others which are more common but can be adapted to suit different cultural contexts.
2. Conflict is probably inevitable in cross-cultural change facilitation contexts, so having some strategies and skills to minimize and manage conflict across cultures is recommended.
3. Considering the progress and success of change processes through a cultural lens, i.e. in reflection and learning, will help generate more nuanced understanding about how change happens.

The COVID-19 pandemic affects the ability of facilitators to adopt many of the approaches advocated in this book. Restrictions on travel, both globally and locally, have resulted in both reduced opportunities for face-to-face change facilitation and reduced attention to change agendas beyond emergency responses. Just as there are opportunities and challenges with face-to-face intercultural facilitation, there are other opportunities and challenges associated with online processes. Online methods can: enable wider participation; bring people from more contexts together; provide for increased numbers and frequencies of interactions; be undertaken over extended timeframes than would be possible in a single or short visit; and give greater voice and space for local leaders and facilitators. On the other hand, they can: reduce the prospects for building trust and rapport; limit the scope for nuanced conversations; reduce context-specific or place-based collaboration; restrict informal engagement and communications based on body language; and exclude people without internet access.

Development practitioners and organizations are all likely to have examples of their own, illustrating these opportunities and challenges. In one case, an organization focused on mobilizing lawyers to address particular public health issues had planned an intense one-week face-to-face workshop in Australia for 40 participants from various countries. With travel restrictions in place, the workshop was replaced by a series of online events, with participatory and guest speaker elements, over a longer period, for over one hundred participants. While online conversations were probably less 'in-depth', more people, including an increased proportion of women, joined from a broader range of countries, more varied networks were established, and the momentum for change was broadened. In another example, an Asian regional organization had planned an intensive leaders' event to focus on achieving strategic goals. The one-off workshop was replaced by a short online meeting followed by regular facilitated small group coaching over six months, allowing for much more detailed attention to the change agenda as well as deeper collaboration and trust between people who would not regularly meet. Readers are encouraged to learn from and contribute to efforts to maximize opportunities and manage the limitations of online facilitation. Increased attention on supporting local facilitators is an obvious response.

One's views of the world will influence reactions to the frames of reference described in this book, just as they influence openness to any other ideas. Those with a good dose of optimism may find affirmation about the exciting potential for collaboration between people from different cultures. Those more cynical about the possibility of finding accessible solutions to the world's challenging problems may recoil from the complexities described and the levels of uncertainty implied by the strategies proposed. Whatever one's views, there is plenty of evidence that collaboration across cultures can bring about positive change. As a practitioner over decades, the author has witnessed, and maybe even contributed to, a wide variety of good processes and positive changes. Facilitators, whether they be individuals or organizations, have a major and constructive contribution to make. If we can maximize the value of our contribution through being culturally attuned, the world can and should be a better place in future.

ANNEX 1
Facilitation questions to consider through a cultural lens around a program cycle

Program cycle stage and standard purpose	Consideration through a cross-cultural change facilitation lens	Questions to answer	Facilitation steps to take
Conceptualization • To define the purpose of the program. • To broadly define the scope and nature of the program. • To describe the expected connection between planned activities.	Consider the purpose through different cultural lenses. Consider the validity of the expected connection through a different cultural lens (e.g. will A lead to B in that context?)	Are we aware of the cultural values that influence perceptions of change generally and this particular change in the particular context? Is the expected change prioritized in the cultural context? Do most people share this interest, or is it an elite or minority group? Is there alignment between the program and the cultural values (as well as the official plans)?	Analyse the values that shape perceptions of change and the particular change and how these perceptions are likely to shape engagement in the change process. Listen to people who deeply understand the context. Seek to co-conceptualize as far as possible. Reframe the concept to maximize its cultural relevance and thus its likelihood of success
Feasibility assessment • To assess whether the program is politically, practically, and financially feasible,	Add consideration of whether the program is culturally feasible. Consider whether existing strengths are known, recognized, and able to be used as a means to generate motivation towards expected change.	Does the 'program logic' really apply in a different culture? What strengths already exist and how can they be mobilized to achieve positive change? How feasible is it for the program to work inclusively? If the program will not be inclusive, how will power issues be engaged with and accounted for?	Ensure people with deep knowledge of the cultural context are involved in the analysis and listened to during the feasibility assessment.

(Continued)

Continued

Program cycle stage and standard purpose	Consideration through a cross-cultural change facilitation lens	Questions to answer	Facilitation steps to take
Design • To develop details of all aspects of the program.	Consider **all** aspects of program through a cultural lens, e.g. plan, implementation, governance etc.	Will the planned implementation be appropriate in the cultural context? How will implementers be selected and supported to work in culturally attuned ways? How will governance reflect potentially different priorities, cultural values, and decision-making practices?	Design all aspects of implementation in ways which reflect understanding of existing/diverse cultural values, so the program is more likely to resonate, be implemented respectfully, and succeed in achieving objectives.
Implementation • To ensure plans are applied to achieve the overall objectives, taking account of lessons learned through ongoing experience.	Consider **all** aspects of implementation through the lens of cultural value differences.	Examples include: • Is governance/decision-making culturally inclusive? • Are plans culturally informed? • Are different perceptions of time, process, and change reflected in day-to-day administration?	Ensure people with deep cultural knowledge are involved in informing all aspects of implementation, from decision-making at strategic levels to practical day-to-day management and task organization. Use methods which maximize alignment with existing systems and norms, or if they are expected to be changed, then ensure people responsible for systems and norms are active participants in leading and supporting the change process.
Monitoring • Check progress during implementation.	Consider different cultural perspectives about time, progress, and definitions of success.	Is the program responding to learning about what works well in each context?	Ensure people with deep understanding of the cultural context are involved in monitoring processes (designing M&E plans, data collection, analysis etc.).

ANNEX 1 **205**

Program cycle stage and standard purpose	Consideration through a cross-cultural change facilitation lens	Questions to answer	Facilitation steps to take
		Is the program reflecting understanding about the values which dominate in each context? How is the program supporting respectful discussions and reflections about whether values are still 'fit for purpose' and, if not, how they might realistically change over time and in collaboration?	Ensure that culturally attuned analysis applies to determining what monitoring data is showing. Promote the development of culturally appropriate monitoring and evaluation capacity in each context.
Evaluation • Assess whether intended results have been achieved. • Collate lessons learned.	Consider different cultural perspectives about 'success' and the connections between program contributions and any high-level changes.	Are there different perceptions of success for the program? May different perceptions of success shape the likelihood that benefits will be sustained?	Use culturally relevant evaluation methods (see chapter 12). Ensure that culturally relevant analysis is used to assess success of the program. Promote the findings of evaluations in culturally relevant ways.

References

ABC news (2019) 'Australia's climate funding Pacific Islands Forum, Tuvalu' [online] <https://www.abc.net.au/news/2019-08-13/australias-climate-funding-pacific-islands-forum-tuvalu/11408930> [accessed 16 September 2021].

Adapa, S. and Sheridan, A. (2018) *Inclusive Leadership: Negotiating Gendered Spaces*, Palgrave Macmillan, eBook.

Ailon, G. (2008) 'Mirror, mirror on the wall: culture's consequences in a value test of its own design'. *The Academy of Management Review* 33(4): 885–904.

Allen, M. (2016) *Stronger Together: The Cross-Cultural Coalition to Stop a Fossil Fuel Export Terminal in the Salish Sea*, Master's thesis, University of Washington [online], <https://digital.lib.washington.edu/researchworks/bitstream/handle/1773/36738/Allen_washington_0250O_15930.pdf?sequence=1&isAllowed=y> [accessed 29 May 2020].

Allen, M.G. (2020) 'Covid 19 development and a green new deal', Devpolicy Blog [blog], <https://devpolicy.org/covid-19-development-and-a-green-new-deal-20200827/?utm_source=rss&utm_medium=rss&utm_campaign=covid-19-development-and-a-green-new-deal-20200827> (posted 27 August 2020) [accessed 16 September 2021].

Anderman M. and Anderman, L.H. (eds) (2009) 'Bloom's Taxonomy' in *Psychology of Classroom Learning: An Encyclopedia*, vol. 1, Macmillan Reference, Gale eBooks.

Andrews, M. (2013) *The Limits of Institutional Reform in Development: Changing Rules for Realistic Solutions*, Cambridge University Press, <https://doi.org/10.1017/CBO9781139060974>.

Andrews, M., Pritchett, L. and Woolcock, M. (2012) *Escaping Capability Traps through Problem-Driven Iterative Adaptation (PDIA)*, HKS Faculty Research Working Paper Series RWP12-036, John F. Kennedy School of Government, Harvard University, Cambridge, MA.

Ang, S. and Van Dyne, L. (eds) (2008) *Handbook of Cultural Intelligence: Theory, Measurement and Applications*, M. E. Sharp, Armonk, New York.

Argyris, C. (1977) 'Double loop learning in organisations', *Harvard Business Review*, September-November. 2(2): 113–23.

ASEAN, (2016) 'ASEAN Qualifications Reference Framework' [PDF] <https://asean.org/wp-content/uploads/2017/03/ED-02-ASEAN-Qualifications-Reference-Framework-January-2016.pdf> [accessed 8 November 2021].

Ashkanasy, N.M. (2004) 'Emotion and performance', *Human Performance* 17(2): 137–44 [online], <https://doi.org/10.1207/s15327043hup1702_1>.

Augsburger, D.W. (1992) *Conflict Mediation Across Cultures: Pathways and Patterns*, Westminster John Knox Press, Louisville, KY.

Australian Council for International Development (ACFID) (2015) *Guidelines for Ethical Research and Evaluation in Development* [online], <https://rdinetwork.org.au/effective-ethical-research-evaluation/principles-guidelines-ethical-research-evaluation/#:~:text=The%20Principles%20and%20Guidelines%20function%20as%20an%20applied,and%20practitioners%20seeking%20to%20implement%20ethical%20research%20practice> [accessed 8 November 2021].

Australian Evaluation Society (AES) (2010) 'Guidelines for the ethical conduct of evaluation' [online], <https://www.betterevaluation.org/en/resources/example/aes_ethical_guidelines#:~:text=AES%20Guidelines%20for%20the%20Ethical%20Conduct%20of%20Evaluations,and%20decision%20making%20are%20incorporated%20into%20evaluation%20practice> [accessed 16 September 2021].

Avruch, K. and Black, P.W. (1993) 'Conflict resolution in intercultural settings: problems and prospects', in D.J.D. Sandole and H. Van der Merwe (eds), *Conflict Resolution Theory and Practice: Integration and Application*, pp. 131–45, Manchester University Press, Manchester.

Barder, O. (2012) 'The implications of complexity for development' The Kapuściński Lecture [online], <https://www.cgdev.org/media/implications-complexity-development-owen-barder> [accessed 16 September 2021].

Barefoot Guides (n.d.) Barefoot Guide Connection [website], <https://www.barefootguide.org/> [accessed 16 September 2021].

Barr, C. and Huxham, C. (1996) 'Involving the community: collaboration for community development', in C. Huxham, *Creating Collaborative Advantage*, pp. 110–25, SAGE, London.

Basu, S. (2018) 'Talanoa and the Pacific dialogue on climate change' <https://sei.sydney.edu.au/opinion/talanoa-pacific-dialogue-climate-change/> [accessed 8 November 2021].

Battiste, M. and Henderson J.Y. (2000) *Protecting Indigenous Knowledge and Heritage*, UBC Press, Purich Publishing.

Bennett, F. and Roberts, M. (2004) *From Input to Influence: Participatory Approaches to Research and Inquiry into Poverty* [PDF], <https://www.participatorymethods.org/sites/participatorymethods.org/files/From%20input%20to%20influence_bennett.pdf> [accessed 16 September 2021].

Bens, I. (2005) *Advanced Facilitation Strategies*, Jossey-Bass, eBook.

Bens, I. (2016) *Advanced Facilitation Strategies: Tools and Techniques to Master Difficult Situations*, Wiley, eBook.

Bergh, S.I. (2009) 'Traditional village councils, modern associations and the emergence of hybrid political orders in rural Morocco', *Peace Review* 21(1): 45–53.

Bernardo, B.I., Rosenthal, L. and Levy, S.R. (2013) 'Polyculturalism and attitudes towards people from other countries', *International Journal of Intercultural Relations* 37(3): 335–44, <https://doi.org/10.1016/j.ijintrel.2012.12.005>.

Bernardo, A.B.I., Salanga, M.G.C, Tjipto, S., Hutapea, B., Khan, Q. and Yeung, S.S. (2019) 'Polyculturalism and attitudes toward the continuing presence of former colonizers in four postcolonial Asian societies'[online], Frontiers in Psychology, (posted June 2019), <https://doi.org/10.3389/fpsyg.2019.01335>.

Bhabha, H. (1994) *The Location of Culture*, Routledge, London.
Bicchieri C. and Mercier H. (2014) 'Norms and beliefs: how change occurs', In M. Xenitidou and B. Edmonds (eds) *The Complexity of Social Norms*, Computational Social Sciences. Springer, Cham, <https://doi.org/10.1007/978-3-319-05308-0_3?>.
Blank, W. (1982) *Handbook for Developing Competency-based Training Programs*, Prentice-Hall, Englewood Cliffs, New Jersey.
Blunt, P. (1995) 'Cultural relativism, good governance and sustainable human development', *Public Administration*, 15: 1–9, <https://doi.org/10.1002/pad.4230150102>.
Boal, A. (1974) *Theatre of the Oppressed* [PDF], <https://warwick.ac.uk/fac/arts/english/currentstudents/undergraduate/modules/fulllist/first/en122/lecturelist2019-20/theatre_of_the_oppressed.pdf> [accessed 16 September 2021].
Boje, D.M. (2014) *Storytelling Organizational Practices*, Routledge, London.
Bolman, L.G. and Deal, T.E. (2013) *Reframing Organizations: Artistry, Choice and Leadership* (Fifth edition), Jossey-Bass, San Francisco. CA.
Booth, D. and Unsworth, S. (2014) Politically Smart, Locally Led Development, ODI discussion paper, [PDF], <https://odi.org/en/publications/politically-smart-locally-led-development/> [accessed 8 November 2021].
Booth, D., Harris, D. and Wild, L. (2016) *From Political Economy Analysis to Doing Development Differently: A Learning Experience*, ODI [PDF], <https://www.effectiveinstitutions.org/en/resource-library/216> [accessed 8 November 2021].
Bortini, P., Paci, A., Rise, A. and Rojnik, I. (2016) *Inclusive Leadership Theoretical Framework* [PDF], Poland School for Leaders Foundation. <https://inclusiveleadership.eu/il_theoreticalframework_en.pdf> [accessed 8 November 2021].
Bourke, J. (2018) 'The diversity and inclusion revolution: eight powerful truths' [online], *Deloitte Review* 22, <https://www2.deloitte.com/us/en/insights/deloitte-review/issue-22/diversity-and-inclusion-at-work-eight-powerful-truths.html#endnote-sup-11> [accessed 16 September 2021].
Brear, M. (2020) 'Silence and voice in participatory processes – causes, meanings and implications for empowerment', *Community Development Journal* 55(2): 349–68, <https://doi.org/10.1093/cdj/bsy041>.
Brinkerhoff, R. (2003) *The Success Case Method: Find Out Quickly What's Working and What's Not* Berrett-Koehler, San Francisco, CA.
Brownlee, T. (n.d.) 'Multicultural collaboration', Community Toolbox [website], <https://ctb.ku.edu/en/table-of-contents/culture/cultural-competence/multicultural-collaboration/main> [accessed 16 September 2021].
Bushe, G.R. (2013) 'Generative process, generative outcome: the transformational potential of appreciative inquiry', in D.L. Cooperrider, D.P. Zandee, L.N. Godwin, M. Avital and B. Boland (eds) *Organizational Generativity: The Appreciative Inquiry Summit and a Scholarship of Transformation (Advances in Appreciative Inquiry, Volume 4)*, pp. 89–113, Emerald Group Publishing Limited,.
Canadian Observatory on Homelessness (n.d.), 'Strength-based approach' [website], <https://www.homelesshub.ca/toolkit/strength-based-approach> [accessed 16 September 2021],

Carothers, T. and de Gramont, D. (2013) *Development Aid Confronts Politics: The Almost Revolution* New York: Carnegie Endowment for International Peace, Washington, DC.

Carter, B. (2015) *Benefits to Society of an Inclusive Societies Approach*, GSDRC Helpdesk Research Report [PDF], <https://gsdrc.org/wp-content/uploads/2015/09/HDQ1232.pdf> [accessed 16 September 2021].

Castellani, B. (2018) '2018 Map of the complexity sciences' Art and Science Factory [website], <https://www.art-sciencefactory.com/complexity-map_feb09.html> [accessed 16 September 2021].

Chambers, R. (1983) *Rural Development: Putting the Last First*, Longman, London.

Chambers, R. (1994) 'Participatory rural appraisal (PRA): analysis of experience' *World Development*, 22(9): 1253–68.

Chambers, R. (2002) *Participatory Workshops: A Sourcebook of 21 Sets of Ideas and Activities*, Earthscan, London.

Chambers, R. (2005) *Ideas for Development*, Earthscan, London.

Chambers, R. (2008) *Revolutions in Development Inquiry*, Earthscan, London.

Chambers, R. (2013) 'Participation for development: a good time to be alive', Introduction to *Challenges for Participatory Development in Contemporary Development Practice*, Development Bulletin No 75 [PDF], <https://crawford.anu.edu.au/rmap/devnet/devnet/db-75.pdf> [accessed 16 September 2021].

Chang, W. (2007) 'Cultural competence of international humanitarian workers' *Adult Education Quarterly* 57(3): 187–204, <https://doi.org/10.1177/0741713606296755>.

Chatterjee, S. (2014) 'Role of Panchayati Raj in facilitating the process of social change', *International Journal of Social Science & Interdisciplinary Research* 3(7): 32–39.

Chilisa, B. (2012) *Indigenous Research Methodologies*, Sage, Thousand Oaks, CA.

Chouinard, J.A. and Bradley Cousins, J. (2007) 'Culturally Competent Evaluation for Aboriginal Communities: A Review of the Empirical Literature', *Journal of MultiDisciplinary Evaluation*, 4(8), [online], <https://eric.ed.gov/?id=EJ800317> [accessed 8 November 2021].

Christie, A. and Green, D. (2018) *Adaptive Programming in Fragile, Conflict and Violence-Affected Settings, What Works* and *Under What Conditions?: The Case of Pyoe Pin, Myanmar* [online], Itad and Oxfam in association with IDS for the Action for Empowerment and Accountability Research Programme <https://www.ids.ac.uk/publications/adaptive-programming-in-fragile-conflict-and-violence-affected-settings-what-works-and-under-what-conditions-the-case-of-pyoe-pin-myanmar> [accessed 16 September 2021].

Chua, E.G. and Gudykunst, W.B. (1987) 'Conflict resolution styles in low- and high-context cultures' *Communication Research Reports* 4 (1): 32–7.

Clark, M.K. and Koster, M.M. (2014) *Hip hop and social change in Africa: Ni Wakati*, Lexington Books.

Climate Action Network International (2017) 'Pacific COP23 announces "Talanoa Dialogue", sets into motion Paris Agreement' <https://climatenetwork.org/2017/11/17/pacific-cop23-announces-talanoa-dialogue-sets-into-motion-paris-agreement/> [accessed 8 November 2021].

Cohen, J., Schrimper, M. and Taylor, E. (2019) 'Elephant in the room: making a culture transformation stick with symbolic actions' [blog], McKinsey organisation blog, <https://www.mckinsey.com/business-functions/organization/our-insights/the-organization-blog/elephant-in-the-room-making-a-culture-transformation-stick-with-symbolic-actions#> (posted 29 July 2019) [accessed 16 September 2021].

Conn, C., Said, A., Sa'uLilo, L., Fairbairn-Dunlop, P., Antonczak, L. Andajani, S. and Blake, G.O., (2016) Pacific Talanoa and Participatory Action Research: *Providing a Space for Auckland Youth Leaders to Contest Inequalities*, Auckland University of Technology [PDF] <https://ccep.crawford.anu.edu.au/rmap/devnet/devnet/db-77/db-77-vcc-2.pdf> [accessed 8 October 2021].

Cooke, B. and Kothari, U. (eds) (2001) *Participation: The New Tyranny?* Zed Books, London.

Cooperrider, D. (1986) *Appreciative Inquiry: Toward a Methodology for Understanding and Enhancing Organizational Innovation*, Unpublished Ph.D. dissertation, Case Western Reserve University, Cleveland, OH.

Cooperrider, D. Whitney, D. and Stavros, J. (2003) *Appreciative Inquiry Handbook*, Lakeshore Communications, Bedford Heights, OH.

Cooperrider, D, and Whitney, D. (2007) 'Appreciative Inquiry: A positive revolution in change', Chapter 5 in P. Holman, T. Devane, and S. Cady (eds), *The Change Handbook*, pp. 73–88, Berrett-Koehler, San Francisco, CA.

Corbett, J. (2019) 'Where do leaders come from?' [online], DLP Foundational Paper, <https://www.dlprog.org/publications/foundational-papers/where-do-leaders-come-from> [accessed 16 September 2021].

Cornwall, A. (2006) 'Historical perspectives on participation in development', *Commonwealth and Comparative Politics* 44(1): 62–83, <https://doi.org/10.1080/14662040600624460>.

Cornwall, A. and Coelho, V.S. (2007) 'Spaces for change? The politics of participation in new democratic arenas' [online], <https://www.researchgate.net/publication/289986868_Spaces_for_change_The_politics_of_participation_in_new_democratic_arenas> [accessed 16 September 2021].

Corritore, M., Goldberg, A. and Srivasta, S.B. (2020) 'The new analytics of culture' [online], *Harvard Business Review*, January–February 2020, <https://hbr.org/2020/01/the-new-analytics-of-culture> [accessed 16 September 2021].

Costin, A. (2015) 'Negotiating in cross-cultural contexts', *Knowledge-Based Organization International Conference*, <https://doi.org/10.1515/kbo-2015-0030>.

Craney, A. and Hudson, D. (2020) 'The hard truth about supporting local leadership: three dilemmas for those who want to' [online], Developmental Leadership Program, <https://www.dlprog.org/opinions/the-hard-truth-about-supporting-local-leadership-three-dilemmas-for-those-who-want-to> [accessed 16 September 2021].

Dean, P. (2013) *The Power of Symbols*, 4 Square Books, London.

Denney, L. and McLaren, R. (2016) 'Thinking and working politically to support developmental leadership and coalitions: the Pacific leadership program' [online], DLP Research Paper, <https://www.dlprog.org/publications/research-papers/thinking-and-working-politically-to-support-developmental-leadership-and-coalitions-the-pacific-leadership-program> [accessed 16 September 2021].

Denney, L. (2018) 'Walking the adaptive talk' [blog], Development Policy Blog, 11 September 2018, <https://devpolicy.org/walking-the-adaptive-talk-20180911/> [accessed 16 September 2021].

Denzin, N.K. (1997) *Interpretive Ethnography: Ethnographic Practices for the 21st Century*, SAGE Publications, London, <http://dx.doi.org/10.4135/9781452243672>.

Denzin, N.K., Lincoln, Y.S. and Smith, L.T. (eds) (2008) *Handbook of Critical and Indigenous Methodologies*, Sage Publications, Thousand Oaks, CA.

Developmental Leadership Program (DLP) (2020a) 'Leadership observatory: issue 11' [online], <https://www.dlprog.org/opinions/leadership-observatory-issue-11> [accessed on 11 September 2020].

Developmental Leadership Program (DLP) (2020b) 'How is leadership understood in different contexts' [online], DLP Foundational Papers, <https://www.dlprog.org/publications/foundational-papers/how-is-leadership-understood-in-different-contexts> [accessed on 25 May 2020].

Diaz-Veizades J. and Chang, E.T. (1996) 'Building cross-cultural coalitions: a case-study of the Black-Korean Alliance and the Latino-Black Roundtable', *Ethnic and Racial Studies* 19(3) 680–700, Taylor and Francis, <https://doi.org/10.1080/01419870.1996.9993930>.

Dilling, L. and Moser, S.C. (2007) *Creating a Climate for Change : Communicating Climate Change and Facilitating Social Change*, Cambridge University Press, Cambridge.

Dinh, K., Worth, H. and Haire, B. (2019) 'Buddhist evaluation: applying a Buddhist world view to the most significant change technique', *Evaluation* 25(4): 477–95 Sage.

Dinh, K., Worth, H., Haire, B. and Hong, K.T. (2019) 'Confucian evaluation – re-framing contribution analysis using a Confucian lens', *American Journal of Evaluation* 40(4): 562–574, Sage.

Dolan, S. and Kawamura, K. (2015) *Cross Cultural Competence: A Field Guide for Developing Global Leaders and Managers*, Emerald Publishing.

Dolton, P., Marcenaro, O., De Vries, R. and She, P-W. (2018) *Global Teacher Index 2018* [PDF], Varkey Foundation, University of Sussex, <https://www.varkeyfoundation.org/media/4790/gts-index-9-11-2018.pdf> [accessed 16 September 2021].

Dweck, C.S. (2008) *Growth Mindset: The New Psychology of Success*, Random House, New York.

Dwonczyk, M. (2015) 'Diversity as an essential partnership ingredient' *Betwixt and Between Journal of Partnership Brokering* [online], <https://partnershipbrokers.org/w/journal/diversity-as-an-essential-partnership-ingredient-2/> [accessed 16 September 2021].

Earley, P.C. and Ang, S. (2003) *Cultural Intelligence: Individual Interactions Across Cultures*, Stanford University Press, Stanford, CT.

Elgstrom, O. (1990) 'Norms, culture, and cognitive patterns in foreign aid negotiations, *Negotiation Journal* 6(2): 147–159, <https://doi.org/10.1111/j.1571-9979.1990.tb00565.x>.

Eslake, S. (2017) 'How can we use music to achieve social change?' [online], Cut Common <https://www.cutcommonmag.com/how-can-we-use-music-to-achieve-social-change/> (posted 25 March 2017) [accessed 16 September 2021].

Felder, R.M. (1998) *Learning Styles and Teaching Styles* [PDF], Proceedings of the 1998 Annual Conference of the American Society for Engineering Education, <https://www.engr.ncsu.edu/wp-content/uploads/drive/1vRjpenyeO5BbV6VLWBx4ebL8u2C_wUry/1998-ASEE-LS.pdf> [accessed 16 September 2021].

Ferreira, P. (2018) 'Power of theatre in social change' [online] <https://www.iol.co.za/entertainment/movies/power-of-theatre-in-social-change-14536350

Fine, M. (1994) 'Working the hyphens: reinventing self and other in qualitative research', in N.K. Denzin and Y.S. Lincoln (eds), *Handbook of Qualitative Research* pp. 70–82, Sage Publications, Thousand Oaks, CA.

Fine, M., Tuck E. and Zeller-Berkman, S. (2008) 'Do you believe in Geneva? Methods and ethics at the global-local nexus', Chapter 8 in Denzin, N. et al., *Critical and Indigenous Methodologies*, pp. 157–80, Sage, Thousand Oaks, CA.

Fowler, A. (1997) *Striking a Balance: A Guide to Enhancing the Effectiveness of Non Governmental Organisations in International Development*, Earthscan, London.

Fox, J. (2010) *Coalitions and Networks* [PDF], UC Santa Cruz Working Papers, <https://escholarship.org/content/qt1x05031j/qt1x05031j.pdf> [accessed 16 September 2021].

Freire, P. (1970) (first English version) *Pedagogy of the Oppressed*, Continuum, Herder and Herder, New York.

Gay, G. (2015) 'The what, why, and how of culturally responsive teaching: international mandates, challenges, and opportunities' *Multicultural Education Review Journal*, 7(3): 123–9

Gaulee, U., Sharma, S. and Bista, K. (eds) (2020) *Rethinking Education Across Borders: Emerging Insights and Critical Issues on Globally Mobile Students*, Springer, Singapore.

Gelfand, M., Gordon, S., Chengguang, L., Choi, V. and Prokopowicz, P. (2018) 'One reason mergers fail: the two cultures aren't compatible' [online], *Harvard Business Review*, <https://hbr.org/2018/10/one-reason-mergers-fail-the-two-cultures-arent-compatible> [accessed 16 September 2021].

Gesteland, R., (2005) *Cross-Cultural Business Behaviour: Negotiating, Selling, Sourcing and Managing Across Cultures*, Copenhagen Business School.

GLOBE Project (2020) [website], <https://globeproject.com/studies> [accessed 8 November 2021].

Green, D. (2016) *How Change Happens*, Oxford University Press, Oxford.

Grown, C. Addison, T. and Tarp, F. (2016) Aid for gender equality and development: lessons and challenges, *Journal for International Development* 28(3): 311–9 <https://doi.org/10.1002/jid.3211>.

Guild, P. (1994) 'The culture/learning style connection', *Education for Diversity* 51(8): 16–21.

Gulrajani, N. (2018) *Merging Development Agencies: Making The Right Choice* ODI Briefing Note, [online], <https://odi.org/en/publications/merging-development-agencies-making-the-right-choice/> [accessed 8 November 2021].

Guthrie, G., (2021) *Foundations of Classroom Change in Developing Countries* Vol. 1 Evidence [PDF}, <https://www.researchgate.net/profile/Gerard-Guthrie> [accessed 8 November 2021].

Hagen, E. and Bryant G. (2003) 'Music and dance as a coalition signaling system', *Human Nature* 14: 21–51 <https://link.springer.com/article/10.1007/s12110-003-1015-z> [accessed 16 September 2021]/>.

Haidt, J. (2012) *The Righteous Mind: Why Good People are Divided by Politics and Religion*, Pantheon, New York.

Hailey, J. (2001) 'Beyond the formulaic: process and practice in South Asian NGOs', Chapter 6 in B. Cooke and U. Kothari (eds), *Participation: The New Tyranny*, pp. 88–101, Zed Books, London.

Hall, E.T. (1976) *Beyond Culture*, Anchor Press, New York.

Halley, S. and Fox, J. (2007) 'Playback theatre', Chapter 60 in P. Holman, T. Devane, and S. Cady (eds), *The Change Handbook*, pp. 561–72, Berrett-Koehler, San Francisco, CA.

Hammer, M.R. (2005) 'The intercultural conflict style inventory: a conceptual framework and measure of intercultural conflict resolution approaches, *International Journal of Intercultural Relations*, 26(6): 675–95, <https://doi.org/10.1016/j.ijintrel.2005.08.010>.

Hammer, M. and Wiseman, R. (1978) 'Dimensions of intercultural effectiveness: an exploratory study', *International Journal of Intercultural Relations*, 2(4): 382–93.

Hansen, E., Torkler, A-K., Covarrubias Venegas, B. (eds) (2018), *Intercultural Training Tool Kit: Activities for Developing Intercultural Competence for Virtual and Face-to-face Teams*, SIETAR Europa Intercultural Book Series.

Harari, Y. (2014) *Sapiens: A Brief History of Humankind*, Harper, New York.

Harrison, L. (2000) 'Why Culture Matters', in L. Harrison and S. Huntington, *Culture Matters*, Basic Books, New York.

Harrison, L. and Huntington, S. (2000) *Culture Matters*, Basic Books, New York.

Hartley, J. and Potts, J. (2014) *Cultural Science: A Natural History of Stories, Demes, Knowledge and Innovation*, Bloomsbury Academic, London.

Haslam, N. (2017) 'Cultures fuse and connect, so we should embrace polyculturalism [online],' *The Conversation*, <https://theconversation.com/cultures-fuse-and-connect-so-we-should-embrace-polyculturalism-78876> (posted 6 June 2017) [accessed 16 September 2021].

Hearn, S. and Mendizabal, E. (2011) *Not Everything that Connects is a Network*, [online] Background Note, ODI <https://odi.org/en/publications/not-everything-that-connects-is-a-network/> [accessed 8 November 2021].

Hofstede, G. (1980) *Culture's Consequences: International Differences in Work-Related Values*, Sage, Beverley Hills, CA.

Hofstede, G. (2020) Hofstede Insights [website], <https://www.hofstede-insights.com/country/australia/> [accessed 16 September 2021].

Hofstede, G. and Hofstede, G.J. (2005) *Cultures and Organisations: Software of the Mind*, McGraw Hill, New York.

Hollander, E.P. (2012) *Inclusive Leadership*, Taylor and Francis, New York.

Holman, P. (2007) 'Preparing to mix and match methods', Chapter 3 in P. Holman, T. Devane and S. Cady (eds), *The Change Handbook*, pp. 44–58, Berrett-Koehler, San Francisco, CA.

Holman, P., Devane, T. and Cady, S. (eds) (2007) *The Change Handbook*, Berrett-Koehler, San Francisco, CA.

House, R.J., Hanges, P.J., Javidan, M., Dorfman, P.W. and Gupta, V. (eds) (2004) *Culture, Leadership, and Organisations*, Sage, Thousand Oaks, CA.

Hudson, D.J. (2017) 'On "diversity" as anti-racism in library and information studies: a critique', *Journal of Critical Library and Information Studies*, 1(1) <https://doi.org/10.24242/jclis.v1i1.6>.

Hudson, D. and McLoughlin, C. (2019) 'How is leadership understood in different contexts?' [online], Developmental Leadership Program <https://www.dlprog.org/publications/foundational-papers/how-is-leadership-understood-in-different-contexts> [accessed 16 September 2021].

Hudson, D., McLoughlin, C., Margret, A., Ardiansa, D., Panjaitan, Y. and Novitarsari, M. (2019) *'Identity Matters: Unpacking the Effects of Prototypicality on Perceptions of Leadership in Indonesia'* [online], Developmental Leadership Program Paper <https://res.cloudinary.com/dlprog/image/upload/identity-matters-prototypicality> [accessed 16 September 2021].

Hult, M. and Lennung, S. (1980) 'Towards a definition of action research: a note and bibliography', *Journal of Management Studies* 17(2): 241–50 <https://doi.org/10.1111/j.1467-6486.1980.tb00087.x>.

Hunt, V., Layton, D. and Prince, S. (2015), 'Why diversity matters' [online], <https://www.mckinsey.com/business-functions/people-and-organizational-performance/our-insights/why-diversity-matters> [accessed 8 November 2021].

Hyatt, M., Belden-Charles, G. and Stacey, M. (2007) 'Action learning', Chapter 48 in P. Holman, T. Devane, and S. Cady (eds), *The Change Handbook*, pp. 479–83, Berrett-Koehler, San Francisco, CA.

Jackson, K.F. and Samuels, G.M. (2011) 'Multiracial competence in social work: recommendations for culturally attuned work with multiracial people', *Social Work* 56(3), <https://doi.org/10.1093/SW%2F56.3.235 f>.

Janakiraman, M. (n.d.) 'Inclusive leadership critical for competitive advantage' [online], <https://mobilityexchange.mercer.com/insights/article/inclusive-leadership-critical-for-competitive-advantage> [accessed 17 September 2021].

Javidan, M. (2007) 'Forward Thinking Cultures', *Harvard Business Review*, July–August, [online] <https://hbr.org/2007/07/forward-thinking-cultures> [accessed 8 November 2021].

Jelavic, M. and Salter, D. (2014) 'Managing facilitation in cross-cultural contexts: the application of national cultural dimensions to groups in learning organisations', *Transformative Dialogues: Teaching & Learning Journal* 7(1), <https://www.kpu.ca/sites/default/files/Transformative%20Dialogues/TD.7.1.6_Jelavic%26Salter_Managing_Facilitation_in_Cross-Cultural_Contexts.pdf> [accessed 17 September 2021].

Jones, A. with Jenkins, K. (2008) 'Rethinking collaboration: working the indigene-colonizer hyphen', Chapter 23 in N.K. Denzin, Y.S. Lincoln, and L.T. Smith (eds), *Handbook of Critical and Indigenous Methodologies*, Sage Publications, Thousand Oaks, CA.

Jordan, K. and Elsden-Clifton, J. (2014) *Through the Lens of Third Space Theory – Possibilities for Research Methodologies in Educational Technologies*, in Proceedings of the 6th International Conference on Computer Supported Education (CSEDU-2014), pp. 220–4, <https://www.scitepress.org/Papers/2014/47924/47924.pdf> [accessed 17 September 2021].

Kabigting, J. (2017) 'Avoiding mindless cultural training with cultural mindfulness,' https://globisinsights.com/career-success/avoiding-mindless-cultural-training-with-cultural-mindfulness/> [accessed 17 September 2021].

Kali, J.M. (2019a) 'Australian aid to PNG: transparency, accountability and the partnership environment – Part 1' [blog], Devpolicy Blog, <https://devpolicy.org/australian-aid-to-png-transparency-accountability-and-the-partnership-environment-part-1-20200409/> (posted 9 April 2020) [accessed 17 September 2021].

Kali, J.M. (2019b), 'Australian aid to PNG: transparency, accountability and the partnership environment – Part 2' [blog], Devpolicy Blog, https://devpolicy.org/australian-aid-to-png-transparency-accountability-and-the-partnership-environment-part-2-20200409/> [accessed 8 October 2021].

Kawamura, K. (2013) *Consensus and Democracy in Indonesia: Musyawarah-Mufakat Revisited'* IDE Discussion Paper No. 308. Institute of Developing Economies (IDE-JETRO).

Kelley, C. and Myers, J. (1995) 'Cross Cultural Adaptability Inventory', National Computer Systems, Minneapolis, MN.

Kelley, R.D.G. (1999) 'The people in me', *Utne Reader* 95: 79–81.

Khan, C. and Chovanec D. (2010) 'Is participatory action research relevant in the Canadian workplace?' *Journal of Contemporary Issues in Education*, 5(1): 34–44 [online], <https://journals.library.ualberta.ca/jcie/index.php/JCIE/article/view/9485> [accessed 8 November 2021]

Khan, M.A. and Ebner, N. (2019) *The Palgrave Handbook of Cross-Cultural Business Negotiation*, Palgrave, London.

Kirkhart, K.E. (1995) 'Seeking multicultural validity: a postcard from the road', *Evaluation Practice*, 16(1) 1–12.

Kirkhart, K.E. (2005) 'Eyes on the prize: multicultural validity and evaluation theory', *American Journal of Evaluation* <https://doi.org/10.1177/1098214010373645>.

Kohls, L. R. and Knight, J. M. (1994), *Developing Intercultural Awareness: A Cross-Cultural Training Handbook*, Intercultural Press Inc.

Knowles, M.S. (1970) *The Modern Practice Of Adult Education*, New York Association Press, New York.

Knowles, M.S. (1978) 'Andragogy: adult learning theory in perspective' *Community College Review* <https://doi.org/10.1177/009155217800500302>.

Korten, D.C. (1980) 'Community organization and rural development: a learning process approach', *Public Administration Review* 40(5): 480–511.

Krznaric, R. (2007) *How Change Happens: Interdisciplinary Perspectives for Human Development*, Oxfam Publishing, Oxford.

Land, C. (2015) *Decolonising Solidarity: Dilemmas and Directions for Supporters of Indigenous Struggles*, Zed Books, London.

Landis, S., Plaut, T., Trevor, J. and Futch, J. (1995) *Building a Healthier Tomorrow: A Manual for Rural Coalition Building* [PDF], Kellogg Foundation, Kendall/Hunt Publishing Company, <https://files.eric.ed.gov/fulltext/ED432415.pdf> [accessed 17 September 2021].

Lane, H.W., Maznevski, M., Dietz, J., DiStefano, J.D. (2010) *International Management Behavior: Leading with a Global Mindset*, John Wiley, 6th edition, New York.

Lastennet, C. (2015) 'Leading change internationally: 3 key cross-cultural factors [online], LinkedIn, <https://www.linkedin.com/pulse/leading-change-internationally-3-key-cross-cultural-lastennet/> [accessed 17 September 2021].

Leask, B. and Carroll, J. (2013) 'Learning and Teaching Across Cultures: Good Practice Principles and Quick Guides', <https://www.ieaa.org.au/documents/item/397>.

Lee, K. (2009) 'The importance of culture in evaluation: a practical guide for evaluators' [online], The Colorado Trust, <https://www.coloradotrust.org/find?search_api_views_fulltext=The%20importance%20of%20culture%20in%20evaluation%3A%20a%20practical%20guide%20for%20evaluators%E2%80%99> [accessed 17 September 2021].

Leftwich, A. (1995, published online 2007) 'Bringing politics back in: towards a model of the developmental state', *Journal of Development Studies*, 31(3) <https://doi.org/10.1080/00220389508422370>.

Leftwich, A. (2009) 'Bringing agency back in: politics and human agency in building institutions and states' [online], DLP Research Paper 6, <https://www.dlprog.org/publications/research-papers?page=8> [accessed 17 September 2021].

Leftwich, A. (2011) 'Developmental states, effective states, and poverty reduction: the primacy of politics', *Indian Journal of Development*, 5(2).

Leftwich, A. and Wheeler, C. (2011) 'Politics, leadership and coalitions in development: findings, insights and guidance' [online], DLP, <https://www.dlprog.org/publications/research-papers/politics-leadership-and-coalitions-in-development-findings-insights-and-guidance> [accessed 17 September 2021].

Leggatt, R. (2018) 'Developing the coalition – can we do more?'[online], The Force, Australian Defence College <https://theforge.defence.gov.au/publications/developing-coalition-can-we-do-more> [accessed 17 September 2021].

Lensu, M. (2003) *'Respect for Culture and Customs in International Humanitarian Assistance: Implications for Principles and Policy'* [PDF], Ph.D. thesis, <https://core.ac.uk/download/pdf/46519656.pdf> [accessed 17 September 2021].

Leonard, R.H., Kilkelly A. and Burnham, L. F. (2006) *Performing Communities: Grassroots Ensemble Theaters Deeply Rooted in Eight U.S. Communities*, New Village Press, New York.

Lewin, K. (1946) 'Action research and minority problems'. *Journal of Social Issues* 2(4): 34–46. <https://web.archive.org/web/20111030120737/http:/www.comp.dit.ie/dgordon/Courses/ILT/ILT0003/ActionResearchandMinortyProblems.pdf> [accessed 17 September 2021].

McAdam, D. (1994) 'Culture and social movements', Chapter 3 in E. Laraña, H. Johnston and J.R. Gusfield, *New Social Movements: From Ideology to Identity Book*, Temple University Press, Philadelphia, PA.

McEvoy, P., Brady, M. and Munck, R. (2016) 'Capacity development through international projects: a complex adaptive systems perspective', *International Journal of Managing Projects in Business* 9: 528–45, <https://doi.org/10.1108/IJMPB-08-2015-0072>.

McKenzie, F., Beaudoin, Y., Birtles, J., Chatterton, P., Gillinson, S., Killick, S., Mannov, A., Munk, J., Roberts, A., Rose, V., Seneque, M., Siodmok, A., Trebeck, K. and Van den Broeck, D. (2017) 'A wayfinder's guide to systems transformation: 18 insights for catalysts and convenors' Report from the workshop 'How might we approach transformational change for complex challenges in the future?' pp. 30-31, London <https://oecd-opsi.org/toolkits/a-wayfinders-guide-to-systems-transformation-18-insights-for-catalysts-and-convenors/> [accessed 7 November 2021].

McSweeney, B. (2002) 'Hofstede's model of national cultural differences and their consequences: a triumph of faith – a failure of analysis', *Human Relations* 55(1): 89–117.

McTaggart, R. (1999) 'Reflection on the purposes of research, action, and scholarship: a case of cross-cultural participatory action research' *Systemic Practice and Action Research*, 12(5): 493–511.

Margulies, N. and Sibbet, D., (2007) 'Visual recording and graphic facilitation: helping people see what they mean', Chapter 61 in Holman, P. et al. The Change Handbook, pp. 573–87, Berrett-Koehler, San Francisco. CA.

Marika, R., Ngurruwutthun, D. and White, L. (1992). 'Always together, Yaka gana: participatory research at Yirrkala as part of the development of Yolngu education'. *Convergence* 25(1): 23–39 [online], <https://www.proquest.com/openview/810f908ff4a694ea32f71221a9050989/1?pq-origsite=gscholar&cbl=2030445> [accessed 8 November 2021].

Mathie, A., Cameron, J. and Gibson, K. (2017) 'Asset-based and citizen-led development: using a diffracted power lens to analyze the possibilities and challenges', *Progress in Development Studies* 17(1): 1–13.

Maznevski, M.L. and Di Stefano, J. (2003) 'Developing global managers: integrating theory, behavior, data and performance', W. Mobley and P. Dorfman (eds), *Advances in Global Leadership*, Vol. 3, JAI Press, New York.

Mendenhall, M., Osland, J. and Bird, A. (2008) *Global Leadership: Research, Practice, and Development*, 2nd edition, Routledge, New York.

Mertens, D. (2012) *Program Evaluation Theory and Practice: A Comprehensive Guide*, The Guildford Press, New York.

Mertens, D., Kram, F. and Chilisa, B. (2016) *Indigenous Pathways into Social Research*, Routledge, Oxford.

Milheim, K.L. (2014) 'Facilitation across cultures in the online classroom', *International Journal of Learning, Teaching and Educational Research* 5(1) 1–11.

Mohammed, A. (2019) 'Delivering on sustainable development goals requires transformational, inclusive leadership' [online], speech by the UN Deputy Secretary-General to the World Government Summit's SDGs in Action, Dubai, February 2019, <https://www.un.org/press/en/2019/dsgsm1249.doc.htm> [accessed 17 September 2021].

Moller, H., O'Blyver, P., Bragg, C., Newman, J., Lucas R., Fletcher D., Kitson J., McKechnie S., Scott D. and Rakiura Titi Islands Administering Body (2009) 'Guidelines for cross-cultural Participatory Action Research partnerships: a case study of a customary seabird harvest in New Zealand' *New Zealand Journal of Zoology*, 36: 211–41.

Moore, J. (1993) *Visions of Culture: An Introduction to Anthropological Theories and Theorists*, Altamira Press, Lanham, MD.

Mor Barak, M.E. (2000) 'The inclusive workplace: an ecosystems approach to diversity management' *Social Work*, 45(4): 339–53, <https://doi.org/10.1093/sw/45.4.339>.

Mor Barak, M.E. (2015) 'Inclusion is the key to diversity management, but what is Inclusion?' *Human Service Organisations: Management, Leadership and Governance*, Routledge 39(2): 83–8.

Morris, M.W., Chiu, C. and Liu, Z. (2015) 'Polycultural psychology', *Annual Review of Psychology* 66: 631–59, <https://www.annualreviews.org/doi/abs/10.1146/annurev-psych-010814-015001 [accessed 17 September 2021]>.

Munk, J., Roberts, A., Rose, V., Seneque, M., Siodmok, A., Trebeck, K. and Van den Broeck, D. (2017) *'A Wayfinder's Guide to Systems Transformation: 18 Insights for Catalysts and Convenors'* [online], Report from the Workshop 'How might we approach transformational change for complex challenges in the future?' 30–31 August 2017, London <https://oecd-opsi.org/toolkits/a-wayfinders-guide-to-systems-transformation-18-insights-for-catalysts-and-convenors/> [accessed 17 September 2021].

ODI (Overseas Development Institute) (2014) Doing Development Differently [PDF], <https://cdn.odi.org/media/documents/5149.pdfodi.org/media/documents/5149.pdf> [accessed 8 November 2021].

O'Keefe, M. (2015) 'The strategic context of the new Pacific diplomacy', Chapter 11 in G. Fry and S. Tarte, *The New Pacific Diplomacy*, <http://doi.org/10.22459/NPD.12.2015>.

O'Keefe, M., Sidel, J., Marquette, H., Roche, C., Hudson, D. and Dasandi, N. (2014) *Using Action Research and Learning for Politically Informed Programming*, DLP Research Paper 29.

Oetzel, J.G. and Ting-Toomey, S. (2003) 'Face concerns in interpersonal conflict: a cross-cultural empirical test of the face negotiation theory' *Communication Research*, 30(6): 599–624, <https://doi.org/10.1177/0093650203257841>.

Okada, A. and Riedl A. (1999) *When Culture does not Matter: Experimental Evidence from Coalition Formation Ultimatum Games In Austria and Japan* [PDF], <https://papers.tinbergen.nl/99043.pdf> [accessed 17 September 2021].

Olbrecht, A. (2019) 'Adaptive management and programming: the humanitarian perspective' [online], Groupe URD, <https://www.urd.org/en/review-hem/adaptive-management-and-programming-the-humanitarian-perspective/> [accessed 17 September 2021].

Padilla, Y.C., McRoy, R. and Calvo, R. (2020) Rethinking Social Work Practice with Multicultural Communities, Routledge, Oxford.

Palus, C. J. and Horth, D.M. (2008) 'Visual explorer', chapter 65 in Holman, P. et al. *The Change Handbook*, pp. 603–8, Berrett-Koehler, San Francisco, CA.

Pamphilon, B. (2015) 'Weaving knowledges: the development of empowering intercultural learning spaces for smallholder farmers in Papua New Guinea' *Multicultural Education Review* 7(1–2): 108–21 [online], https://www.tandfonline.com/doi/abs/10.1080/2005615X.2015.1061921?journalCode=rmer20 [accessed 8 Novembe 2021].

Parkin, M. (2015) *Tales for Change: Using Storytelling to Develop People and Organizations*, Kogan Page, London.

Partnership Brokers Association (2019) *Brokering Better Partnerships* [PDF], <https://partnershipbrokers.org/w/wp-content/uploads/2020/05/Brokering-Better-Partnerships-Handbook.pdf> [accessed 17 September 2021].

Pataranutaporn, P. (2017) 'Prototyping future society through theatre for social change' [blog], <https://medium.com/@patpataranutaporn/prototyping-future-society-through-theatre-for-social-change-1d78b776d88e#:~:text=Even%20thought%20the%20scope%20of,issues%20through%20community%20engagement%20process>. (posted 15 June 2017) [accessed 17 September 2021].

Peng, K., Ames, D.R. and Knowles, E.D. (2001) 'Culture and human inference: perspectives from three traditions', in D. Matsumoto (ed.), *The Handbook of Culture and Psychology*, pp. 245–64, Oxford University Press, Oxford.

Pettigrew, T.F. and Tropp, L.R. (2006) 'A meta-analytic test of intergroup contact theory', *Journal of Personality and Social Psychology*, 90(5): 751–83, <https://doi.org/10.1037/0022-3514.90.5.751>.

Pipi, K. (2016) 'Maramatanga (enlightenment): a creative approach to connecting facilitation and evaluation', *New Directions for Evaluation* 2016(149) 43–52, <https://doi.org/10.1002/ev.20178>.

Polley, B. (1989) 'Coalition, mediation, and scapegoating: general principles and cultural variation' International Journal of Intercultural Relations 13(2): 165–81, <https://doi.org/10.1016/0147-1767(89)90004-7>.

Pon, G. (2009) 'Cultural competency as new racism: an ontology of forgetting', *Journal of Progressive Human Services*, 20: 59–71.

Prasetyo, Y.E. (2017) 'From storytelling to social change: the power of story in the community building', *SSRN Electronic Journal*, Community Development Academy III <https://www.bvsc.org/from-storytelling-to-social-change-the-power-of-story-in-the-community-building> [accessed 8 October 2021].

Prashad V. (2001) *Everybody was Kung Fu Fighting: Afro-Asian Connections and the Myth of Cultural Purity*, Beacon Press, Boston, MA.

Pretty, J., Guijt, I., Thompson, J. and Scones, I. (1995) *Participatory Learning and Action: A Trainer's Guide*, International Institute for Environment and Development, London.

Quinn Patton, M. (2011) *Developmental Evaluation: Applying Complexity Concepts to Enhance Innovation and Use*, The Guildford Press, New York.

Ramalingam, B. (2013) *Aid on the Edge of Chaos*, Oxford University Press, Oxford.

Ramsey, C. (2006) *Introducing Reflective Learning* [PDF], The Open University, <https://www.open.edu/openlearncreate/pluginfile.php/159274/mod_resource/content/3/Introducing%20Reflective%20learning%20Ramsey,%202006.pdf> [accessed 17 September 2021].

Randel, A.E., Dean, M.A., Ehrhart, K.H., Chung, B. and Shore, L. (2016) 'Leader inclusiveness, psychological diversity climate, and helping behaviors', *Journal of Managerial Psychology* 31(1) 216–34 <https://doi.org/10.1108/JMP-04-2013-0123>.

Randel, A., Galvin, B., Shore, L., Ehrhart, K.H, Chung, B., Dean, M. and Kedharnath, U. (2018) 'Inclusive leadership: realizing positive outcomes through belongingness and being valued for uniqueness', *Human Resource Management Review* 28(2) 190–203.

Rao, V. and Walton, M. (eds) (2004) *Culture and Public Action*, Stanford Social Sciences, Stanford, CA,.

Rathod, S. (2020) 'Response to "Impact of culture on response to COVID 19"', *BMJ* 2020: 369 <https://www.bmj.com/content/369/bmj.m1556/rr> [accessed 17 September 2021].

Reason, P. and Bradbury, H. (2008) *Action Research: Participative Enquiry and Practice*, Sage, Thousand Oaks, CA.

Reese, A. (2015) 'How can music inspire social change' [blog] <https://facingtoday.facinghistory.org/how-can-music-inspire-social-change> (posted on 12 April 2015) [accessed 17 September 2021].

Reiner, C. and Willingham, D. (2010) 'The myth of learning styles', *Change: The Magazine of Higher Learning* 42:5 32–5, <https://doi.org/10.1080/00091383.2010.503139>.

Reis, C. and Bernath, T. (2017) *Becoming a Humanitarian Aid Worker*, Butterworth Heinemann, Oxford.

Reynolds, K. (2018) '13 benefits and challenges of cultural diversity in the workplace' [blog], Hult International Business School, <https://www.hult.edu/blog/benefits-challenges-cultural-diversity-workplace/> [accessed 17 September 2021]>.

Rhodes, D. (2014) *Capacity Across Cultures: Global Lessons from Pacific Experiences*, Inkshed, Ballarat.

Rhodes, D. (2016) 'Relevance of cross-cultural understanding for evaluations in development practice', *Evaluation Journal of Australasia* 16:2 15–21.

Rhodes, D. and Antoine, E. (2013) *Practitioners' Handbook for Capacity Development: A Cross-Cultural Approach*, Inkshed Press, Ballarat.

Rhodes, D. and Antoine, E. (2019) 'Leadership for all: is it culturally feasible?' *Development Bulletin*, 81: 53–7.

Robertson, Q.M. (2006) 'Disentangling the meanings of diversity and inclusion in organizations', *Group and Organisation Management* 31: 2 212–36, Sage Publications, <https://pdfs.semanticscholar.org/56d9/e2b708137906af2a6bb00cbf929fd87c5298.pdf> [accessed 17 September 2021].

Rocha Menocal, A. (2014) 'Getting real about politics: from thinking politically to working differently', ODI Research Paper, ODI [online], <https://odi.org/en/publications/getting-real-about-politics-from-thinking-politically-to-working-differently/> [accessed 8 November 2021.

Roche, C. (2019) 'Leadership for inclusive development' *Development Bulletin* 81: 4–7.

Roche, C. and Kelly, L. (2012) 'The evaluation of politics and the politics of evaluation' [online], Background Paper 11, Developmental Leadership Programme, <https://www.dlprog.org/publications/research-papers/the-evaluation-of-politics-and-the-politics-of-evaluation> [accessed 17 September 2021].

Rogers, P.C., Graham, C.R., Mayes, C.T., (2007) 'Cultural competence and instructional design: exploration research into the delivery of online instruction cross-culturally', *Education Tech Research Dev* 55: 197–217.

Rowlands, J. (1997) *Questioning Empowerment: Working with Women in Honduras* [online], Oxfam <https://policy-practice.oxfam.org/resources/questioning-empowerment-working-with-women-in-honduras-121185/> [accessed 8 November 2021].

Ruben, D.J. (1989) 'The study of cross-cultural competence: traditions and contemporary issues' *International Journal of Intercultural Relations* 13(3): 229–40.

Ruben, D.J. and Keally, B.D. (1979) 'Behavioral assessment of communication competency and the prediction of cross-cultural adaptation', *International Journal of Intercultural Relations* 3: 15–47.

Runde, C. and Armon, B. (2016) 'Conflict competence in a multicultural world', in *Critical Issues in Cross Cultural Management* pp. 61–72.

Rutherford, J. (1998) 'The third space, interview with Homi Bhabha', in *Identity: Community, Culture, Difference*, p 211, Lawrence & Wishart, London.

<https://www.scribd.com/document/358684105/The-Third-Space-Interview-With-Homi-Bhabha> [accessed 8 November 2021].

Sakamoto, I. (2007) 'An anti-oppressive approach to cultural competence', *Canadian Social Work Review* 24(1): 105–114.

Sakkir, N.B. (2021) 'Musyawarah-Mufakat: Indonesian diplomacy through the Jusuf Kalla experience' [online], Jenggala Institute for Strategic Studies, <https://www.jenggalacenter.org> [accessed 8 October 2021].

Saltmarshe, E. (2018) 'Using story to change systems' [online], Stanford Social Innovation Review, <https://ssir.org/articles/entry/using_story_to_change_systems> [accessed 17 September 2021]/

Sanga, K. and Reynolds, M. (2018) 'Melanesian tok stori in leadership development: ontological and relational implications for donor-funded programmes in the Western Pacific' *International Education Journal, Comparative Perspectives*, 17(4): 11–26.

Sarabhai, M. (2009) 'Dance to change the world' [video], Ted Talk, https://www.bing.com/videos/search?q=Ted+Talk+Mallika+Sarabhai%3a+Dance+to+Change+the+World&docid=607995497360854900&mid=418E736 98DE791F74F03418E73698DE791F74F03&view=detail&FORM=VIRE> [accessed 17 September 2021].

Sauer, N. (2018) 'The Talanoa dialogue explained'[online], Climate Home News, <https://www.climatechangenews.com/2018/12/10/talanoa-dialogue-explained/> [accessed 17 September 2021].

SBS (n.d.), Cultural Competence [website], <https://www.cultural-competence.com.au/> [accessed 17 September 2021].

Sebenius, J.K. (2002) 'The hidden challenge of cross-border negotiations', *Harvard Business Review* 80(3): 76–85.

Secretariat of the Pacific Community (SPC) (2020) *Pacific Monitoring, Evaluation and Learning Capacity Strengthening Rebbilib*, SPC [online] <https://www.spc.int/updates/blog/2020/08/pacific-mel-rebbilib-report-on-mel-capacity-available-for-download> [accessed 8 October 2021].

Seelye, H. N. (editor) (1996), *Experiential Activities for Intercultural Learning*, Intercultural Press Inc.

Sen, A. (2004) 'How does culture matter?' Chapter 2 in V. Rao, and M. Walton, *Culture and Public Action*, pp. 37–58, World Bank, Washington, DC.

Sen Gupta, S., Hopson, R., Thompson-Robinson, M., (2004) 'Cultural competence in evaluation: an overview,' *New Directions for Evaluation*, 102, Summer, Wiley Periodicals [online] <https://onlinelibrary.wiley.com/doi/abs/10.1002/ev.112> [accessed 8 November 2021].

Serrat, O. (2017) 'Political economy analysis for development effectiveness', *Knowledge Solutions: Tools, Methods, and Approaches to Drive Organizational Performance*, Springer, 207–222, <https://link.springer.com/chapter/10.1007/978-981-10-0983-9_21> [accessed 17 September 2021].

Shulman, L. (2013) 'How art creates social change in 5 TED talks' [blog], Cloudhead, <http://cloudhead.org/2013/09/03/the-power-of-art-to-affect-social-change-shown-in-5-ted-talks/> (posted 3 September 2013) [accessed 17 September 2021].

Siler, T. (2003) 'Think like a genius: realizing human potential through the purposeful play of metaphorming', Chapter 30 in Holman, P. et al. *The Change Handbook*, pp. 288–93, Berrett-Koehler.

Sinha, A. and Jaiswal R. (2020) 'Positioning panchayats as India's agents of change' [online], *Hindustan Times*, <https://www.hindustantimes.com/analysis/position-panchayats-as-india-s-agents-of-change/story-6qBRbyPSsEn2r2dYH7exjP.html> (posted 24 April 2020) [accessed 17 September 2021].

Sloman, A. (2012) 'Using participatory theatre in international community development', *Community Development Journal* 47: 1: 42–57.

Snowden, D. (2011) 'Cynefin, a sense of time and place: an ecological approach to sense making and learning in formal and informal communities' [online], <https://www.researchgate.net/publication/264884267_Cynefin_A_Sense_of_Time_and_Place_an_Ecological_Approach_to_Sense_Making_and_Learning_in_Formal_and_Informal_Communities> [accessed 17 September 2021].

Soja, E.W. (1996) 'Margin/alia: social justice and the new cultural politics', in A. Merrifield and E. Swyngedouw (eds), *The Urbanization of Injustice*, pp. 180–99, Lawrence and Wishart, London.

Song, K-H, 2016, *Multicultural and International Approaches in Social Work Practice*, Hamilton Books, Lanham, MD.amilton

Star-Glass, D. (2013) 'Learning through learning: experiential resonance in an online management course', *International Journal of Management, Knowledge and Learning* 1: 65–82.

Stephan, U. and Pathak, S. (2016) 'Beyond cultural values? Cultural leadership ideals and entrepreneurship' *Journal of Business Venturing* 31: 505–23.

Sugden, J. (2016) *Adaptive Management for Resilient Communities: Development in a Volatile Environment*, Practical Action Publishing, Rugby.

Tapenes, M.A., Smith, G.G. and White J.A. (2009) 'Cultural diversity in online learning: a study of the perceived effects of dissonance in levels of individualism/collectivism and tolerance of ambiguity', *The Internet and Higher Education*, 12(1): 26–34.

Tendy, S.M. and Geiser, W.F. (1997) *The Search for Style: It All Depends on Where You Look* [PDF], <https://files.eric.ed.gov/fulltext/ED410029.pdf> [accessed 17 September 2021].

Teskey, G. and Tyrrel, L. (2021), *Implementing Adaptive Management: A Front-Line Effort. is There an Emerging Practice?* [PDF] Abt Associates, Government and Development Practice note <https://abt-associates_adaptive-management_a-frontline-effort_digital-1.pdf> [accessed 17 September 2021].

Tett, G. (2021) *Anthro-Vision: How Anthropology Can Explain Business and Life*, Random House Business, London.

Thompson, J. (1996) 'Moving the indigenous knowledge debate forward?', *Development Policy Review* 14:1 105–12.

Ting-Toomey, S. (1994) 'Managing intercultural conflicts effectively', in L. Samovar and R. Porter *Intercultural Communication*, 7th edition, Wadsworth, Belmont, California, pp. 360–371, <https://www.talent.wisc.edu/home/Portals/0/ManagingInterculturalConflicts.pdf> [accessed 17 September 2021].

Ting-Toomey, S. and Oetzel, J.G. (2001) Communicating Effectively in Multicultural Contexts: Vol. 6. Managing Intercultural Conflict Effectively, Sage Publications, Inc, Thousand Oaks, CA.

Ting-Toomey, S. and Oetzel, J.G. (2013) *The SAGE Handbook of Conflict Communication*, 2nd edition, Sage, Los Angeles, CA.

Trompenaars, F. and Hampden-Turner, C. (1997) *Riding the Waves of Culture*, Nicholas Brealey Publishing, Boston, MA.

Tunufa'i, L. (2016) 'Pacific research: rethinking the talanoa 'methodology', *New Zealand Sociology* 31(7): 227–39

UN Women (n.d.) 'Global norms and standards' [website], UN Women <https://www.unwomen.org/en/what-we-do/youth/global-norms-and-standards> [accessed 17 September 2021].

Vaioleti, T.M. (2006) 'Talanoa research methodology: a developing position on Pacific research,' *Waikato Journal of Education*, 12 (1): 21–34.

Valters, C., Cummings, C. and Nixon, H. (2016) 'Putting learning at the centre Adaptive development programming in practice' ODI Report [online], <https://odi.org/en/publications/putting-learning-at-the-centre-adaptive-development-programming-in-practice/> [accessed 8 November 2021].

VeneKlasen, L. and Miller, V. (2007) *A New Weave of Power, People & Politics: The Action Guide for Advocacy and Citizen Participation*, Practical Action Publishing, Rugby.

Walker, P. (2013) 'Storians: building on indigenous knowledge to enhance Ni-Vanuatu mediative capacity', *Conflict Resolution Quarterly, Special Issue: Colloquy on Indigenous and Local Conflict Resolution Processes* 30(3): 309–28, <https://papers.ssrn.com/sol3/papers.cfm?abstract_id=2254759> [accessed 17 September 2021].

Wang, C. and Burris, M.A. (1997) 'Photovoice: concept, methodology, and use for participatory needs assessment', *Health Education Behaviour*, 24(3): 369–87.

Wang, J. (2018) 'Strategies for managing cultural conflict: models review and their applications in business and technical communication', *Journal of Technical Writing and Communication* 48(3): 281–94.

Wang, J. and Farmer, L. (2008) 'Adult teaching methods in China and Bloom's Taxonomy' *International Journal for the Scholarship of Teaching and Learning* 2(2) DOI: 10.20429/ijsotl.2008.020213.

Wang, T.P. (2007) 'The comparison of the difficulties between cooperative learning and traditional teaching methods in college English teachers', *The Journal of Human Resource and Adult Learning* 3(2): 23–30.

Warren, D.M., Slikkerveer, J., Brokensha, D. and Dechering, W.H.J.C. (1995) *The Cultural Dimension of Development*, Practical Action Publishing, Rugby.

Weeks, W., Hoatson, L. and Dixon, J. (2003) *Community Practices in Australia*, Pearson Education Australia.

Wehipeihana, N., Davidson, J., McKegg, K. and Shankar, V. (2010) 'What does it take to do evaluation in communities and cultural contexts other than our own?' *Journal of Multidisciplinary Evaluation*, 6(13): 182–92.

Wiest, D. (2010) 'Interstate dynamics and transnational social movement coalitions: a comparison of Northeast and Southeast Asia', Chapter 3 in N. Van Dyke and H. McCammon (eds), *Strategic Alliances: Coalition Building and Social Movements*, University of Minnesota Press, Minneapolis, MT.

Winterford, K. and Laqeretabua, A. (2019) '*Mid-term Evaluation of the Strengthening Feminist Coalitions and Partnership for Gender Equality: We Rise Phase 2 Project*' [PDF], <https://www.dfat.gov.au/sites/default/files/we-rise-2-mid-term-evaluation.pdf> [accessed 17 September 2021].

Winterford, K., Rhodes, D. and Dureau, C. (forthcoming) *Re-framing Aid: A Strengths-based Approach for International Development*.

Wright, K. (2018) 'Helping our beneficiaries tell their own stories, International aid agencies and the politics of voice within news production', *Global Media and Communication* 14(1): 85–102.

Wright, S. and Neimand, A. (2018) 'The secret to better storytelling for social change', *Stanford Socal Innovation Review* <https://ssir.org/articles/entry/the_secret_to_better_storytelling_for_social_change_better_partnerships#> [accessed 8 October 2021].

Wuffli, P.A. (2016) *Inclusive Leadership: A Framework for the Global Era*, Springer, Switzerland AG.

Yukl, G., Fu, P.P. and McDonald, R. (2003) 'Cross-cultural differences in perceived effectiveness of influence tactics for initiating or resisting change', *Applied Psychology: An International Review*, 52(1): 68–82.

Ziegahn, L. (2001) Considering Culture in the Selection of Teaching Approaches for Adults [PDF], ERIC Digest, <https://files.eric.ed.gov/fulltext/ED459325.pdf> [accessed 17 September 2021].

Zingaro, L. (2009) Speaking out: Storytelling for Social Change, Left Coast Press, California. <https://books.google.com.au/books?hl=en&lr=&id=wt3LyW2Cw18C&oi=fnd&pg=PA5&dq=storytelling+for+social+change&ots=8ecr-OqQMy&sig=9yxJXBk36gkRL5KTsGVexx9bPWs#v=onepage&q=storytelling%20for%20social%20change&f=false> [accessed 17 September 2021].

www.ingramcontent.com/pod-product-compliance
Lightning Source LLC
Chambersburg PA
CBHW070921030426
42336CB00014BA/2489